Strategic HR

Strategic HR

Building the Capability to Deliver

PETER REILLY AND TONY WILLIAMS

Routledge
Taylor & Francis Group

LONDON AND NEW YORK

First published in paperback 2024

First published 2006 by Gower Publishing

Published 2016 by Routledge
4 Park Square, Milton Park, Abingdon, Oxon OX14 4RN

and by Routledge
605 Third Avenue, New York, NY 10158

Routledge is an imprint of the Taylor & Francis Group, an informa business

British Library Cataloguing in Publication Data
Reilly, Peter A. (Peter Andrew), 1952-
  Strategic HR : building the capability to deliver
  1. Personnel management
  I.Title II.Williams, Tony
  658.3

Library of Congress Cataloging-in-Publication Data
Usability success stories : how organizations improve by making easier-to-use software and web sites / edited by Paul Sherman.
    p. cm.
  Includes bibliographical references and index.
  ISBN-13: 978-0-566-08656-4
  ISBN-10: 0-566-08656-5 (alk. paper)
  1. New products--Management. 2. Customer relations. 3. User interfaces (Computer systems) I. Sherman, Paul, 1966-

  HF5415.15.U73 2006
  005.068--dc22

                                                                2006013672

ISBN 13: 978-0-566-08674-8 (hbk)
ISBN 13: 978-1-03-283773-4 (pbk)
ISBN 13: 978-1-315-61091-7 (ebk)

DOI: 10.4324/9781315610917

Contents

List of Figures

Foreword

There are surprisingly few books which are about the HR function itself, rather than its policies, and which are set in a UK rather than North American context. There are very few good ones. This book is definitely one of them, primarily I think because of the depth, the breadth and particularly the balance of the observation and analysis it contains.

The obituary of the HR function has been written many times since Peter Drucker famously questioned the role and contribution, the future existence, of the then personnel departments 50 years ago. Academic articles continue to split definitional hairs and lament the conflicting identities of the function's roles, while the authors wryly observe that sometimes practitioners can justly be accused of being better at analysis and fault-finding than action and implementation.

For the last decade we have been inundated with superficial and normative admonishments to avoid the modern-day version of Drucker's fate, an administrative and outsourced purgatory in which we are progressively replaced by line managers and MBAs. We must 'get strategic', reinvent ourselves, lose our administrative and employee-friendly baggage and all follow Dave Ulrich's supposed miracle recipe of partnering with the business to achieve boardroom presence and success.

Ulrich himself, of course, in reality describes a 'cacophony' of value-adding roles for HR to apply and crucially adapt in their own setting. The authors rightly caution us to avoid being 'obsessed with a narrow and outdated concept of the strategic', as well as with the 'me too' supposed best practice contained in much of the literature. 'The aim [of the book] is to get one and all to think through why they are taking a particular approach and the consequences.' Context is king.

But Peter and Tony do much more in this book to help us pursue the appropriate pathways to success. Displaying their own multiple roles as leading thinkers, consultants, practitioners and writers they delve beneath the superficial and above the narrowly over-analytical to observe and infer from what is actually happening to HR in many different UK organizations and settings. They generally see not a required or actual 'radical transformation' but 'an evolutionary process' of building on traditional strengths and melding on new and enhanced responsibilities and contributions. And, overall, their findings give them 'much reason to be optimistic'.

HR outsourcing? Exaggerated in extent and tough to deliver in practice. Replacement by the line managers? They generally have not the time, the skills nor the inclination. Business partners? An essential role for HR functions but one in which there has been too much focus on job titles and aspirations and not enough on delivery. The obsession with strategy? HR has to find a balance between its still valuable day-to-day operational role and the 'big-picture' transformational initiatives, and the two in reality can't be neatly segmented. Employment legislation? A powerful reinforcement to an influential regulatory role for HR. Understanding and identifying with employees? Also a continuing and key aspect of HR's USP.

A function in terminal decline? Look at the Institute for Employment Studies' (IES) research for the Chartered Institute of Personnel and Development (CIPD) showing significant growth in the numbers of HR staff since 2001. Are talent and human capital management the latest in a long line of faddish straws we clutch at? No, they are both crucial and indicative of a fundamental shift in the global economy towards service and knowledge-based work which means people really are an organization's most important asset. And, for HR, the function that should know more about the people aspects of the organization and how to deliver performance through them than anyone else, they are a fantastic opportunity.

But optimism is combined with realism, and this book is far from being an HR whitewash or love-in. It combines a full description of the evolving role and purpose of HR in the first part, and of this visionary potential contribution in the second, with a powerful and challenging critique of current practice and the very real obstacles to delivering on this potential in the third. Lack of vision and optimism; a bias towards inaction and progressive retreat from an essential front-line presence and impact ('for many employees HR has become remote and irrelevant'); and, perhaps most critically, an over-focus on HR structures, roles and processes rather than on developing and what the authors call 're-contextualizing' our skills and capabilities. 'Lack of the right skills', the authors write, 'will continue to be the principal reason for HR not meeting its own aspirations.'

The CIPD continues to adapt and expand the professional development it provides to tens of thousands of HR practitioners each year to help to address this challenge. We are currently working with IES to examine the shifting career and development pathways in HR, and the broader evolution of the function. But at its heart it's down to the personal commitment each of us makes to continually question, learn and re-learn so as to be ever better at linking the people and performance agendas in the specific settings each of us works in.

A recent CIPD survey found that HR professionals are only devoting half the time they feel they need to their own personal development. Only if we make this commitment will more of us realize the magnificent vision of the function's future the authors hold out, where 'far from being Human Remains, HR is the part of the organization that orchestrates employee performance, conducting … playing the employee engagement notes'.

Everyone at whatever level and role in HR, or with studies or interests in people management more generally, should find plenty in this book to help them develop and improve significantly on this score.

Duncan Brown, Assistant Director General, CIPD

Introduction

According to the 2001 Census, there were then some 320,000 people working in HR and training in the UK. Statistics from the Labour Force Survey in 2004 suggest that the numbers in the function have grown by over 12 per cent since then. Despite this apparent robust good health, the HR function continues to lack confidence in its role and purpose. Navel gazing is a near-continuous activity. The views of customers, especially senior management ones, are canvassed to test opinion on whether HR is doing a worthwhile job. For example, in a CIPD survey of HR practitioners (2003a), only a third thought that others in the organization believed it was a good place to work. This puts off quality people from joining the function and dispirits those working in it. There is the gloomy report that, of HR staff in the UK surveyed, as high a proportion as 39 per cent claimed to be unhappy or very unhappy in their work (*Personnel Today*, 2005a). A wider SHRM (Society for Human Resource Management in the USA) survey of 23 countries reported HR professional's low sense of self esteem (*People Management*, 2005).

There is the self-flagellation of repeating the critical comments of colleagues that HR is a dead-end place. There is frequent anxiety over whether HR is making the right sort of organizational contribution or even whether it has a future at all. At the HR Forum in 2005 (Dempsey, 2005) it was claimed that HR faced a double bind. There is the risk, according to Larry Hochman, of HR becoming 'human remains' if its role does not change, with Vance Kearney of Oracle arguing that if it were successful at organizational transformation, it would do itself out of a job.

To fight back, HR is keen to promote research that establishes the connection between HR and the 'bottom line', to emphasize its relevance. Phrases such as 'the war for talent', 'employer of choice' and 'employee value proposition' have entered business parlance as means to emphasize the importance of employee attraction to organizational success. The concept of 'human capital' has also been the subject of much recent debate, not least because it allows HR to present the value of people management in strategic terms – as a source of competitive advantage.

As is often said, the finance function does not seem to have this sense of insecurity. It claims its rightful place and gets on with the job. Part of the difficulty for the HR function seems to stem from an uncertainty over what role it should play. For some critics the very renaming of the function, from personnel to human resources, was no more than a rebranding exercise, a matter of spin not substance. Whilst many may now adopt the term 'HR' rather than 'personnel' because the abbreviated HR trips off the tongue more easily, there are those though who want to assert a real difference between the two and a freshly defined position for the function. As we will discuss later, this goes back to the development of the concept of 'human resource management' in the late 1980s. HRM appeared to offer a new philosophy of people management that sought to find ways to release the potential of the workforce. This encouraged the shift in HR's role definition from welfare or administrative officer to business strategist. Opponents saw this less positively as a means to exploit the value of staff and considered the term HR as demeaning to employees, counting them as resources no different from money or machinery.

But change in the role of HR has also been driven by real change in the context within which it has had to operate. Briefly put, more intense and globalized competition has pushed organizations to be both more effective and efficient. Private sector companies have had to respond to stock market demands for a quick return on investments. Those in the public sector have had to cope with similarly impatient government requirements for cost reduction and improved delivery. This has driven many companies into mergers or new partnership arrangements; others have been the subject of takeovers. Reconfiguration, perhaps more for political than efficiency reasons, has similarly affected public sector bodies. At a more micro level, structures have adjusted to meet organizational imperatives. Delayering, matrix management, broader roles in place of jobs, project team working, decentralization of responsibility to business units and the centralization of administrative activities have all been seen in recent years as means to raise organizational performance. For similar reasons, new forms of service delivery – via call centres, intranets or the like – have been launched. Tasks may, as before, be subcontracted to specialist outsiders, but talk (and sometimes action) is of whole functions being outsourced, or even offshored. There has been internal competition over the investment in resources and the release of funds. Organizations have increasingly paid attention to the customer and to the need for quality, as well as increased productivity. And then there has been the increase in the regulatory burden. Whether emanating from Brussels or from Westminster, over the last ten years there has been a spurt of employment legislation – from the minimum wage through the working time regulations to the employment of agency workers. Whether this legislative burst is for good or ill is beside the point in this context; what matters is that HR has had to concern itself with its implications. Some have turned out to be less threatening or onerous than expected; others have presented a greater challenge.

This degree of organizational and environmental churn has focused attention on the people element of the business. The HRM notion of getting employees aligned with business goals fitted with the new model of doing business. The current interest in employee engagement and human capital is the latest manifestation of this imperative. Where the labour market has been tight, i.e. where supply hardly matches demand, the emphasis has been on retention. This has been especially true for some specialist skills and for those talented individuals with potential to get to the top. In these situations, for some organizations there has also been a convergence of philosophy and need; employees should be valued to improve their productive capability and must be valued to keep them in their current employment. Indeed, 'human capital' is, in some quarters, even replacing 'human resources' as the term of choice.

By contrast, other organizations have been more concerned with downsizing and redundancy programmes. This may be driven by economic necessity or to meet shareholder requirements. Harder still to manage has been the pendulum swinging between recruitment and reduction, or cutting in some areas and growing in others. This balancing act has been more challenging still for those companies operating on a global scale. The economic situation has varied so much between countries or regions and over time. So we have seen the tiger economies of Asia go from boom to not quite bust and not quite back again. We have seen the growing power of China, but the declining influence of Japan, and the contrast between the sclerotic performance of many European countries and the rollercoaster ride of the USA.

This conflict or tension between retrenchment and growth poses real problems in positioning the HR function in some organizations. The professional leanings of the HR staff are towards engagement and development, yet the exigencies of the business situation may be pushing them towards downsizing and outsourcing/offshoring. They want to assert the value of people as the organization's greatest asset, but the actions required of them reduce the scope of their professional position.

All of this has certainly given HR much to do!

It is an irony that people management is becoming more and more important in many organizations, but that the effectiveness of HR function continues to be questioned.

Against this background, of a changing, and more demanding, organizational environment and an HR function trying to improve its game so that it can make a genuinely strategic contribution, we take time out in this book to look at progress to date and the challenges ahead. The book, like Gaul, is organized in three parts:

Part 1: the story so far. This looks at the changing purpose and role of HR. It reviews the move to devolve more responsibility to line management and to encourage the line to take more of a lead in people management. New structures and delivery mechanisms will be considered next, covering shared services, call centres and business partner models. We will look too at improved HR processes – the move to simplified, standardized and best in class procedures. This section will also include developments in e-HR, outsourcing and measurement and monitoring.

In this part of the book we describe the common features of change and the problems faced. We will also summarize some of the debates about HR's role, activities and ways of organizing itself.

Part 2: where to next? Here we set out our vision of what HR should look like in the context of the big questions faced by the function. What should its purpose be? How can it build the capability to be more strategic? How should it organize itself? What are the skills required for success? We will give our view on HR's role and what activities it should be tackling, organized under the headings of organizational capability, effectiveness and proposition. This leads into a discussion on skill requirements. We will also give our opinion on HR's relationship to its stakeholders: how organizations are pushing line managers more and more to manage their people, and how the function might aim to connect to employees. New structures, processes and delivery will be considered next, including shared services, outsourcing and e-HR. We will also look at the way the function is changing the means by which it relates with the business through the business partner model. Methodologies for measuring the efficiency and effectiveness of HR and people management are discussed.

Part 3: impediments to success. This part of the book confronts the challenges the function faces in meeting the objectives detailed in Part 2 and offers possible solutions. We pick out three particular issues. Firstly, we cover the positioning challenge: the difficulties of building successful relationships with senior managers, line managers and employees. Secondly, we describe problems with the new HR operating model, its structures and roles. Finally, we examine the capability challenge. Against the backdrop of HR's search to be more effective, we ask: what are the skill deficiencies that will be the main impediment to HR's success? Will careers be developed in such a way to bring on talent in the new model?

Under these headings we offer ideas to deal with these challenges. Among the solutions we offer, we suggest that HR looks to other functions (such as finance, marketing and IT) for ideas on the way they have tackled similar issues.

Our conclusion will aim to draw these strands together and we will discuss how HR can best make its strategic contribution, and what obstacles it needs to overcome. We finish with a list of pointers that cover the areas where we believe particular attention is required.

We hope that the book will interest all HR readers, but, depending on the stage the organization is at, HR practitioners may be familiar with the concepts and practices described. We have included at various times reference to issues that we hope should challenge the more sophisticated. The aim is to get one and all to think through why they are taking a particular approach and what the consequences might be. This applies to skills as to structures, content as to roles. But, as we eschew a best-practice style of commentary, we will not be advocating a single approach to people management, rather pointing out the different options – their advantages and disadvantages.

In putting together this book we have drawn on the experience of a number of people in HR roles in large, respected organizations. They have been drawn from the UK public sector (Alan Warner, Director of People and Property Services, Hertfordshire County Council, and Dean Royles, Head of HR Capacity and Employment, Department of Health), from international companies (Neil Roden, Group HR Director RBS; Rick Brown, Vice President of HR Functional Excellence in Shell; Penny Davis, Head of HR, T-Mobile; Trevor Bromelow, Personnel Director of Siemens Business Services; Paul Birt, General Manager, HR Shared Services, and Rob Baston, Head of Compensation and Benefits, Siemens plc) and from those who have had a foot in both camps, i.e. Richie Furlong, ex Unilever and Cabinet Office. In addition, we have spoken to a wide range of people during the course of writing the book – some of whom have been quoted; all of whom have had some influence on our thinking.

In all three parts we will refer to how their organizations have dealt with the challenges we have identified. We hope this will give readers both confirmation that the issues we cover are real rather than imagined and confidence that they can be addressed.

Enjoy!

PART 1

The Story So Far

1 *The Changing Nature of HR*

From welfare to what?

The HR function of today is of course the product of its past. Its history starts in the late nineteenth century with a welfare role which was especially connected with the protection of women. The employment of welfare officers was found in those more paternalistic organizations that felt a moral obligation to improve the lot of their employees. However, it quickly became apparent that welfare officers could aid production by limiting absence and dealing with grievances. A still broader role for them arrived after the First World War when labour management became important. Wartime pressure to deliver unfettered production meant that agreements had to be made with trade unions and the requirement for industrial relations activities continued post war in several sectors of the economy. Dealing with trade unions remained the preserve of line management in many firms, with the emergent personnel function more concerned with recruitment, as well as welfare and absence. Not surprisingly, Personnel put down stronger roots in the new sectors of the economy that best survived the economic depression in the 1920/1930s, where the demand for labour was greatest and the market most competitive. Elsewhere, large-scale unemployment retarded the development of personnel management techniques.

The Second World War again benefited Personnel. The number of practitioners grew as government wanted help with increasing output, securing greater efficiency and smoothing industrial relations. Joint consultation, which had been pioneered by the likes of ICI, before the war, came to the fore during hostilities and afterwards. People management for at least the 40 years after 1945 was dominated by industrial relations and negotiation with trade unions – at least as viewed from the perspective of government (concerned with productivity) and the press (disputes made for good copy). Increasingly, personnel managers came to play a part in industrial relations work. The growth of local bargaining and shop stewards helped develop the site personnel presence. By the 1960s trade unionism had spread from blue collar workers in primary and manufacturing industries to white collar jobs, especially in the public sector, where a high density of trade union membership developed.

Because of the consequential industrial relations problems many organizations faced in the 1960s and 1970s, the industrial relations expert moved centre stage in the unionized parts of the public and private sectors. Personnel departments became dominated by those with skills and experience in this area. The tough-minded individuals that thrived in this environment benefited from the power of the trade unions: it justified their importance. This was particularly true in the 1970s in those areas of the UK economy where the politicization of the workforce, led by trade union militants, meant that disputes extended beyond the usual pay and conditions into wider questions of workers' rights and even into areas outside the employment relationship. In some parts of local government this coincided with the arrival of more ideologically driven council members in place of the more traditional, conservative politicians. Managers in direct service activities were no longer as able as before to cope with the industrial relations on their patch. They needed the support of personnel colleagues, if only to act as the referee between the warring parties. This was a real challenge to the capability and ingenuity of the personnel function.

Another theme in the contribution of the personnel function was that of providing an efficient administrative service within clearly defined procedures. In the public sector, Personnel came out of the 'establishment' office. As the name suggests the function was concerned with manpower numbers and processing work. Recruitment was the high-volume activity, with all the contractual paperwork that followed. Induction and job-related training was a linked task. Many establishment officers, particularly in the NHS, came from military backgrounds and were well suited to providing a well-organized and efficient service. The context was to deliver a very centralized and prescriptive approach to people management. They were not, however, change agents. It was a time of compliance to rules and regulations, not one of challenge.

A third dimension to the development of personnel management (besides industrial relations and efficient administration) was the growth in legal regulation of employment relationships, which fitted with the compliance model. This was nothing new. From the nineteenth-century Factory Acts onwards, government has legislated on workplace conditions and employment practices. The 1960s and 1970s, with entry to the EEC, saw an acceleration and extension of legal provision concerning recruitment, redundancy, pay and protection. As some of these laws were contentious, they would be added to the statute book only to be removed by the next administration. From the Donovan Commission of 1968 (on improving industrial relations) to the Bullock report of 1977 (on industrial democracy), from the Industrial Relations Act of the Heath government in 1971 to the prices and incomes policy of the Callaghan administration that followed, there was heated debate and much for the personnel manager to do by way of response. From commentary on potential legislation to its implementation where it was passed, the personnel function had to be more active and sophisticated.

An area of activity restricted to the larger and more sophisticated companies was the harnessing of the growing interest in business and strategic planning and alignment of the recruitment and development of employment with organizational requirements. The growth in manpower planning, the creation of the government's Manpower Services Commission and the launch of the Institute of Manpower Studies (predecessor of the Institute for Employment Studies) was testimony to this wish to match labour supply more effectively to demand.

Through the 1980s and early 1990s the effects of downsizing and large-scale manufacturing shutdown, legal restrictions on their activities, changing attitudes and symbolic defeats led to a steady decline in trade union membership and collective bargaining arrangements. This meant that industrial relations became less important in the workplace. Or, as Phil Murray of Hewitt (the management consultancy) succinctly put it: 'then along came Mrs Thatcher and made IR redundant'. At the same time high levels of unemployment meant reduced turnover and lower levels of recruitment activity.

So a different skill set was required. Personnel departments were moving beyond conflict management and containment to change management. This involved getting employees to accept new ways of working, to become more productive and to operate in a new performance-oriented setting. At the same time, Personnel was increasingly seen as management's agent in these efficiency programmes, often being on the receiving end of the workforce's frustrations at the effects of redundancy. But critics were concerned that Personnel was ill positioned as 'servants of (management) power', too eager to succumb to its 'overweaning' dominance (Guest, 1994).

There was a time when any aspiring HR director needed to have an industrial relations posting on their CV: no more! The emphasis moved to business credentials and skills in management development and organizational change. There had to be a greater alignment between business strategy and the activities of Personnel. And this grew beyond the very limited ambition for many firms – that of survival.

Enter HRM! The arrival of human resource management in the late 1980s was timely in that it coincided with this change of role and work content. It appeared to offer a distinctive philosophy of people management. It placed a general emphasis on maximizing the contribution of people resources to the success of the organization and on strategic integration of people management initiatives to deliver organizational benefits. It took a *unitarist* view of employment that all should work towards a common business purpose, emphasizing the legitimacy of management's right to be the author of change for the good of the organization.

In practice, HRM philosophy resonated with both the changing political scene, and the swing in the balance of power towards management and away from trade unions on the ground. Managers had a new confidence and a wish to assert their right to manage. The centralized management of the industrial relations dominated world also began to shift towards decentralization of power to business units. In the private sector this coincided with the creation of more complex business models to respond to a more challenging business environment. There was an emphasis on developing managerial skills and competencies, especially communication skills – getting the management message across to the workforce. New or refreshed ideas from the social sciences began to be taken on board, especially theories of motivation. So HR's contribution began to alter towards management education and development in line with HRM thinking. This more positive agenda still had HR at centre stage because the critical changes issues centred on organizational structures and people.

In the public sector, there was decentralization too but on a much bigger scale and with the added impetus of political will behind the changes. The Thatcherite imperative was to reduce the scale of the public sector through privatization and outsourcing, and to weaken trade unions through the decentralization of power. With respect to the latter, pay decisions were increasingly shifted away from review bodies, wages councils or employers associations to the direct employers of labour. For example, the Conservatives delegated responsibility for pay levels for civil servants to individual departments and agencies in the early 1990s. National collective bargaining in local government started to weaken in the late 1980s. Some local authorities in the south-east of England opted out of national pay rates for certain groups of employee in favour of local determination in order to recruit and retain staff in a tight labour market. Individual NHS Trusts arrived in 1988 with the aim of taking managerial decision-making closer to the patients. Trusts became free to set their own terms and conditions from 1992 until stopped by the incoming Labour government in 1997.

Outsourcing entered the service delivery vocabulary via compulsory competitive tendering (CCT), as the means by which it could be pursued in the public sector. The HR community had to learn about transfer of undertakings legislation. TUPE became a well-known term that generated a sense of foreboding in some and loathing in others. Especially in local government, HR practitioners, particularly those at the operational sharp end, found themselves in much more complex situations. The simple compliance model was no longer an option. Decisions had to be made: outsource a swathe of functions (as the likes of Berkshire, Westminster and Wandsworth did) or resist CCT as much as was feasibly possible (the route taken by, for example, Labour-held councils in the north of England). This meant HR had to get much closer to organizational decision-making to have some influence on the outcome. Or, if this was not possible, because the decisions taken were ideologically motivated, then HR had to get close to implementation to ensure that the process went as smoothly as possible. This meant not just simply operating to the letter of the law (TUPE has never been that simple), but interpreting it and deciding where it was safe to take risks. Ironically, despite the complexity of managing CCT, the cost-focused agenda that outsourcing implied led to HR itself being regarded as a financial overhead, not least when its services came under the outsourcing microscope.

The decentralization of power and divestment of 'non-core' activities was accompanied by the adoption of the HRM value set. Movement to this position was variable, often painfully slow, especially in the shift from an administrative to an operational focus, and from a reactive to a proactive approach. It gradually became more evident in public bodies that a greater degree of professionalism was required in HR. This was recognized at central government level with the Hesseltine White Paper of 1995 which argued for more specialization in managerial roles: out was the policy generalist and in were to come HR, finance, procurement experts. This objective is still being pursued. Andrew Turnbull, then head of the UK civil service, demanded greater professionalism. This has led to the Professional Skills for Government project in the civil service. For HR, the Modernizing People Management project is concerned with all the themes of this book – devolution, e-HR, customer focus, business partnership, and structural and process reform.

The Office of the Deputy Prime Minister funded a similar initiative for local government, called 'HR Capacity Building', originally run by the Employers Organisation for Local Government. This had a strong learning and coaching emphasis, but also included the development of a performance framework. The various audit processes, especially the Comprehensive Performance Assessment (CPA), are reinforcing the change. The CPA looks for evidence of workforce planning and development as fulfilment of the sector's pay and workforce strategy.

Devolution has often gone hand in hand with decentralization. The desire to limit the power of the corporate centre over policies and procedures has often been seen as consistent with the aim of maximizing line manager responsibilities for people management. The reasoning behind decentralization to increase local accountability – stripping out bureaucracy, producing faster decision-making, being more attuned to business needs – is similar to the arguments in favour of devolution.

In the late 1990s Hackney Borough Council adopted devolution as one of its most important principles in transforming the organization. Regarding Personnel devolution, the Hackney view was that 'if managers are held to be accountable for achieving their agreed outcomes it is essential they are able to make decisions on all matters relating to the employment of staff in their unit. This is essentially about allowing managers to manage' (Hackney Borough Council policy document).

The balance between what the line manager should do and what Personnel should do 'is as old as the function itself' (Hall and Torrington, 1998). When the latter conducted a survey of personnel managers in 1994/5 the commitment to devolution was evident then. They expected to see, and did see, an increased attempt to devolve given the intention of HRM to make sure that managers take their people management responsibilities seriously. A new role of personnel or HR consultant developed, to facilitate the work of line customers rather than impose a standardized solution. However, in some areas progress was slow. Research by the Institute of Personnel and Development (IPD) from 1995 (Hutchinson and Wood) suggested that many personnel functions had a reputation of being very centralized and controlling in relation to line management.

At the same time as the devolution of tasks to line managers was under debate, HR was being marginalized by the use of business process re-engineering. Where applied, it had the effect of pushing HR to the back seat because the efficiencies it sought were to be achieved by seeking process solutions to problems in ways that often made employees mere bystanders in the search for optimum design.

It was in this context that that US commentators spoke of HR as an 'endangered species', under threat from external consultants' service providers and line management. The view was that there was an opportunity for HR to impact on the business, but that it was not seizing the chance quickly enough to contribute to the change process. Lack of experience was given as one cause; being excluded by CEOs was another explanation (Brenner, 1996). In the UK, around the same time, research from Roffey Park and IPD suggested that HR continued to be overly 'reactive', slow and disjointed (Holbeche, 1998; Hutchinson and Wood, 1995). Academics were posing the question of whether HR could claim the role of strategic 'architect' or whether it was facing 'extinction as a discrete management body or coherent function' (Cunningham and Hyman, 1999). The IPD study worried that Personnel was seen as the 'poor relation with little power or influence,' especially where industrial relations was not important. Similarly, research undertaken in the mid-1990s suggested that HR was 'downstream' of the major business decisions in multidivisional companies; there to implement but not challenge (Purcell and Ahlstrand, 1994). Somewhat later research by Buyens and de Vos (2001) uncovered more positive attitudes amongst senior managers, but the same restricted role for HR. They found that top managers were supportive of HR's role in transformation and change, but it was to 'concretise and translate [management] decisions, taking account of their implications for employees'. Early input from the function was valued, but would not be the basis on which decisions were taken.

But at the same time as these concerns were being raised, HR was itself moving on. Spurred on by business gurus and academics such as David Ulrich, HR was increasingly seeking to play a more proactive role, to get closer to business decisions and have a strategic and longer-term influence. Those companies in the vanguard of change took advantage of the newly emerging organizational models and of the search for efficiency and improved customer service to launch new forms of HR structure. In came shared services, business partners and centres of expertise. Process improvements in HR services were also sought to aid effective delivery, assisted by new technology that both speeded up and simplified administrative processes, and allowed tasks to be further devolved through manager and employee self-service.

The tight labour market of the late 1990s also proved to be a boon for HR. The business requirement was to acquire and retain skills. The 'war for talent' (Michaels et al., 2001) suggested that competitive pressures necessitated new strategies to attract quality recruits. High fliers were in short supply, but so too were able and experienced staff with specialist skills. The demography of the labour market also helped. With an ageing workforce, there was an even greater premium on securing youthful talent, especially since there was a belief that the newer generation of workers was more likely to be fickle in its attitudes to employment: less loyal and more mobile. Moreover, the feminization of the workforce encouraged policy innovation, particularly around working-time flexibility, and posed questions about whether HR policies were sufficiently geared to the female worker.

The intellectual backdrop to these developments was also favourable. The new century has seen a revived interest in human capital and its contribution to business success. Innumerable research papers have sought to prove the connection between employee inputs and business outputs. People can offer more than simply being a passive conduit in the process chain; they can transform the process; they can change the nature of the outcome. The name of the game has moved to harnessing the creative capabilities of the workforce, as we grow the knowledge economy. HRM (at least in the soft version) has helped this development by seeing people as an asset, not a cost.

Lessons from history

The history lesson just delivered had a purpose: it should have demonstrated that HR's role has been continually changing, along with its name. It has had to be responsive to the changing context within which it has been operating and to key events in the external environment. There have been longstanding tensions in the nature of the role. In the early days of personnel management there was a strong thread of paternalistic protection of employees' welfare needs, but this was balanced by the aim to maximize productivity and efficiency. Using more contemporary language: is HR the social conscience of the organization? Can it be the employees' 'champion', to quote Ulrich (1997)? Or is it to be the business partner, linking organizational strategy to people management? Are these roles necessarily in conflict?

A similar distinction can be drawn between 'administrative expert' (Ulrich again) who ensures an effective bureaucracy and the change agent aiming to be innovative in employment practice. No one would deny that both activities are important and should be performed, but can they be combined effectively in an integrated function?

Then there is the content of the role. As we have seen, personnel tasks have broadened from predominantly welfare into resource planning and recruitment, industrial relations and legal expertise, training and organizational design/development. There is also the move away from personnel generalists to increasing specialization as the sub-disciplines of HR have become more complex in theory and execution.

Frequently too, HR seems to have felt under a degree of threat, though this has varied both over time and between organizations. For example, in 1989 British Airways halved its HR department, devolving much of its activities to line management. Today, it is the BBC axing over half of HR jobs. In 1994, Industrial Relations Services reported cuts to central personnel function: 'hands-on' administrative tasks were devolved to managers freeing up time for the corporate HR department to take on 'policy making and an advisory function' (Industrial Relations Services, 1994). Is this so different an ambition compared with now, even if the terms used have altered somewhat? Similarly, an IPD report (Hutchinson and Wood, 1995) stated that the drivers for change for HR then were the need for cost control in a more competitive environment, having a stronger customer orientation, greater decentralization of decision-making and the poor past performance of Personnel: a set of challenges that still would be recognized by many organizations today.

Some HR directors have been confident that their contribution has been valued. Yet it has also been true that, from being key colleagues, other HR directors have fallen from positions of power as the world has left them behind. Sometimes this has been the result of seismic shifts in the world of work, such as in the industrial relations climate. At other times, change has been more gradual, or more parochial – a cost-cutting exercise in HQ.

During HR's journey to the present day, the skill requirements and personal attributes demanded of the HR community have adjusted with the role changes. The refocusing of HR has occurred at variable speeds and in a variety of ways in the different sectors. Now, there seems to be a greater degree of convergence. Naturally, there are still differences between organizations, but these seem to be less to do with sector, more to do with size and complexity.

Writing in 2006, we feel there is much reason for HR to be optimistic in the UK. There is a stable economy, healthy demand for labour and competition for talent. Investment in human capital seems to be worth the money, not just for reasons of recruitment and retention, but also to improve organizational performance. Organizational change, often in a global setting, is offering both new and familiar challenges.

So where does the function stand now?

2 *The HR Function Now*

Its role

One might think that with the now widespread use of the term 'HR' and the dominance of the market, extending into more and more aspects of life, that HRM would hold centre stage. However, things are more complicated than that. Despite the theory, in practice HRM has not proved to be a single, unified concept, but a varied approach to people management – or, as described by Keenoy (1989), 'a patchwork-quilt concept'. Some versions, according to Williams (1993), emphasize the *human* part of the equation (by talking of the importance of employee development); others concentrate on *resources* (emphasizing their utilitarian role as part of the corporate business strategy). A similar distinction (Storey, 1989) has been drawn between *soft HRM* (concentrating on communication, motivation and leadership) and *hard HRM* (emphasizing the economic, numerical and calculative aspects). So in one set of models of HRM, people are seen as a cost to be controlled, whereas in the other they are an asset to be exploited.

The distinction between the different schools of HRM seems to be more about the means to achieve these goals than any challenge to the primacy of the organization's will. Yet the means are important. In the UK there has been a shift from a sense in which within personnel management efficiency and social justice could be reconciled to the HRM position that employers and employees have mutual goals. In personnel management of the 1960s and 1970s, differences between the stakeholders could be accommodated or negotiated. It was acceptable in this more pluralist model for commitment from employees to be conditional (e.g. we will stay with this organization if it delivers against its promises). In HRM there are no such half measures or ambiguities. The people management aspects of organizational life are combined with the organizational to deliver an integrated and strategic approach. Organizational values are in step with business needs. All are required to sign up to the shared goals. And in the more individualist orientation of HRM, it is employees themselves who are expected to share the vision. There is less room for a collectivist perspective, certainly for a trade union view that subscribes to any other economic philosophy than capitalism.

These differences between personnel management and HRM help both describe and explain the multifaceted nature of HR's role within organizations. Whilst the somewhat sterile debate on the meaning of HRM has, one hopes, finished, the various views on the best way to achieve efficiency remain, and these hark back to this earlier debate on soft versus hard approaches to people management.

What we are left with is a wide variety of conceptions of HR's role. It may be a permanent *advisor* to the line or to the organization more generally. It may be a *consultant* engaged to assist where a need is identified by a management customer. It may be a *partner* sharing in the development of solutions. It may a *guardian* of policies and practices. It may be a *leader* creating change or a *representative* of employees' views. These roles are in part driven by the wide range of expectations of HR from a variety of stakeholders — senior management, line managers, employees — who inevitably try to influence what the function should be doing and how it should be doing it. There has been a greater tendency under HRM to give more attention to senior management's wishes because of the imperative to align HR policies and practices to strategic business objectives. By contrast, HR has become less and less employee-centred as time has moved on. Many senior HR managers have taken to heart the Personnel Lead Body's injunction, given as long ago as 1993, that 'Personnel directors have to behave as GMs with personnel specialism rather than personnel people with GM tendencies.' This business orientation and the effects of devolution of activities to line management have, as we shall see, led to some companies putting significant distance between HR and employees.

HRM thinking has affected the HR function, beyond its name, in other ways. A self-conscious move from old-style Personnel to new wave HR has developed in many organizations, aiming to re-orientate the role. Oversimplifying things, there is an intended shift from:

tactician	to	strategist
firefighter		risk manager
short-term operator		long-term visionary
navel gazer		lookout
controller		facilitator
soloist		integrator
passenger		driver
reactor		creator
off-the-shelf distributor		bespoke tailor
police officer		advisor
traditionalist		innovator
welfare officer		diagnostician

So there is a self-conscious, 'modernization' process that wants to see HR as playing a more strategic, business-aligned role which means it has to look over longer-term horizons and be more of a change agent. This aspiration was well expressed by a senior manager at Hewlett Packard (HP) who described his role as being to 'steer this organization along a winding and unpredictable road. We have to be sufficiently agile to adapt as the road winds, and be foresightful about what might be ahead' (quoted in Gratton, 1998). This adjustment is not just because HR wants to reposition itself, it is because it is operating in a faster-moving, highly competitive and increasingly global environment. Speed of thought, flexibility of response and imagination of the future are all required to survive and prosper. Could the HR man from HP have imagined the merger with Compaq four years later?

In reality, some of this adjustment is not as straightforward as it might seem, and certainly not as black and white. All seem to be agreed that HR has a strategic role to play. This has to be done as an integral part of the business activity. The relationship with employees is more contentious. These days any self-respecting HR professional would run a mile rather than be called a welfare worker, and many private sector companies have either outsourced or externalized activities such as counselling and occupational health. Nonetheless, the renewed interest in employee well-being means that the relationship between, say, health and absence, or health and working hours, is very much back on the agenda. This means that HR has to have an approach to stress, work–life balance, etc., even if some services handling specific tasks are externally provided. It is no longer sufficient to say that XYZ company provides our employee counselling service: it is important to know whether employee well-being has improved as a result. And, indeed, it is necessary for HR to work with the provider to get feedback on themes and emerging issues in a structured way so that it may still protect employee interests without having to undertake the task itself.

There is a similar tale with respect to HR administration. Some organizations have sought to marginalize the activity by outsourcing it on the basis that it is non-core and/or can be more efficiently undertaken elsewhere. Moving administration into a shared services centre has also been done for efficiency reasons. But the aim of these decisions in many instances is to ensure that HR concentrates on (or only performs in-house) the high 'added-value' activities. This means HR is always playing the strategic business partner role, never the 'clerk of the works' role (Tyson and Fell, 1986). Other organizations take the view that getting administration right is a core business in itself. It gives permission to tackle higher value-added tasks. Failure to perform denies HR access to a strategic role. As an HR director from a manufacturing company argued against some of his team, it is not a case of moving up the value chain or emphasizing the top half of Ulrich's quadrants (see Figure 2.1), but of being competent in all aspects of the role, including administration. Again, even if HR has stepped away from the doing, it still needs to get in place good feedback mechanisms so that it understands any issues or trends, as the senior manager will still hold the business partner accountable for the whole HR service – even if the function no longer has involvement in all its activities.

This may only be a debate about means. All surely agree that there needs to be a smooth running administrative activity. The difference of view could be between those organizations that believe this objective can best be achieved through externalization of service delivery and those that think that in-house delivery is more effective. Yet, the manner in which the marginalization of HR administration has taken place suggests that some feel like Henry II: 'who will rid me of this turbulent priest?' They think of HR administration as the king did of Thomas Becket – obstructing progress towards a desirable goal. Certainly, many HR staff have been on the receiving end of downsizing and job redesign (even if they haven't been murdered at their workplace). If the comparison seems a little extreme, there is a real contrast in the language used between those fervent in their belief that getting the HR 'basics' right is essential and those who talk of 'getting rid' of 'transactional' activities in a sort of 'out of sight, out of mind' way. Those who take the latter position, though, will have been reminded by the British Airways catering dispute in the summer of 2005 of the risks involved in taking such an approach. Outsourcing something that is meant to be no longer critical to core operation still warrants management time in overseeing the service provision. Failure to give such attention can come at quite a cost!

Source: Ulrich (1997)

Figure 2.1   Ulrich's HR role structure model

A third area of debate, and perhaps more contentious, or at least not so clear cut, is the degree of operational support HR gives to line management. One view is that HR's expertise is really in its technical professionalism and this is what managers want from HR. Put simply, it is HR's USP. According to those who hold this view, managers want professional skills in recruitment, employee relations or training and development. Sure, they require HR to be business-savvy, but they don't want HR so much in the clouds that it can't contribute to the day to day operational business. Penny Davis of T-Mobile, for example, believes line customers want HR's operational support and expertise. As a function responsive to customer needs, she believes the line should receive what it asks for. The alternative view is that such an approach draws HR back into the responsive, firefighting role it has been trying to escape. It means holding the line's hand in recruitment interviews and disciplinary hearings rather than devolving these activities to where they should be performed. The risk is that line managers do not develop their people management skills; they continue to rely on HR.

Again, for many HR functions, this argument is a matter of degree – how much operational HR support is given – not a theological dispute. It is, as we will soon describe, a matter for many organizations of how these tasks are performed and by whom. Some organizations have structured themselves precisely to control (and in some cases, certainly, minimize) the type of operational involvement HR has with day-to-day people management tasks. In others, the devolution discussion has led to a greater degree of HR involvement than might be expected.

A fourth matter of dispute concerns HR's governance role. Oversimplifying, in some organizations HR does not want to be seen as a policeman in any way. The extent of devolution of responsibilities to line management, its positioning as an agent of line management and its customer service orientation have really precluded HR from having a governance function. HR facilitates what management wants to do; it does not challenge it. It advises, not directs. The role of 'prop and cop' (an American manager quoted in Eisenstat, 1996) supporting the line to solve its problems and acting as the corporate enforcer to prevent managers breaking the rules is rejected. This view is well expressed by Richard Allen, at the time head of HR at Defra: 'personnel had the reputation of being the police and being unhelpful. That's not good when your purpose should be to provide a service' (Griffiths, 2004).

Although HR directors in other organizations would not wish to deny the facilitation or advisory role, they would want to assert the right of HR to prevent managers damaging the organization or contravening agreed rules. This may come sharply into focus over legal issues. Proponents of this view would say that in some cases it is not advice that is being given but direction: managers cannot be allowed to act in an unlawful manner. In other words, a policeman role is still being performed. It would probably not be described that way: it is more likely to be called the guardian of agreed rules, standards or values. The key question is when HR would intervene and how. The circumstances can vary from handling incidents of managerial bullying or whistleblowing (where HR might be more proactive) to decisions on outsourcing or downsizing (where HR might be more hesitant to challenge, even if it felt the decision misconceived). To what extent is HR *always* servant to the line master? The answer to the question goes back to the beginning of the debate: if HR is such an integral part of the management activity, does it need to have an independent voice to warn or object? In this discussion, HR's relationship to the employees is key.

The legal role can be interpreted more broadly to include an auditing and review function. This would be seen as legitimate in organizations where maintaining legal compliance and conforming to organizational standards is seen as important. It tends to be more commonplace in public sector organizations where the public interest requires frequent audits and where there is an assumption that organizations should be whiter than white in their observance of legislation. Conducting periodic equal pay reviews is an example of ensuring compliance. The private sector is less concerned with compliance, as it gives more emphasis to managerial flexibility. Managers are expected to manage pay or performance in a way that achieves corporate objectives. Whilst managers are of course expected to keep within the law, the HR function is less likely to be asked to check whether strict observance is being achieved. Adherence to standards may be more important in multinational companies where observance of corporate rules and values may need to be more explicitly encouraged in locations where what is or is not acceptable behaviour is more ambiguous.

A final area of contention to report is the composition of the HR function itself – how far does it extend? We are not talking about add-on activities – such as responsibility for catering, cleaning, health and safety, etc. – we are interested in the definition of the core function. For example, some companies exclude organization development (OD) from HR, seeing it as an independent change agency. By contrast, in others, HR is called OD in order to assert a different kind of animal – a more business-focused, problem-solving function.

Practice has also differed with respect to training and development. In some organizations it is integrated into HR; in others it is quite separate; whereas in a third model technical training has been separated from management development with the latter in HR. The CIPD director general claimed recently (Pickard, 2005a) that the move was towards greater integration of HR and development. He of course has a vested interest in hoping that this integration takes place. However, there is a good reason why the separation between HR and development is becoming less common, and that is the increasingly holistic approach being taken to people management. This would suggest that artificial barriers between, say, training and development and resourcing or reward are unhelpful if the employment proposition is based on a combination of people management elements. ASTD (the American Society of Training and Development) is taking the same approach. It has shifted its activities away from technical training and towards the strategic impact of learning and development (linked with other people management functions) on business performance. It is influenced by the fact learning and development functions in leading companies are spending an increasingly proportion of their time on such things as organizational effectiveness, OD and performance improvement. According to the views of training and development specialists reported at the CIPD 2005 HRD conference, there is also a shared need of HR and development to demonstrate relevance. In fact, research by the Institute for Employment Studies (IES) (Carter *et al.*, 2002) suggests that in a large majority of organizations training and development reports to the HR director, but under a whole range of different organizational structures, from centralized to devolved, from largely in-house to largely outsourced. A key factor is what is the content of the training and development work. How much is it training delivery (generic or technical)? How much is the role concerned with design and evaluation? And how much is it about advice or facilitation?

So much for the changes and issues for HR in performing its role, but what of the key relationships it has with its various stakeholders?

Its relationships

WITH LINE MANAGERS

Despite the rhetoric of devolution as a primary goal for HR over more than 20 years, in practice what has been devolved has varied greatly. Research by Torrington (1998) suggested that on some subjects it was already common for management to develop strategy without HR participation (especially regarding work design or quality initiatives). In only a small proportion of organizations did HR continue to take the lead principally on recruitment and employee relations. On the vast majority of subjects and in a majority of organizations, there was a clear line/HR partnership at work in a wide variety of areas, including training and development.

Industrial Relations Services' 1998 survey similarly illustrated the growth in devolution over the previous three years, with aspects of recruitment and performance management processes in the vanguard. The survey also showed partial devolution on many activities.

Since then, new technology has been pushing out the boundaries of what line managers can do. Organizations are making use of e-HR to enable managers to conduct administrative tasks online (e.g. booking training courses) or to make independent decisions (e.g. changing subordinates' salaries, recruiting staff, etc.). HR may set the rules of the game, but it allows managers to make the decisions. This keeps HR out of the day-to-day issues, in terms of both operationalizing policies and administering them; for example salary updates bypass HR, being entered from the manager's desk straight to payroll.

Despite the opportunities e-HR presents, more up-to-date evidence suggests that the devolution position is relatively unchanged. The line and HR continue in partnership over people management. On some issues one party may take more of a lead; on other issues it is the reverse, with shared responsibility for a third set of activities. Thus, according to a CIPD survey (2003a), half the organizations reported that recruitment and selection are shared, whereas in nearly a third the line was reported to be in control. By contrast, though employee relations is shared in 40 per cent of companies, in half of them HR takes the lead. Reward is even more HR–biased, training and development more shared.

These figures suggest a consolidation of the previous position of partial devolution, rather than a step change. The boxed example may be typical.

> Rolls-Royce has gradually strengthened line responsibility for HR, but really follows a partnership model. The company believes this to be more effective than abrupt devolution. A lot of focus has been given to key HR processes and explicit guidance has been given on how managers should approach them.

Why might devolution have not gone further? The research of the 1990s (e.g. Bevan and Hayday, 1994; McGovern *et al.*, 1997; Thornhill and Saunders, 1998; Cunningham and Hyman, 1999) gives some pointers to reasons why progress has been slower than hoped. The research suggested problems with:

- line management disposition to take on these tasks
- absence of senior management encouragement

- fears of work overload
- lack of people management skills
- absence of people management training
- lack of support from HR colleagues
- lack of line interest in people management policy-making.

Tackling the first question, there are a number of dimensions on whether managers are sufficiently disposed to discharge the people management aspects of their role and they link in with the other points. The research suggested that not all managers accepted that people management was an important component of their job. Many remained unwilling to accept that devolved staff management responsibility is a legitimate part of their job. They would rather concentrate on the technical aspects of their work. They had plenty enough on their plate and people management was often regarded as difficult. They did not see the relevance of working with their staff to achieve business goals, except in a narrow, instrumental sense. They were more concerned with the 'whats' of achieving business success than the 'hows'. There was little inclination to engage staff or encourage their participation, or, if there was, it was too piecemeal in nature. The research suggested that where neither senior management nor HR gave managers contrary direction, managers sought the easiest route to achieve their objectives. In some cases senior management, far from leaving a vacuum, inhibited their managers from exercising their people management duties. Cunningham and Hyman (1999) reported that even where managers were better disposed to take their people management tasks seriously, they were handicapped by 'the dominance of "harder" priorities'. And Gratton's research (1997) with 'leading edge' companies found that even in such organizations HR issues were a low priority.

Another reason why devolution developed more slowly than intended was because, it was alleged, there were no incentives for managers to demonstrate their interest in employee issues. Studies pointed to the absence of people management responsibilities in performance objectives and the lack of reward incentives regarding people management. Hitting business targets gave managers a payback rather than motivating staff (other than indirectly). McGovern *et al.*, (1997) suggested, that in these circumstances, management involvement in people management practices was 'often a matter of personal, rather than institutional motivation'.

The third critical impediment to devolution was that managers felt they had insufficient time in relation to the rest of their workload to give proper attention to performance management, training and development or even simple 'one-to-one contact'. Some of their difficulties stemmed from the effects of downsizing, delayering and even globalizing business activities, leaving managers with large spans of control. It is hard to give time to people issues if you have the responsibility for so many staff.

The next limitation to devolution was found to be that line managers did not feel they had the skills to perform people management tasks, even if they had the time. Weak skills and limited experience also led to a shortage of confidence. Managers were concerned about accepting responsibility for people management issues where they felt exposed through inexperience or lack of knowledge or capability. A lack of training and competence among managers and supervisors seemed to be partly the result of low prioritization, partly through a belief that formal training was unnecessary because skills were 'best picked up through experience' (Cunningham and Hyman, 1999) and partly due to a shortage of time to train.

Resistance to devolution from some in HR was reported to have slowed the devolution process still further. The causes seem to have varied:

- a sense of the function losing power and control
- giving up activities that staff felt confident to perform, were good at and were appreciated by the line
- fears over job security if line managers were proficient in operational HR
- concerns that managers were ill equipped to deal with people management issues.

The combination of disposition, skills, time and management pressure not only inhibited managers from taking on tasks from HR or from effectively managing their staff, it also limited their participation in HR policy-making. The research we are reporting suggested that managers were not adequately participating in the formulation of HR policies or were not in tune with what the function wished to do with the development of people management. This seemed to be either because of workload pressures or through a breakdown in communication (Bevan and Hayday, 1994). Where HR itself was doubtful about devolution, it seemed that it had 'a strong desire to control the design and implementation of personnel policies and practice, while at the same time emphasising the critical role of line managers in delivering them' (Bevan and Hayday, 1994). In other words, the function was trying to have its cake and eat it!

There is a separate but related point: whether line management was satisfied with the contribution from HR, whatever the devolution deal. Again the research evidence suggests that it many cases it has not been. Only half the respondents in a Watson Wyatt survey in 2002 rated HR favourably (Pfau and Cundiff, 2002). Where views were more positive they related to the provision of administrative services, rather than to leadership or advice. Whittaker and Marchington (2003) summarized the complaints under four headings:

- HR is insufficiently in touch with business realities.
- HR unduly constrains line management autonomy.
- The function is unresponsive and slow.
- Policies developed by HR are good in theory but difficult to implement in practice.

Cunningham and Hyman (1999) reported some line reaction to HR services in even starker terms. Managers saw HR as uninterested and remote, even obstructive, leading a number to question the value of the function.

Management frustration with HR has been one of the drivers for devolution. This frustration may have resulted either from the line's irritation at the competence of HR in delivering a service or from restrictions placed on its ability to manage staff in the way it wishes. The combination of these two factors has been behind much of the philosophical repositioning of HR and behind the justification for restructuring the function.

Devolution should indeed be giving managers more freedom to manage. HR, through backing out of day-to-day matters, would then have the space to help shape the strategic direction of people management. As the research showed, however, the aspiration to devolve is ahead of the practice in many organizations. Progress seems to have been inhibited both because of reservations in the line community and in HR. HR may not wish to let go, hoping to continue to control people management. The line may not want to pick up the baton. It could be, too, that, for all the talk of e-HR, the simplification of administrative tasks is not taking place as rapidly as one would suppose. We will return to these points in the section on new relationships with line management in Chapter 5.

WITH SENIOR MANAGEMENT/BUSINESS LEADERS

Over many years surveys have been conducted to ascertain the proportion of HR directors on the main boards of companies, since having a 'seat at the top table' is an indication of functional vitality. They have not always proved happy reading. They demonstrate the poor standing of the HR function in the eyes of CEOs (see e.g. Guest, 2000), with its attachment to 'cuddly' or 'pet' theories or 'gimmicks' (Syedain, 1999). HR leaders may find themselves reporting to chief operating officers or administrative general managers, not to the CEO. They are denied access to the top team on either a formal or a regular basis.

Yet, whilst there are reasons to be discouraged in some organizations, in others the role of HR with respect to senior decision-makers has been changing for the better. With a younger breed of executives, more attuned to the requirement to sell the organization to employees in a consumerist society with a tight labour market, there is a greater acceptance of the importance of people management. Whereas once the senior HR director would be called in to 'mop up' strategic business decisions, it is expected in the more enlightened organizations that the senior HR professionals now contribute to the debate on what the strategic aims of the organization are in the first place. At least the hope is that HR has moved on from the position of being the 'handmaidens' (Storey, 1992) of the business. The reality is that there is likely to be a wide spectrum of relationships between HR and senior management: from HR directors as true business partners to HR leaders without a seat on the executive committee, let alone the board, with limited influence.

Where an individual organization's HR sits on this spectrum is a consequence of the personal credibility of the HR director, the stance taken by the CEO and senior colleagues, and the culture of the organization. CEOs can be hostile to HR, obstructive or indifferent to it, helpfully supportive or suffocating in their interest. It is a good HR leader who can persuade the top team to operate in the way that suits the function best.

WITH EMPLOYEES

As we described in the section on the changing nature of HR, there has long been a tension between HR in its role as support to employees and HR as an agent of management. With the advent of HRM, and to some extent with the decline in importance of industrial relations, the emphasis seems to have decisively shifted towards HR as unequivocally integrated with other management activities. This is true whether one applies the soft HRM model (employees and management share common goals) or hard model (where employees are merely one set of resources to be utilized). In many ways, one could argue that this is a non-debate: HR was and always will be a management entity, pursuing business objectives whether that be through negotiations with trade unions, downsizing or, even, management development programmes.

And yet, the issue is subtler than that. Part of the reason that employees cannot be treated just like any other resource is that they have minds of their own. They can leave the company, go on strike, speed up or slow down production, decide to stay in bed one day more after an illness, etc. This means they need to be managed in a different way. A *raison d'être* for HR (maybe the *raison d'être*) is its ability to understand what motivates and demotivates employees. In that context, according to Ulrich (1997), one of the roles for HR is to be the 'employee champion'. Yet in many organizations HR has tended to disengage from the relationship with employees. This has come about for a number of reasons.

With its desire to get closer 'to the business' and to ditch any sense that it is a welfare function, HR has put more distance between itself and staff. There is no question of on what side of the fence HR sits. Time was when HR was seen as being too close to employees or, more particularly, too cosy with their representatives. One of the authors was described as a 'snake in the grass' by his management colleagues for being too pally with employee representatives. The risk of HR falling into the trap of being the people's champion has receded with the decline of industrial relations. Then the boundaries between HR's role as management representative and employee advocate were deliberately blurred in order that HR could exercise influence with both 'sides'. Now, with its position as management member even clearer than it was, HR conversely may not now be seen as such an effective conduit between management and employees. The business partner role we will describe below reinforces HR's participation in the management team as an equal member, but increases the likelihood that HR is one of 'them', not sympathetic to 'us'.

The manifestation of HR as a management agent was particularly seen in HR's central role in the downsizing exercises of the 1980s and 1990s. The significance of these and future exercises is that they went beyond cutting jobs to achieve survival to cutting jobs to increase profitability – to satisfy shareholders. This made some staff feel that HR was a 'management stooge'. This impression was reinforced by a change philosophy that suggested that not only was the concept of jobs for life dead, but that workplace survival was down to the employee. Paternalism was gone, replaced by individual resilience – a sort of social Darwinist survival of the fittest. HR articulated this new approach, talking about employability instead of job security, portfolio careers in place of continuity of employment.

This perception that HR is merely there to do management's bidding is emphasized by the tendency of some line management to blame disagreeable, or even merely contentious, people-related business decisions on HR. Instead of seeing their role as defenders of management policy, it is too easy for some managers to shirk responsibility and transfer it to HR. The scapegoating of the function thereby reinforces the negative impression in the minds of some employees.

This is linked to the above-mentioned transfer of people management responsibility from HR to line management. In many organizations, it is a cardinal principle that line managers are the party that deals with the needs and problems of employees. HR's role is one of business support, offering a policy and procedural framework with advice and guidance when required.

The physical consolidation of HR into centralized, shared service centres, furthermore, has meant that employees do not come into physical contact so much with HR colleagues. Those organizations that have the service centres at one of the larger employee sites understandably report much higher interaction with employees, and it should be said much greater mutual satisfaction. In other organizations, employees have to be satisfied with contact down the telephone wire or via computer. The advent of e-HR means that more communication with employees is done in this way. As an Apple employee pithily put it: 'my HR representative is not a human being but a floppy disk' (Eisenstat, 1996). For some tasks, this lack of face-to-face interaction may not matter. On sensitive topics employees may prefer human contact.

So a redefinition of HR's role, together with the impact of physical distancing by means of technology and centralization of services, has meant that there is a strong perception that HR is less connected with employees. Those who are most concerned with this direction of travel include those who, as we shall see, are the most doubtful about e-HR and the new HR structural model.

WITH EX-EMPLOYEES

Increasingly, the organization (and often the HR function) is having to spend more time on its relationship with former employees, perhaps driven by two fundamentals. Firstly, the fact that many ex-employees remain consumers (and, one hopes, positively so) of the organization's products or services and bad treatment beyond employment can lead to lost business. Secondly, with the UK certainly experiencing a tightening of the labour pool, especially in terms of clerical 'white collar' roles, the need to attract back past employees is becoming an increasingly important imperative.

There are many good examples of both factors at work. Financial institutions such as RBS spend time and effort in maintaining relationships with their pensioner population by proactively offering them services like insurance discounts. This activity is led by the HR function. Many retail companies such as M&S, B&Q and Tesco have created innovative ways of keeping in touch with past employees (especially given the peak periods which demand seasonal cover) to make the process of resourcing easier.

Relationships with ex-employees will be affected by the pensions debate. Those who have enjoyed final salary schemes know what pension to expect. Those on money-purchase schemes are less certain, as it depends on investment returns and annuity rates. What will relations be like with pensioners whose income has fallen below 'acceptable' levels? Will there be a comeback on their former employers? And, if so, what will be the organization's stance?

WITH EXTERNAL STAKEHOLDERS

An additional element in the broadening expectations of senior management is that increasingly many HR directors and business partners are being asked to contribute to the management of external stakeholders. Many financial institutions, for example, now expect the HR director to meet the Financial Services Authority (FSA) in response to increasing questions on management capability and 'bench strength', as regulation and concerns over controls of high-powered firms increase in the wake of past failures. HR has to demonstrate that the necessary succession planning is in place, along with appropriate risk management and governance processes. This may include working with the board's remuneration committee to frame reward arrangements that will satisfy shareholders, which seems to be an increasingly difficult challenge because scrutiny of executive pay has grown with the size of the pay packet and with the complex nature of the link to performance.

We reported in the section on HR's role in Chapter 1 on HR's need to be involved in external affairs. This consists both of lobbying for the right regulatory frameworks or participating in the debate. Many HR directors believe that active participation is required through *ad hoc* membership of relevant commissions (like Kingsmill) or standing membership of the appropriate committees of bodies like the CBI or EEF. Others will be active in sectoral or professional bodies.

Trends in structures and delivery mechanisms

Under the twin pressures of becoming more efficient and becoming more effective, HR functions in many large, complex organizations have moved (or intend to move) to new organizational structures. In some cases they have followed the lead of other parts of the business or indeed been an integral part of the change. In other cases the HR function has been in the vanguard.

Led by the HR director, it has had its own reasons to reform. One of these reasons has been a realization that the function has to be more customer focused in the way it delivers its services – and this might be a matter of time, manner or cost. The other is the point made earlier that HR wishes to reposition itself. Modernization of service delivery has allowed the function to focus on its strategic and change management activities.

> In Unilever, HR drove the introduction of HR shared services. There was a recognition that cost needed to be taken out of the business, as margins were being driven down, and that HR needed to make its contribution. Moreover, HR was out of kilter with the new operating business model. This had moved to cross national structures, whilst HR was still nationally aligned. This meant that HR was in the wrong place to influence business decisions. The shared services and business partner model achieved the twin objectives of greater efficiency and better fit with business structures.

A key facilitator of these developments has been the arrival of more sophisticated technology that has speeded up processing and allowed remote and integrated operation. We will cover this in more detail shortly.

So, how have these changes been achieved? There are three elements to the new model. These are the creation of:

1. shared service operations
2. business partner roles
3. centres of expertise/excellence/competence (with or without a 'consultancy pool').

These elements have been added to the traditional HR corporate centre. The idea behind shared services is that activities performed locally by business units are re-engineered and streamlined and then combined so that the business units 'share' the service delivery solution. So, there is a common provision of services with (in theory) the nature of the services determined primarily by the customer. The 'user is the chooser' to use Ulrich's graphic expression (1995). In practice, many shared service operations have been introduced as cost-saving measures. As a result, they have taken on more the form of centralization than customization of services (Reilly and Williams, 2003). Although cost may more often than not be the primary driver to launching shared services, there are often secondary benefits that organizations are hoping to realize, especially improving quality.

What is included in the HR shared services ambit varies considerably from organization to organization. The principal components are the undertaking of administrative tasks and the provision of information and advice through intranets and call centres. Some companies add consultancy or project support from a shared services centre. In another variation, individual casework may form part of the shared services' responsibilities.

The bread-and-butter activities of the shared services function include:

• payroll changes (on/off/variation)
• administration of employee records
• relocation services
• recruitment administration
• administration of benefits (including flexible systems and share schemes)
• company car provision

- administration of pensions
- employee welfare support
- training administration
- absence monitoring
- management information.

Not all these services are included in every shared service centre. Some are outsourced. Others, as a matter of choice, are excluded because they are aligned with delivery activities that do not form part of the shared services operation – recruitment administration might sit with a separate recruitment function or training administration with the training and development service.

Services centres mostly provide information or advice to managers and, sometimes to employees. Most systems these days try to steer users to the corporate intranet to have their questions answered. As shown in Figure 2.2 at British Telecom, for example, 95 per cent of questions are dealt with by the web and, in a less technological organization, the Department of Work and Pensions' new delivery model assumes 80 per cent of queries are satisfied at this stage. Helplines are supposed to be restricted to non-standard problems or to interpretation of more common problems. More complicated issues are escalated to a more experienced or skilled operator. For those of a more fundamental policy nature, the centre of expertise is brought in. To give an idea of the difference: at IBM's Ask HR, the average routine phone call was dealt with in two minutes, whilst the target time for a more complex question passed to a specialist was two days (Industrial Relations Services, 1999).

The name of the unit that receives incoming calls, contact or call centre, can indicate difference of orientation. Those that emphasize effective customer handling will tend to staff up with those with the same skill set as is to be found in call centres. They will probably pass on a higher proportion of calls than those contact centres that use professionally trained HR people, where knowledge is more at a premium than telephone skills. The choice between the two models partly depends on what sort of service structure the organization wants (how many calls are expected to be escalated) and partly on the customer base – how sophisticated it is.

It is now commonplace to have an HR person in a customer-facing role; this is usually described now as a business partner or sometimes advisor, account manager or relationship manager. Business partners may either report to a line manager or to a senior HR manager,

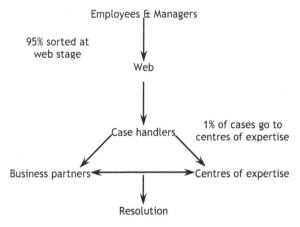

Figure 2.2   BT's problem-solving model

usually, but not always, separately from the shared services organization. This individual, or at most small team, is expected to support their line clients in terms of strategic development, organizational design and change management. This is described by some as offering 'transformational' activities, to be contrasted with transactional services. HR administrative services in support of the business units are, of course, provided from the shared service centre, leaving the business partner to act as a broker between line customers and the shared services operation. The business partner will confirm the service provision, perhaps, or may even be involved in the commissioning process, but will not take part in the delivery of services. Neither managers nor employees are expected to trouble the HR business partner with day-to-day operational issues—this would divert them from concentrating on strategic issues. They are redirected to the shared services centre.

The idea of having a project or consultancy pool of advisors is that they are able to tackle longer-term problems. Having a pool of consultants offers greater resourcing flexibility than would be found in conventional structures where staff are tied to a business unit HR team. Consultants are available to all of the organization. They are usually accessed by business partners, but they can be deployed to support policy projects run by the centres of expertise. The pool can be structured in a number of ways. Do you choose to have consultants with specialist knowledge in particular people management areas with the benefit that they can give quality support, but with the drawback that this can be an inefficient resourcing model? The same problem occurs with the pool organized by business unit – it is inflexible and limits shared learning. A general, undifferentiated pool has resourcing and learning advantages, but disadvantages in terms of depth and breadth of knowledge, skills and experience.

> British Airways opted to have a general pool of consultants when it first set up the model, but then decided that their service would be improved if consultants were dedicated to particular businesses. It had experienced the difficulty that its consultants were insufficiently aware of local issues. The knowledge of individual businesses was found to be essential for effective support.

Consultancy or project pools can be standalone functions or organizationally connected to the centres of expertise. The advantage of the latter approach is that they can tune into policy development work. Clearly, this makes more sense if the consultants are structured by work content area.

A lot of attention has focused on business partners; far less has been devoted to centres of expertise. This may be because the challenges faced are fewer. Centres of expertise build on the importance of specialist knowledge, something that is revered by many HR professionals. As we have seen, the professionalization of HR has brought with it the idea that expertise is required not just in training and development or employee relations, but in reward, resourcing and OD. The concept of centres of expertise builds on this notion. Business partners can be generalists supporting their line clients. When they need in-depth know-how, they can call on colleagues in the centre of expertise.

Typically, centres of expertise or excellence are organized around such areas as resourcing, employee relations, reward and training. Their role can be threefold:

- To offer immediate advice, usually to shared services colleagues (e.g. as the next or final tier on a problem escalation ladder) and/or to business partners. In some organizations guidance is also provided to line managers directly.

- To give assistance over a more extended period in supporting projects with consultants or business partners.
- To develop policy or solutions to problems in their area, normally commissioned by either the corporate centre or a cross-business-unit HR team.

In some organizations the centre of expertise is located in the corporate office along with the work undertaken on policy direction. In other companies it is part of the shared services operation. The location of the activity depends upon the extent to which the organization gives emphasis to being customer responsive (placing it in the shared service centre) or gives more weight to the need for clear corporate direction. Centres of expertise are also sometimes combined with the consultancy pool to integrate the activities described above.

Improved processes

Poor processes delivering poor outcomes have threatened the credibility of the function. Problems arose because, if it was hard enough for HR insiders to manage the spaghetti that was the HR process system (as shown in Figure 2.3), it was impossible for customers. There were simply too many process hand-offs between different groups. Documents would circle a building looking for signatures, passing through too many people on the way.

> One European bank was still asking for five signatories to a staff loan, including the member of staff, their line manager, the HR function (confirming salary), the credit function and the department head. As a result of questioning the added value of the process it was replaced with the same approach as that used for customers – namely, an application form, sanctioned by the credit function based on its usual approval processes.

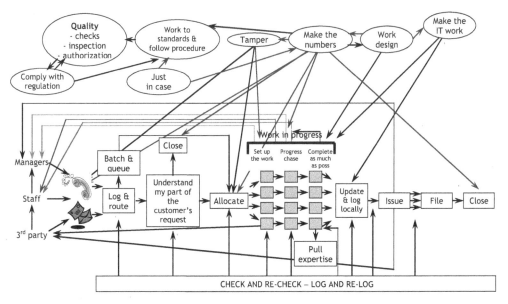

Figure 2.3   A process map in an 'unreformed' HR function

So, change in processes has been driven by the requirement for HR to become more efficient and effective. This has meant not just delivering services at a lower cost, but also giving better quality to customers. In practical terms, this has involved:

- improving connections between activities
- removing unnecessary tasks
- reducing the number of handovers
- simplifying tasks
- measuring performance to check that standards are being met.

Where modernization has occurred, HR has delineated the key processes and looked critically at all the links in a process chain to establish inefficiencies. HR then removed duplication between the line and HR or within HR, exited from situations where it was merely a 'post box', decided who best should undertake the process (leading to increased devolution to the line), benchmarked its performance against competitors or industry norms, and strove to produce easier processes to manage. Indeed, HR started to apply best practice from other business functions to improve processes. Standards, such as ISO 9000/1, have become more prevalent as a 'stamp of approval' to establish broader credibility.

As we will see in the next section, technology facilitated much process change, but organizations have also sought a change in attitude from HR. In some organizations the customer service ethic was insufficiently evident. Rather than find the best means to satisfy customer requirements, staff would adopt 'standard practice'. This might be itself defined in terms of what is most convenient to the function. It was a producer-first not a customer-first mindset. Much of the process change, therefore, concerned how HR could give customers what they wanted and then working backwards to deliver this. Indeed, it could be argued that organizations wanted to move beyond customer service to a focus on customer needs over the longer term, being more proactive than responsive.

Linked to this point, organizations defined new performance standards for each of their re-engineered processes (in a customer-centric manner) and then sought delivery against them. HR intoned the mantra 'getting it right first time' as a means of both being more efficient and being more attuned to customer needs. In multinational companies, standardization of processes has had a global dimension. Real economies of scale can be achieved if there is worldwide adherence to corporate process standards. Rooting out the 'not invented here' syndrome and 'this does not apply to us, we're unique' response has been a requirement in getting to the objective of common approaches. For other organizations, standardization has been a step too far (at least for now) and they have contented themselves with simplification of processes.

> By means of process improvement Standard Life HR cut the time taken to process a season ticket loan from 4.3 days to 2.7. It cut the number of process steps in handling a leaver by a third.

A third characteristic of the attitudinal shift sought by organizations was to imbue a sense of continuous improvement. Again, rather than rest on one's functional laurels, the demand was to seek ways of operating at a higher standard of service at a lower cost. Process improvement is then not a one-off exercise, but a constant imperative. Productivity levels can be driven up through process efficiency and new technology, but also through staff searching ways of doing things better.

Use of technology

According to Alan Warner, in an interview with the authors, the main change over the last ten years has been that 'technology can now do what it says on the tin'. Before, not only was there a large initial outlay, there was also a big cost in getting the system to work. Even five years ago, organizations would need to spend extra to ensure the HRIS (HR information system) was able to function effectively in their own organizational setting. As the new breed of records and payroll systems and e-HR applications mature, it is easier to get them to run in a wide variety of environments.

Increasingly too, the quantum of tools available is helping address a wide variety of HR applications. These include:

- better data capture at the point of the transaction (such as allowing staff to update their own address when they move house or inputting their own overtime/sickness details) improving data quality and reducing errors;
- improved data management allowing more meaningful management information to be provided to line managers and business partners and in time driving better HR solutions to identified issues (such as detailed reports on why staff leave the company);
- employing predictive analysis tools to forecast HR trends such as likely staff turnover based on historic trends;
- the use of interactive voice response telephony in service centres to get the required service to the right employee/line manager or, in some cases, asking the employee to enter their personnel number into the telephone system, allowing the service representative to instantly know what division the caller is based in and bringing up their records on screen as the call switches into the call centre;
- more sophisticated document management systems, e.g. allowing paper to be scanned so as to feed electronic files, to transfer material electronically and to permit multiple access by HR staff;
- the introduction of workflow systems that guide and prompt the user as to the next steps to be taken;
- the use of an 'extranet' that provides computer links to other service providers, e.g. employment lawyers or counsellors;
- the application of intranet and internet services to undertake actual transactions or services such as online payslips, online training materials, online pension quotes, performance reviews, and so on;
- using the corporate intranet to offer online policy advice and access to knowledge repositories;
- employing modular IT systems that can sit either on internal platforms or be outsourced as a managed service, and be applied to standalone business processes such as e-learning or e-recruitment.

In this mixture of tools, organizations can move from read-only systems to systems that can deal with more complex interactions. One description (Kettley and Reilly, 2003) of this hierarchy would look like this:

1. Posting of purely static information on the intranet.
2. Simple transactions.
3. Workflow and external transactions.

4.   Fully web enabled.

Figure 2.4 shows how e-HR can become more complex, as new features are added, but also much richer in terms of functionality. Some of this activity is aimed at making processes within HR more efficient. Some are concerned with communication: to inform the organization on policies and procedures. Others are externally focused, like e-recruitment, better engaging with prospective candidates. Another cluster is designed to transfer work from HR to line managers and employees, or to automate paper-based processes to bypass HR. Manager self-service and employee self-service describe the latter. In this world, users are able to complete transactions such as amending personal details and booking training courses without having to involve HR. Beyond administrative improvement, this technology allows better data capture (e.g. on skill profiles) and devolved decision-making (e.g. managers uprating salaries directly into payroll).

Of course, organizations are at different stages of development along this path. Most organizations of reasonable size have intranets with HR information contained within them, but still only the most IT sophisticated are pushing out the boundaries to stage four on the list above. E-HR costs money and requires expertise. Many organizations find it hard to justify the investment in HR tools against competing business demands. Indeed, some are still struggling to find the money to permit the introduction of a modern HRIS or the combination of employee records and payroll into a single system. Some organizations have been able to rationalize multiple systems to save money. For example, a US company, Carlson, had six time-recording systems. This could be collapsed in one system, saving on resources and maintenance. Other organizations have been forced or have chosen to outsource some HR administration in order to get access to decent technology. Part of the reasoning behind the BAE Systems outsourcing deal was the need to integrate diverse HR IT systems that had come from a merger. Similarly, access to technology (as well as cost saving) was behind Procter & Gamble's outsourcing move. 'For Procter & Gamble, outsourcing parts of our human resources organization was a strategic move to further deploy state-of-the-art processes and related technology in order to better serve our internal customers,' said Luigi Pierleoni, HR director, Procter & Gamble (www.sap.com).

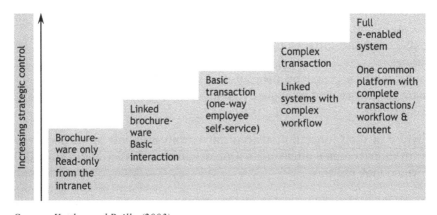

Source: Kettley and Reilly (2003)

Figure 2.4   Key steps to e-enablement

> One retailer reported that it has been suffering from a lack of IT investment for HR. For example, it still has a 'primitive' HR intranet. This means HR is drawn into administrative activities that it would like to exit from. It is still engaged in paperchasing. Manager self-service, however, has just started, but employee self-service is difficult because of the lack of access for many staff. The organization is asking itself whether outsourcing part of its administrative function is the solution, which would fund the necessary step up in technological provision, and whether such a move is justified. In other words, is e-HR important enough to warrant outsourcing its administrative activity?

Other organizations have used the justified cuts in manpower to fund the purchase of kit. The difficulty is that some applications (like e-recruitment) may well lead to staff reductions, but for others (like extranets or performance management online) the savings are less obvious. The advantages are in improved ease of operation, access or benefit to employees. For these applications funds may be denied precisely because the cost savings are not so self-evident. The function is thereby prevented from developing the integrated architecture for which it was aiming.

> The e-working strategy (Kettley and Reilly, 2003) of one organization was rolled out under five propositions or streams:
>
> 1. Employee self-service with a series of web-enabled applications including e-pay, e-personnel details, e-learning and e-travel.
> 2. A communications suite, which includes intra- and inter-organizational e-mail, an interactive online newsletter, video links, e-surveys and webmail.
> 3. Connectivity to ensure the infrastructure is in place to ensure a highly dispersed workforce can easily access the intranet via kiosks as well as PCs and remotely where necessary.
> 4. A web-enabled workplace that includes a mix of offices for privacy, shared workspaces, social facilities and resource centres. Hot-desking and homeworking are facilitated by 'flood-cabled' telecommunications and power for laptops etc. and online room booking via a central 'concierge' service.
> 5. Business intelligence and knowledge management applications that include collaborative tools such as online meeting rooms, secure virtual workspaces, personalized dashboards and newsfeeds.

As to the need for expertise, even the likes of BP felt that outsourcing was required to get the skills because it wanted to act quickly. Other organizations might take more time over e-HR, adding features as resources permit and using external consultants to help build internal capability.

Outsourcing status

As the last section suggested, another big decision for an organization to make is who carries out its HR activities, or, more accurately, what is the balance between in-house and outsourcing.

It is very hard to get a handle on the nature and extent of outsourcing in the UK, not least because the suppliers of outsourced services talk up the market and the press seizes on the major deals that are concluded by such companies as BT, BP, Boots and BAE Systems. What independent research there is suggests that between a half and three quarters of organizations outsource at least one HR activity. As to which are the most common to be outsourced, The Work Foundation's (2003), an independent piece of research, but on a very small response rate, reported that they were:

- occupational health services – 54 per cent
- pensions administration – 44 per cent
- training – 37 per cent
- payroll – 32 per cent.

Salary and benefits administration was the area least often outsourced by respondents (2 per cent). No organizations reported outsourcing strategic activities and only a few indicated that policy work was done externally.

In the 2004 Workplace Employee Relations Survey (WERS), training (37 per cent) was by far the most common HR activity to be undertaken externally. Payroll and resourcing of temporary positions were outsourced by about a quarter of respondents and recruitment by only 14 per cent.

On another small sample (200 organizations) from a survey by recruitment consultancy Digby Morgan, payroll is the most likely to be outsourced (45 per cent), followed by administration (25 per cent) and recruitment (24 per cent) (*People Management* online, 21 September 2005).

A CIPD survey (2003a) of HR practitioners concluded that the outsourcing market was static. Some organizations had increased their use of external providers over the previous three years whilst others had cut back. The growth areas of outsourcing were reported to be in the areas of training and development, recruitment and employee counselling, but even here there was a sizeable proportion of organizations that had reduced the outsourcing of training and recruitment.

In general, research suggests that organizations outsource for the following main reasons (Reilly and Tamkin, 1997):

- Cost reduction
  - achieving economies of scale
  - higher labour productivity
  - more efficient deployment of labour
  - numbers reduction through attrition
  - erosion of old terms and conditions.
- Shift from fixed to variable costs.
- Improved service
  - access to specialist skills
  - access to up-to-date technology
  - advantages in size or geographic spread
  - product or market knowledge
  - avoidance of internal controls.
- Focus on core business.
- Reduced exposure. Protection against:

- the costs of downsizing
- adverse publicity
- changes in regulation and legal requirements
- changing career expectations.
- Avoidance of headcount-based manpower controls.
- Flexibility to meet fluctuating supply and demand.

The 2004 WERS survey supported the view that cost saving is the principal driver for outsourcing. It found that over half of its respondents contracted out to save money. The focus on service improvement also featured — a third of the respondents outsourced in order to improve the quality of service. Some organizations (a further 30 per cent) choose to outsource non-essential activities in order to concentrate on the core business – a significantly higher proportion than in the 1998 survey.

A survey by the International Data Corporation in 2003 gave the top three benefits of HR business process outsourcing (BPO) as:

- cost savings
- technological expertise
- process expertise.

Given the emphasis on business process in the question, these results are not surprising. Nor are the findings of a survey by RebusHR 2001 (now Northgate HR Outsourcing) that also put cost as the principal driver, followed by the buying-in of specific expertise and the need to comply with employment legislation. Their market is in the small and medium-sized organizations where HR expertise is lacking.

A study by Accenture and The Conference Board (2002) came to roughly the same conclusions. The three most significant drivers in HR outsourcing reported were:

- cost reduction
- improving the quality of HR services provided to employees
- maximizing resource availability.

The Work Foundation's survey confirmed that the quality and resourcing point also applies to bigger organizations:

- 63 per cent of respondents who outsourced one or more function did so 'to harness specialist knowledge'
- 44 per cent cited a key reason as 'maximizing resource availability'.

In a SHRM survey, provision of services they could not offer in-house was second only to cost as the reason for outsourcing (Murray, 2004). A survey from the Shared Services and Business Process Outsourcing Association (SBPOA) (2005) added the repositioning of the HR function as a key driver to HR outsourcing. It was cited by 68 per cent of respondents, more than cost or quality of service. It is surprising that other surveys reported here did not produce a similar focus on this point, as it has been behind much of the drive to introduce shared services.

Other reasons advanced for HR outsourcing include:

- process standardization and 'tidying up' (especially after mergers)
- policy harmonization, especially in decentralized organizations
- better understanding of costs of service delivery

- access to good process tools.

The picture that emerges is that HR outsourcing for most organizations is restricted to externalizing service supply in very specific areas where there is an efficiency or effectiveness gain. Pressure on costs or workforce numbers continues to drive interest in outsourcing, but there is a quality and expertise consideration relation to specific activities. Few organizations move beyond the tactical to strategic outsourcing, despite the suppliers moving up the value chain. Even the big outsourcing deals reported largely cover the transactional activity. Few go as far as Liverpool Victoria (which only retains two in-house HR staff) or Blackburn and Darwen Borough Council (where the whole function was outsourced). In these cases the decision to outsource seems to be about more than efficiency: it concerns focus and quality.

As to the results of outsourcing, cost reduction seems to be achieved. For example a Towers Perrin survey (2005) reported that 88 per cent of its respondents felt that short-term savings had been delivered and, more surprisingly, 92 per cent claimed long-term cost benefits. The box below indicates one particular example.

> In 2004 Procter & Gamble outsourced the running of its HR services to IBM. This has included IBM taking responsibility for, amongst other things, payroll, recruitment and training. IBM took over 800 staff in 28 countries to run the service from three centres. P&G did not see HR administrative activities as part of the core business and wanted to reduce costs and improve service. Over the ten-year contract costs are due to be cut by 30 per cent (www.sap.com).

But outsourcing is not without its problems. Here is a sample of the evidence of the success or failure of HR outsourcing:

- 'Fewer than half of HR professionals believe that their role has improved following the outsourcing of functions in their organization' according to a survey of 200 HR professionals by Digby Morgan (People Management online, 21 September 2005).
- The study conducted by Accenture and The Conference Board (2002) discovered that only 50 per cent responded that their objectives had been fully met, although 90 per cent felt that they would continue to outsource more HR activities despite the inherent challenges. Of those who did outsource one or more HR activity, fewer than 1 per cent had chosen to move these back in-house, suggesting a high level of satisfaction with the outsourcing experience.
- The same Towers Perrin survey (2005) which described cost advantages with outsourcing also reported that only 40 per cent of those that had outsourced a while ago reported improvements in service quality. A majority of respondents also failed to improve productivity from HR or the line, and to 'speed the transformation of the function from tactical to strategic'.
- Lawler and Mohrman (2003) similarly found no association between outsourcing and HR becoming more strategic. Though HR might have the idea that by removing non-core activities it would move up the value chain, this research found no empirical support for this happening in practice.

The impression given by this research is consistent evidence on outsourcing generally, with, depending upon the survey, only around a third of respondents positive about the results (e.g. Lonsdale and Cox, 1998; Booz Allen Hamilton, 2004; Wigham, 2005). It is also worth noting that the latest WERS research discovered that 16 per cent of organizations had brought activities back in-house after outsourcing them. This was for cost and service reasons equally.

The conclusion one should draw from this material is that outsourcing can offer benefits in cost saving or quality improvement, but only if it is executed correctly. Problems have occurred with respect to:

- managing the contractor (made harder by the loss of internal content expertise or the lack of commercial skills in HR)
- legal (contractual) disputes
- service difficulties
- customer complaints
- employee relations
- poor communication
- unexpected costs.

Illustrating these points by way of example, Pickard (2004a) describes communication failings in the BT/Accenture deal, a tendency for customers to blame outsourcing for any service deficiency and weak account management on the part of both parties. Jenny Arwas of BT more recently admitted (Scott-Jackson *et al.*, 2005) that better performance criteria and metrics could have been in place for the first deal – something that has been rectified in the renewed contract. The same message came from the Hays/Liverpool Victoria contract. Lawrence Hoefkens, Hays' business sector director, reflecting on how their arrangement had gone, said: 'we should have paid more attention to service-level agreements, processes and policy. It didn't seem that relevant at the time. Integration seemed more important' (Smethurst, 2003).

In the early days of its outsourcing arrangement (late 2001), BP was concerned that Exult had gone too far and too fast in automating HR activities. Employees seemed reluctant to use the new e-HR technology. Managers were concerned with the standardization of some policies that they did not believe to be achievable or even desirable. Costs rose because there was duplication of service — electronic and personal (Higginbottom, 2001).

Problems of growing costs, especially of internal HR numbers growing back after outsourcing, and poor vendor account management (frequent changes in staffing) are also reported by The Conference Board research (2004).

Anecdotal evidence suggests that suppliers will not invest in the relationship where returns will only be seen beyond the contract termination date. Thus, if you are two years into a six-year deal, the contractor will not look to train or develop staff if the benefits take a while to come through. Similarly, the relationship with the supplier can be very transactional and contract driven. The supplier will only carry out the tasks specified, unless paid for by the client. In other words, clients have to realize that this is a commercial arrangement, however close the 'partnership'.

Doubts about outsourcing have led some organizations to reject the idea. Some of The Work Foundation's respondents seemed to take this position. Of the 66 organizations which did not outsource any HR activities, nearly half were not 'convinced that a third party would add value' (The Work Foundation, 2003). These points are consistent with two of the objections to outsourcing Reilly and Tamkin (1997) found. These were:

- an underlying difference in outlook between profit maximization on the part of the contractor and cost minimization for the vendor

- damage to business performance through a loss of control through being locked into inflexible contracts
- we can perform the work as well in house — what value does the contractor have?

OFFSHORING

Offshoring business process activities is the movement of tasks or business functions to locations overseas. Newspaper headlines have screamed explosive growth in offshoring, and business research firms have predicted continued expansion over the coming years. Offshoring became an election issue in the USA during the 2004 presidential campaign, out of all proportion to its effect thus far on employment levels. Similarly, in December 2003, the UK government reacted to the disclosure that high-profile organizations intended to transfer a significant number of jobs overseas by launching a review. The study by the Department for Trade and Industry (DTI) was unable to report on the extent of jobs transfer. The DTI, however, rejected protectionism and competition for low-paid jobs, favouring instead an emphasis on skills, innovation and productivity. It argued that the UK exported more services than it imported and that offshoring 'brings benefits and challenges' (Department for Trade and Industry, 2003a). The message was that UK plc should be more positively disposed towards offshoring.

Its prime driver is to achieve significant cost savings through access to lower labour and accommodation costs. A survey conducted by PricewaterhouseCoopers/Economist Intelligence Unit (2005) on offshoring in financial services found that 79 per cent of those surveyed said that they expected to achieve cost savings, and nearly all reported that they did. The sort of cost savings involved might be as high as 65 per cent to 70 per cent, depending not just on wage differentials and cheaper accommodation (rents in Bangalore were half those of Sheffield, one of the cheaper UK call centre locations), but whether process improvements can be achieved during the change. Higher management and telecom costs need, however, to be factored in (Hawksworth, 2005).

The IT service sector has led the way towards offshoring. Companies have been able to access a large pool of skilled, English-speaking workers and advanced telecom/networking infrastructures. Since 1998, governments in countries as diverse as Vietnam, Ireland, Guatemala and Ghana have promoted new offshore BPO processing centres. For example, the South African minister for trade and industry expressed the hope that his country will become 'the back office to the world' (Reilly, 2004a). Despite competition, India has emerged as the dominant offshore BPO provider. Only the Philippines is a near-term market share competitor (Dalal, 2003). India's BPO prominence is based on several factors – a first mover lead in the offshoring market, initial cost advantages (total labour costs being five times cheaper in India than in the UK), skills' profile, language and relatively stable social and political environment. However, there are now signs that in cost and quality terms India is losing its allure because of rising costs and staff turnover, running at between 40 per cent and 60 per cent, according to PricewaterhouseCoopers/Economist Intelligence Unit (2005).

Will HR services follow the IT lead and get involved in offshoring? According to some observers (e.g. Dalal, 2003), there are reasons for doing this that are very similar to those that have encouraged outsourcing within the same country. These include:

- the search for lower operational costs
- aiming for higher productivity levels, resulting in further cost reductions
- seeking quality improvement in operational processes
- enabling more strategic focus on key issues/activities

- using it as a tool for evoking culture change
- searching for product/service improvement.

There are some advantages that may be peculiar to offshoring:

- tax incentives on offer in some developing countries
- labour subsidies (e.g. as available in Ireland and parts of Canada)
- a 'follow the sun' model of service delivery
- access to skilled and available labour pools.

Thus far, despite the headline-grabbing deals, there has been limited HR offshoring. The Offshoring Survey 2004, conducted by the CBI/Alba, reported only 2 per cent of the 45 firms offshoring had included HR. As the boxed examples show, IBM is a notable example of HR offshoring from the UK. For Standard Chartered, given their significant existing presence in India, it may not be even appropriate to use the term 'offshoring'.

> IBM has moved its HR shared services centre from Portsmouth to Budapest. The choice of location was based on cost, language and political stability.
>
> In 2002 Standard Chartered set up its own shared services centre in Chennai, India to cover four out of the 50 countries in which it operates, with plans to aggressively migrate other operations over time. This was part of a group-wide drive for economies of scale, common processes and lower operating costs. Specifically, with respect to HR, the decision was aimed at upgrading the quality and nature of the function's performance.

Why might there be this dearth of HR examples? Is it just that HR is, as ever, behind IT, in developments that will come in due course? Is it the conservatism of the HR function that suppliers complain about? Is it that there are too many risks involved — political instability, technological breakdowns, customer resistance, public relations objections — that deter HR directors? Or are they not convinced by the cost savings or quality improvements?

It is likely that some HR activities will be deemed more suitable for offshoring than others where cost saving advantages are obvious and the downside effects likely to be limited. Clearly those that require deep local knowledge or face-to-face contact are ruled out. More appropriate will be back office processing or employee help-desk facilities. Even here, companies are more likely to offshore work themselves if they operate internationally and have a physical presence already in the country concerned. Offshoring as part of an outsourcing deal will probably be more common. An international service provider will seek lower costs by moving processing abroad.

Measurement and monitoring

MEASUREMENT

Recent developments in management information systems have resulted in a great deal of progress being made in providing better quantification of the inputs and outputs that HR produces. However, too much of the emphasis has been on 'HR measures', not enough on 'people management measures'; on input rather than outputs; and on 'lag' not 'lead indicators'. It might be useful at the outset to explain these distinctions.

Quite simply, the 'lag' measures focus on things that have already happened, whereas 'lead' indicate potential future performance. An example of a lead measure would be the result of asking staff in an opinion survey whether they intended to leave the organization over the next six months. A lag measure would be to report the number of people who actually have left in the last six months. The former allows issues to be addressed before they have crystallized. The latter, at best, can only give a data item that could form part of a trend. That information might encourage action to stem an outward flow, but after it had started.

Lag indicators are easier to identify and to measure. Many of the commercial measures of performance fall within this category and, unfortunately for HR professionals, can excessively preoccupy business leaders. Quite often they are the subject of management targets, and hence disproportionate time is spent on them. They suffer from the fact that, at the time of reporting, they are often some weeks or even months out of date. As they are measures of what has happened, other than helping indicate trends and allowing for benchmarking with like-minded organizations, they are of limited value.

'People management measures' can be distinguished from 'HR measures' in that 'people measures' are those metrics that provide information about employees, rather than the performance of the HR function, that help business leaders make decisions about what management processes need to be improved, introduced or removed to maximize the productivity of their staff. They can include such key measures as staff:

- morale
- turnover
- sickness and other forms of absence
- qualifications or measures of skill and learning
- productivity (e.g. cost/full time equivalence (FTE) or in commercial enterprises income/ FTE).

Some of the above represent inputs to business success (e.g. qualification levels) whereas others are outputs of it (e.g. productivity rates). These people management indicators also contain both 'lead' and 'lag' measures, as the illustration earlier indicated.

Measures of HR performance, by contrast, are the factors by which the contribution of the HR function can be determined. These typically include metrics that report on the productivity and efficiency of the HR function itself, such as:

- HR staff numbers/total organizational headcount
- HR FTE/payroll cost
- HR administrative cost/payroll cost
- proportion of rework
- distribution of time spent on different activities
- productivity measures (number of calls taken, number of files processed, number of records opened, number of referrals made, etc.)
- client feedback on key performance indicators
- time taken to process certain tasks.

Some of the above measures concern inputs (e.g. the processing ones), others describe efficiency (the cost-based ones) or quality (rework); a fourth group report how well HR is doing against its intent to reposition itself (e.g. the activity analysis).

In relation to this list, the concentration has been on inputs, looking at measures of process efficiency, such as time taken to process an application form, to issue a new contract of employment, to amend a payroll entry, etc. Much of the push to achieve HR efficiency and effectiveness came from improving simple, transactional processes. So reducing the time taken to issue a contract letter, respond to phone calls, deal with an overtime claim, etc. was a key measure to illustrate improvement in efficiency. Cutting out errors and rework was tracked to point to the growing effectiveness of the function.

When looking at output metrics, many organizations in our view confuse the issue by describing people management measures as HR ones, and holding HR accountable. Thus, HR would be challenged over morale or sickness. This seems to us to fly in the face of the aim to devolve responsibilities to the line. If managers are to be held accountable for, say, staff productivity, how can HR be charged with meeting metrics that precisely indicate whether employee productivity is improving or not? It is the line that primarily influences resignation, absence, morale, etc. It is these managers who should be measured against the relevant metrics.

MONITORING/BENCHMARKING/BEST PRACTICE

Another area of growing interest is the move to compare performance data of both people measures and HR measures between organizations and indeed between parts of the same organization. These developments probably fall into three distinct camps: monitoring or regular reporting, benchmarking in general and identification of best practice. For clarity's sake we describe each below:

- Monitoring/reporting – the regular recording and reporting to appropriate stakeholders of Key Performance Indicators (KPIs) both in respect of people measures and HR measures.
- Benchmarking – the comparison of KPIs between similar business units or organizations.
- Best practice – the identification of the highest performer in the comparator group (be it internal or external), suggesting the adoption of similar policies and processes.

Monitoring   It has become increasingly common practice over the last ten years for organizations to define KPIs. With the coming of a greater service ethos, the HR function has given a great deal of attention to identifying the right sort of KPIs. These have formed a key part of service-level agreements (SLAs) between service providers and customers. These 'contracts' usually specify the services offered, their frequency and the quality standards to be expected. Some companies have gone further and attached a monetary value to the services. KPIs will specify deadlines (on say payroll entries), turnaround times (e.g. at RBS 48 hours for a new hire contract, 48 hours for a reference response etc.), and targets (e.g. on accuracy of management information). Whilst managers trot out the adage 'what gets measured gets done', it is equally true to say that 'what can (easily) be measured, gets measured'. Hence there is the emphasis on inputs rather outputs and lag rather than lead indicators.

The development of IT solutions and the increasing move to standardized and centralized people data within organizations have helped get better measures into the reporting processes. This is especially true where the data is provided by outsourced providers (such as Xchanging for BAE Systems). The suppliers are usually contracted to provide data in a systemized way, not least because part of the rationale for outsourcing has been to get a handle on service performance in the first place.

If care is not exercised, the new breed of management information systems can, however, produce forest-fulls of data. One of the worst offenders is the shared services or outsourced operation. Increasingly over the last five years, they have been providing a mesmerizing array of measurement from telephone answering times, to process completion times; from feedback on the competence of line managers/employees, to the period taken to complete process steps in an accurate manner. As the manager of an HR contract told us: 'we have got quite anal about measuring everything that moves in our department'. But again the emphasis is on HR processes, not people management outcomes.

Some data collection is done to measure the performance of the HR function from the customer's perspective. The centres of excellence/expertise, shared services centre or, with more difficulty because their performance is harder to measure, business partners may ask their own clients to complete surveys to provide feedback on HR performance. A wide variety of subjects may be covered, including technical knowledge (remuneration, training solutions, change management expertise and so on), service (data reporting, query turnaround times etc.) or general statements of competence (value added, professionalism etc.).

Clearly some of this information gathering is useful, and organizations have got better at being more selective in what they present, or in helping the reader by formatting it in an informative way. The use of traffic lights to signal where management should focus attention is one example. However, our concerns remain that the effort spent on producing the material can far outweigh the benefits derived from it, particularly if attention is not given to doing something with the results.

Where greater progress has been made, it has been in getting acceptance that people management measures should be better reported as part of overall business performance. Kaplan and Norton (1996) did an enormous service to people management by proposing the balanced business scorecard. It has moved the emphasis in measurement away from the obsession with financial performance, and brought consideration to other performance aspects, including those relating to employees. Thus in the original balanced business scorecard there is a four-box structure to present data to stakeholders. The four categories are: financial, internal business processes, learning and growth, and customers. With respect to the 'learning and growth' box, many organizations have adopted people management measures, and asked the HR function to come up with an appropriate set of metrics to report on. Some organizations have found it hard to populate this box with measures that give a real insight into the employee contribution to the business. Instead, they have used rather unexciting skill or training statistics. It has also been argued that the scorecard approach gives the impression of an equal weighting to the reported elements that may be misleading. Some of the items reported may be far more important than others.

European Foundation for Quality Management (EFQM) models have also been used by some organizations as a way of broadening the focus beyond financial measurement into the appraisal of the people management contribution to organizational performance. This is a structured tool that looks at people, customers, society and key performance results. The latter includes the major indicators of financial and operational good health.

Human capital measurement is a further development that has helped with the definition and description of employee performance. Part of the reason for the renewed interest in human capital is that in the UK, a government-commissioned report (Department of Trade and Industry, 2003b) led by Denise Kingsmill, focused on external reporting of human capital in an operating and financial review (OFR) that aimed to give people assets more of a status in the investment community. Effort has since gone into defining what measures ought to be included and whether these should be mandatory or not. For example, it had been proposed by Kingsmill that the OFR should cover such information in areas such as on the size and composition of the workforce; employee retention and motivation; skills, competencies and training; remuneration and fair employment practice; and leadership and succession planning. In fact, all that the draft OFR regulations did was to encourage organizations to look at the Accounting for People report when deciding what to include. At the time of writing, Gordon Brown suddenly announced the ditching of the statutory OFR. However, instead there will be a requirement for all but small firms to produce a business review. This turns out to be a less prescriptive version of the OFR. Although human capital reporting is not mandatory, the use of non-financial indicators is encouraged, where appropriate. What is unclear is what investors will demand with respect to human capital reporting. So information may be given, but its quality is likely to remain variable.

Economic Value Added is another approach that has its adherents. Like human capital measurement and the balanced business scorecard, it attempts to show how value is created by organizations. Its measures are mainly numerical and financially specified, like revenue per employee. It has a useful application in terms of evaluating the benefit to be derived from different projects. In this respect it offers the same facility as ROI (return on investment). This has been widely used in training evaluation, but has been criticized because the rate of return is frequently hard to specify. It has been more successfully applied to assess the effectiveness of graduate recruitment programmes.

Benchmarking   Both commercial companies and UK public sector bodies are spending more time, effort, and money on benchmarking their performance against similar organizations on both people management and HR measures. Areas looked at have included comparisons of turnover, pay, HR numbers and absence rates, etc. One of the more interesting recent people management benchmarking topics has been the use of employee engagement measures or, more crudely, items from staff survey data. HR consultancies, such as Watson Wyatt, Hewitt Associates, Towers Perrin and Mercer, are providing ever-increasing company comparator material in respect of people performance. Some of this is linked to human capital measurement systems such as Watson Wyatt's Human Capital Index or Mercer's six measures of employee productivity.

Companies such as ISR too have significantly grown business in the last ten years by providing 'norm' groups of data (generally or by sector) on how people practices are received and perceived by employees. Thus, an organization's score on effective communication with employees can be set against the 'norm' in general or by sector.

In respect of HR measures, whilst the context and benchmarks are different, the approach remains the same. HR functions are compared against each other or in league tables (e.g. US company Hackett measures organizational performance on labour, outsourcing and technology against a rank order) on their efficiency and cost. The most frequently quoted measure is the ratio of HR to total staff numbers. Private sector HR ratios tend to be higher than public sector. They are said to average to 1:100 in the private sector, having moved from 1:50 in the last five years. Local government's HR/employee ratio is said to average 1:98 and 1:42 in central government (CIPD, 2005c). A ratio of 1:100 is also 'the rule of thumb' in the USA (Russell and Harrop, 2005), whereas top quintile performance is supposed to be a ratio of 1:173 (www.thecedargroup.com).

The most obvious problem with benchmarking is that organizations are comparing apples with pears and this is true whatever form of benchmarking it is. Are organizations of the same

> Debenhams, before its modernization of HR, stood at 1:60. Its aim is to move to 1:145 (IBM Business Consultancy Services, 2004). Royal Mail altered the ratio from 1:55 to 1:85 in two years as a consequence of its HR transformation project.

size and sector being compared? Is the same business operating model being used, decentralized or centralized, that will affect the size and shape of the HR function? These health warnings are especially relevant for 'norm' data, league tables or indices of performance. It is less of an issue with bilateral comparisons or benchmarking clubs because these issues should have been sorted out at the outset as part of the information sharing arrangements.

The benefit of a benchmarking review is of course also affected by the quality of measures and reporting in the first place. Again, the more it is under the organization's direct control, the greater the likelihood is that the data will be robust and reliable for its purposes. The more the data is supplied to a distant third party, the greater the risk is that either variations in interpretation or slap dash data entry will occur.

Best (or sometimes better) practice   At one level finding the best performing unit in an organization and adopting its operating model is a sensible approach. Better and, critically, more standardized data has allowed more effective comparisons to be made within organizations. The drive too for efficiency through consolidation has given an impetus to sharing 'best practice'. Perversely, the very fact of consolidation has meant that internal comparisons have become difficult. There is often only one shared services centre, centre of expertise or corporate centre. There may be many business partners, but their alignment with what may be very different business activities makes cross-comparison hard.

This encourages external comparisons. These can work well in the public sector where the aim is to encourage performance improvement. The strategy in the NHS is to showcase the best performers amongst the Trusts as exemplars for others to follow. An 'Improvers Club' has been set up in local government to encourage sharing of good practice. The title is something of a misnomer as participants are skilled and successful practitioners, but it does emphasize the importance of continuously building knowledge and skills. Auditing in local government offers both a statement of the absolute standard and a relative reference point in how well any particular authority is doing. Elsewhere, if the aim is merely to see how well the organization is performing on any particular activity, then all well and good (though there are limitations to benchmarking we described above). If the aim is to identify the best in class and then emulate it, there are the more serious problems.

The same limitations apply to the search for best-practice exemplars as the search for the ideal approach to benchmarking. Best-practice reviews are especially dependent on the openness of an organization (or indeed between competing parts of the same organization!) to share details of how it performs better than others. Critical too is the way HR reacts to the evidence. Does it take the 'not invented here' attitude or, of equal concern, have the opposite reaction of adopting the practice wholesale without thought for whether it will fit with their own organization's culture and values. Some have criticized decisions to outsource or set up shared services as being on a 'me too also' basis, rather than through a proper study of the pros and cons. The recent scramble to implement shared services in the public sector organizations in the UK might, at least initially, have an example of this point, although more considered guidance is now appearing, to help steer organizations towards effective implementation.

Instead, HR should critically examine the way other organizations manage HR and employees. They need to start to understand why another similar organization is performing especially well. A real best-practice exercise would look at underlying causes, be they policies, practices or processes. For example, does one pharmaceutical company retain more women than the rest of the sector because of more favourable maternity policies? Or, has one bank got a lower cost payroll per capita because it is outsourced? HR management then has to have an open mind to see if there appear to be useful lessons to learn. But before simply implementing what has been found, organizations need to decide whether it would work as well in their environment. This can be tested through pilot exercises. So experimentation based on external learning should be encouraged, but not unthinking application of the latest apparently successful fashion.

We will return to these issues in monitoring and benchmarking in Chapter 10.

2 *Where Next for HR?*

3 *New Role*

It is clear from our discussions with organizations that a new role needs to be defined for HR. But this is not in our view a matter of radical transformation from the current situation. Rather, we see an evolutionary process of embedding some recent changes to the activities of the function, whilst at the same time moving into new areas. More work it seems has been done on structures and processes than on skills and capabilities. We believe that this should be rebalanced, but it is not a question of either or – rather and, and.

This journey will be undertaken in the same way as progress to date. There will be some organizations further along the path and moving faster than others, even some mavericks trying something unusual. There will be those lagging behind. There will still be obstacles in the way that will have to be overcome. These will be described in Part 3. Here we will describe the characteristics of the emerging role in terms of purpose, activity and content. We then go on to look at structures and processes before turning to HR's relationships with stakeholders. Last, but no means least, we look at the skills necessary to meet HR's aspiration and the way the function needs to measure success.

Purpose

At the highest level of description, there is not much argument about what HR exists to do. Its aim is to support the organization's management of people in order that the organization's objectives are met. This description makes clear that HR's activity is a means to an end, not an end in itself. The job of HR is not to make employees happy. It is to make employees productive, engaged, creative, etc. These are inputs that connect to outcomes that make organizations successful. So an R&D laboratory needs creative people to invent things. A manufacturing plant requires employees to produce at a fast rate safely. A critical task that frames HR's whole contribution is an understanding of what connects people to the employer: what turns them on (and off), what causes them to join (and leave), and how employee disposition and skills are linked to organizational performance. This is why we give particular attention to the organizational proposition.

How HR achieves this aim will be discussed in more detail below. There is more debate about role and activity than ultimate purpose. What one can say by way of introduction is that HR achieves its purpose at a number of levels – strategic, operational and administrative. It works with senior management, line managers and employees to differing extents and differing ways – hence the sections on relationships below. It devises policies and procedures that conform to the law and cultural norms, but also ones that facilitate the management of people so that change allows them to achieve their best for the organization.

Role and activities overview

The path we have chosen between the differing views of the role of HR we described in Chapter 2 is described below:

- HR should be an integrated people management function covering all aspects of that term. This means, referring back to the debate on page 15, including organizational development (OD) and learning and development within HR, and not seeing them as separate entities. We favour the sort of broad definition offered by Torrington (1989) (albeit it was a description of personnel management!): the activity is underpinned by 'an understanding of one or more the ways in which people, individually and collectively, engage with the need to be employed and the needs of the organisation to employ them'.
- How this role will be played out will vary from organization to organization, and over time. None the less, we see the role as being principally discharged by facilitating line management's direct people management role; by providing the tools, techniques and policies to support this work; and by undertaking some of the necessary administration to ensure staff's proper employment.
- But this role should be proactive, as well as reactive. HR should be involved in influencing the strategic and operational decision-making of the organization by helping to formulate organizational goals and identifying the means to achieve them. This visioning role needs to grow. HR should be helping the organization to understand its organizational purpose, the 'big idea' that drives it forward. It may be too much to hope for these goals to be derived from the capability of the workforce, but at least cognizance should be taken of the numbers, skills and abilities of the workforce. Having an integrated model of human capital development can allow the organization to see how it can build capacity and increase effectiveness through the people it employs. Gratton emphasized that HR should be instrumental in this shift from the short to the long term; from the ad hoc to the integrative (Gratton, 1997). But the model needs to be complex in that, in the increasingly diverse employment world, one size clearly will not fit all. Therefore the model should take into consideration the different ways in which employees are engaged.
- But HR should not be so obsessed with the strategic as it seems currently to be. At least, it should not be obsessed with a narrow (and probably) outdated conception of the strategic. For most practitioners, being strategic means participating in decision-making with the top team in a way that sets out organizational priorities. But, increasingly, it is recognized that strategic actions take place in the day-to-day life of organizations, not just in formal planning sessions. As Purcell (2001) has pointed out, implementation can be regarded as a component of strategy. This suggests that, especially in the business partner role, HR can make its strategic contribution in a broader manner, with a wider deployment of its professional skills than is sometimes conceived. Part of the significance of the Ulrich model after all comes from seeing HR's added value in a number of dimensions: the transactional and transformational. The other distinctive insight from the Ulrich model is that it is set out in terms of customer requirements. It is defined by its 'deliveries' (Buyens and de Vos, 2001), not in terms of its inputs. And if the customers want professional HR support on operational people management issues then they should have it.
- Nevertheless, the customer service imperative should not be taken too far. There are times when the customer is wrong. This may be because the customer is taking too shortsighted or ill–informed a view. HR surely also needs a governance function, despite the reservations

of those who see HR principally as the line's 'handmaidens' (Storey, 1992). There needs to be some internal agency that ensures that the corporate and long-term perspective are taken into account so that short-term operational pressures do not lead to a violation of the law, organizational values or operating principles. HR is in a position to offer this contribution of checks and balances precisely because it has an organization-wide perspective and a requirement to nurture human resources over extended periods. Keenoy (1989) describes HR as being the 'regulator of employment relationship'. In this he talks of HR establishing the 'moral order' of the organization. This can be taken too far, and indeed it can sound rather pious, but it is true that for organizations to be successful they need a set of governing principles to which they adhere. When individuals step out of line somebody has to blow the whistle, and why not HR?

- How this responsibility is performed is not a caricature of the parking warden's behaviour – taking pleasure in catching people without a ticket. It is an activity that helps line managers find appropriate solutions to their problems within these agreed confines. As Maria Di-Sapia, Head of Employment Strategy at Camden Council, put it in an interview with the authors: 'I want the HR function to be less rule bound and more flexible. I want it to wheel and deal to solve managers' problems.' If HR is to have a review function, then its purpose is to discover and disseminate good practice, rather than police the rules. Indeed, HR's contribution may be less in enforcement and more in facilitation. Dean Royles, when talking to the authors, described HR's role to 'champion' a 'value based culture'. This describes how HR should be creating the right climate within which managers and staff operate.

- HR should be regarded as a specialized function with its own distinct professional credentials. As Torrington (1989) has written: 'no matter how skilful line managers become with their competencies, and no matter how exotic the offerings of consultants there will be still a place for an internal HR activity.' And, despite the prophets of doom, as the employment offer becomes more sophisticated and the regulatory environment more complex, so HR's expertise in people management tools and techniques will be seen to be more valuable.

- HR has to continue to develop its professional expertise by taking note of good practice, reviewing evidence of what works, recontextualizing it to fit the changing environment. This means HR should adapt external learning to fit internal circumstances and culture, not simply adopt what others do. HR must therefore be alert to what is happening externally to the organization – in the labour market, in workforce demography, in national and international regulation etc.

- HR derives its specific role, we believe, from its understanding of what motivates employees, how best they can be organized, involved, etc. This is what distinguishes HR from other functions (such as Finance or Marketing). The term 'employee champion' goes too far in its impression that HR asserts employee rights and views *against* the organization. We would prefer to regard HR's role as describing employees' views, wishes, hopes, etc. for management colleagues; interpreting issues from an employee perspective, offering a feedback loop and assessing how proposals for change will 'play' with the workforce. In Dave Ulrich's latest book (Ulrich and Brockbank, 2005), HR's role is described as a bridge between management and employees, making sure employees' wants and needs are heard and understood. This seems to us much closer to what we are suggesting. HR needs to be the eyes and ears of the organization, acting as a listening post, or, mixing our metaphors, the thermometer that takes the temperature of the organization.

- The more sophisticated organizations seek to engage employees at the emotional level, as much as at the transactional, in order that they can boost productivity, improve performance (especially regarding quality and customer satisfaction) and effect change. They realize that bargains simply based on cash for services can only go so far. More can be achieved through relationships based on mutual trust and respect. Evidence suggests that the need for meaning in work, or self-actualization, to use Maslow's term, is on the increase. The new generation of workers is less satisfied with the well-paid career. If this is what it takes to achieve success, then organizations, and the managers within them, need to develop 'emotional intelligence' as much as technical skills in sales, marketing or production. HR should be deeply involved in growing emotional intelligence in the management cadre, helping them develop a trusting relationship with employees based on mutual respect and understanding. This will form a part of the psychological contract between the employer and employee. And a logical role for HR would be to act as 'the guardian of the employment relationship', as Bruce Hedley from Aegon UK put it in an interview with the authors. This is not in the day-to-day sense of managing the relationship – that is the preserve of the line. HR's role is to help provide the people management policies and procedures, to facilitate the appropriate organizational culture.
- The work of improving employment relationships is not just at the individual level, but also at the collective. This means encouraging and supporting consultative and representative mechanisms. Ensuring that employees as a group have a 'voice' will bring business benefits. In a less structural manner it also means building social capital. The organization needs to find ways of facilitating employee networking and interaction. Growing communities of practice is one way of doing this. This can be fruitful in terms of idea generation and knowledge sharing, leading to greater organizational creativity and innovation. Producing positive emotions through developing the right work environment and generating a culture of passion will contribute to employee engagement. HR can stimulate such an approach by itself being passionate about progress through positive thinking and co-operative behaviour at the collective and individual level.
- A key role for HR is to enable managers to behave in ways that support the employment relationship and embrace the culture. Getting the line to 'internalize' the importance of people (Legge, 1995) is critical. This is what will make people management devolution work. If managers do not think it is part of their job to take account of people; if they feel they do not have the skills to manage; if they do not have the time to take their people management responsibilities seriously, then devolution will fail. And employees will be worse off than before with HR more removed from the day to day employment relationship.
- As we have emphasized, the motivation of employees is not just a good thing in itself. Indeed, if motivation is taken to mean happiness, we are not talking about generating a climate of contentment, except in so far as positive well-being leads to organizational well-being. There is a serious risk that HR's interest in employee motivation comes to be understood as the modern version of the welfare worker. No, we want HR's role to be seen as finding the means to improve the bottom line (or public/voluntary sector equivalent). This requires understanding the link between individual and organizational performance, and discovering the ways to unlock the capability and potential of the workforce. It might seem softer than the harder edge of the production or service manager, but its purpose is just the same. It is only the manner of doing this that is different. In dealing with people, organizations have to take account of their emotions, feelings, perceptions.

Concern for employee well-being might seem to be a return to HR's welfare role, but many organizations are now investing in programmes to improve employees' physical and psychological health. This may be for good business reasons (cutting the cost of absence/improving productivity) or to demonstrate the employer is concerned for the employee, thereby strengthening the employment bond. It might be part of organizational branding to attract and retain staff. Failing to give due attention to well-being may lead to psychological withdrawal, which may in turn lead to lateness, absence or even sabotage, as well as resignation.

- Understanding the link between people and business success is not sufficient. HR will need to overcome its 'Achilles heel' (CIPD, 2003a) of poor implementation if it is to be successful. Too often HR has a bias to inaction. It is better at analysis and fault finding than with acting. Thinking may be more fun than doing. As Rick Brown put it in conversation with us: 'HR managers must get their kicks from delivering results.' This will help in taking the temperature of the organizational climate. That knowledge will itself make HR more effective, but its actions will bring further benefits. Some of these actions may be indirect through line managers. Direct actions lie in what will be covered under the 'content' section below: together with its line partners, developing organizational effectiveness and capability, and promoting the organizational proposition.
- To achieve its objectives of competent service delivery and informed insight on organizational health and how to motivate employees, HR requires high-quality measurement systems. This includes, but goes beyond, service process metrics. It covers HR's own performance and especially its value-adding contribution. But it also takes people management data on efficiency and effectiveness (such as employee motivation, well-being and retention) and transforms it into information that drives decision-making on a regular basis. Employee data should be of constant value, not something that is neglected, only to be viewed when there is perceived to be a crisis.

We would therefore argue that HR's *raison d'être* is that it focuses more on the people aspect of the organization than any other function. It does so in the context of understanding the business. Line managers, as we have said, have the primary responsibility for delivering organizational objectives through their employees. But managers will see people as only one of the resources involved in achieving their goals. Through concentrating on how best to mobilize employees to meet organizational ends, HR should develop skills and insights that help line managers and ultimately help their employer. How this capability will be delivered by HR will vary with the business context. This suggests that HR should not spend too long trying to divine an abstract meaning to their work. Rather, in doing their job well – helping connect people and business – they will be adding value, demonstrating their worth and indicating their USP.

How successfully HR performs this role is a matter of the skills deployed, the structures and processes it applies, the relationships with employees and management it builds, and what content (e.g. human capital, engagement, talent management) it emphasizes. These are interlinked points and are discussed later. But first below we need to consider the key aspects of HR's role which require more detailed discussion:

- strategist
- change manager
- professional
- regulator.

Those familiar with Ulrich will observe the same number of categories in his original conception, but note they are only in two respects the same, namely the strategist and change agent. The professional role appears in the new Ulrich conception (Ulrich and Brockbank, 2005). We are also using the 'regulator' description used by Storey (1992). We are not suggesting that these four items cover all that HR does, rather that these are the aspects of the role which are either more contentious or complex. Of the other two parts of the original Ulrich definition, good quality HR administration is incontestably essential and we will cover it as part of the professional role. A key issue is who does it: is it done in-house or outsourced, completely or in part? That will be discussed in Chapter 7. As to the employee champion role, we are covering the relationship with employees later.

HR as strategist

This seems to be the holy grail of organizations at present: how can HR make a strategic contribution? Presumably this ambition is not an end in itself. Strategic influence is sought because it can ensure that people issues are taken seriously in determining critical choices about the organization's future. The complaint in commercial companies is that finance dominates. Decisions are made on the basis of whether the numbers (in pounds, dollars or euros) add up. This is hardly surprising in that satisfying the shareholder is the name of the game. In other sectors, the position is more complicated, but often staff feel their needs are unnecessarily ignored in favour of satisfying the customer, be it a government minister, a hospital patient or a deserving charitable case. Some of these complaints are misplaced. Too many organizations (especially, but not only, in the public sector) have been too producer- and insufficiently customer-centric. Working hours, task flexibility, even services offered, have been determined to suit employees not end-users. Changing this mindset has been one of the major cultural change drivers of the last 25 years. And HR has been as guilty of being customer unfriendly as other functions.

So companies have to satisfy shareholders and all organizations have to satisfy customers and other stakeholders. This means that cost efficiency cannot be the only measure of success. Prahalad and Hamel (1994) complained in the downsizing of the 1990s that too much attention was given to the denominator of the business equation and not enough to the numerator. In other words, should there not be more thinking going into growing the business and less into cutting it. Organizations having gone through the painful exercise of 'rightsizing' cannot unfortunately rest there. Change means that further 'rationalization' will occur. Workforce numbers will reduce. Indeed, this may be a semi-continuous exercise in some companies or a periodic pruning in others. The difference, though, in the twenty-first century, at least from a UK perspective, is the growing realization that employees do matter more than previously thought – certainly in the better-managed firms. This will not stop workforce reductions, where necessary, but it will mean more attention to getting the best out of those who remain.

As the section on organizational capability will show, people can be seen as an asset as well as a cost. As an asset they can improve organizational performance. They can raise productivity, improve quality or deliver superior customer experience. They can grow in knowledge, skills, experience. Thus their value can appreciate and improve the long term prospects of the organization. This allows an organization like the Ministry of Defence (MOD) to begin to talk of getting the maximum return on its investment in its people. There is a lot of research, which will be covered later, that demonstrates this point. HR needs to get into the strategic decision-making process in order that it can argue for the value-adding capability of employees, and warn of the value-depreciating consequences of having a disenchanted workforce. So the prime purpose of HR's strategic contribution is just this: to bring employees into the heart of the business rather than see them as a resource akin to plant and equipment. The human capital argument is one of the reasons why HR can aspire to be strategic, and be taken seriously. Economic changes mean that 'the real foundation of competitive success would no longer be proprietary processes or even distinctive products, but outstanding people' (Connolly *et al.*, 1997).

To achieve the strategic ambition HR has rightly wanted a seat on the board and/or executive committee. As we described earlier, this was to avoid the situation where HR is 'downstream' of the key decisions: only relevant at the third order of business decision-making, operationalizing or implementing business decisions made by other business leaders (Purcell and Ahlstrand, 1994) (see Figure 3.1). Where there was no personnel director on the board, the function seemed to do lower-level tasks and not to be as involved in key decisions (Purcell, 1994) or have less HR influence (Industrial Relations Services, 1998). Where HR was represented at the top table, there was more likelihood of a high-performance working approach and strategic discussion of HR management (Tyson, 1994). This research reinforces what feels intuitively right: if HR has a voice at the top table then the organization is more likely to take human capital, employee engagement, talent management, etc. seriously.

If HR is part of the top team it can both share in the strategic decision-making process and influence the outcome from a people management perspective. It can be inside the proverbial tent, not an outsider looking in. But it is important to consider what sort of role HR has in the boardroom. Is HR a strategic player or partner? In other words, is HR at the top table to give its views and take part in debate – a useful player? Or is HR accorded the same status as other directors, a full partner in business decision-making? It might be unusual for the HR director to lead business decisions – resource-based business strategies are rare in the Anglo Saxon

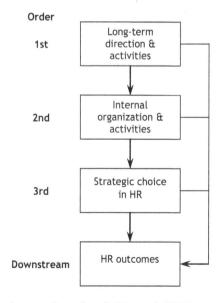

Source: Purcell and Ahlstrand (1994)

Figure 3.1   Purcell/Ahlstrand view on HR strategy

business model (less so in the Japanese) – but at least the people implications would be given due attention in decision-making.

To be effective at the strategic level, HR needs to have a greater understanding of how the strategic process operates. Much of the writing on developing HR's strategic contribution makes the assumption that organizational strategy making is a determinist and rational process, where action follows grand decisions. This has rightly been criticized on two counts. Firstly, strategy making is in the hands of human beings, with their own interests to serve. Strategy making is formed in the 'political hurly burly of organizational life' (Johnson, 1987). It may be carried out informally and be characterized by bargaining, where power and authority are important to the outcome. As a former boss to one of the authors said: 'remember it is always politics before logic in company decision-making.' Secondly, and naturally flowing from the first point, strategy, rather than being developed in a purposive way from top management, instead often occurs unintentionally, through small incremental steps often taken at operational level, as the organization 'feels' its way towards a new position. The strategy then becomes evident in a post hoc rationalization of what has happened. Mintzberg (1994) described this as *emergent strategy*. This blurring between strategy and tactics or plans may well be inevitable, and, in a way, desirable since it means the organization is learning as it carries out its activities or retaining flexibility by framing strategic options, but not deciding between them until it has to.

The implications of this research is that HR must be active in the political and informal processes. It should not think 'now we have a seat on the board we have made it'. The risk is that HR directors may help frame formal positions, yet fail to make an impact where it really counts. This is especially true if the HR director is not part of an 'inner circle', not privy to the key informal decision-making processes, not aware of the political machinations of colleagues. HR should therefore seize opportunities to take part in the informal processes and exploit the ad hoc nature of much strategic execution. This can be done by building alliances with like-minded colleagues; identifying issues where the function can be particularly influential; acting as a personal support – coach, mentor, listening ear – to peers; and not interpreting the field of participation too narrowly, making instead a broad, not just functional, contribution to business affairs. This emphasizes again the importance of the calibre of senior HR people and their business knowledge such that they are seen as vital partners, not bit-part contributors, limited to walk-on roles as deliverers of a message already decided.

It should also be emphasized that many organizations are not that good at strategic thinking or delivery. Criticizing HR's inability to be strategic may be unfair if the whole management team is failing in this task. Goals may be very short term, unconnected to any forward organizational thrust. Tactical solutions to the immediate problems facing the organization may drive out any more reflective thinking on medium- (let alone long-) term issues. This reinforces the criticisms made above, but the difficulty is that some organizations do have formal strategies, it is just that they are not very strategic, not well integrated or thoughtful.

So a key task for HR is to improve the quality of the strategic processes. This means integrating all the functional and business parts so that they form a single organizational strategy. It means looking over a longer time frame at the implications of business decisions and concentrating on the 'big ticket' items that will really affect business success. It means taking proper account of external dimensions be they regulatory, social or economic. It should warn colleagues of the risks of organizational myopia by pointing to the numerous examples of organizations that have fallen from grace through being short term or parochial in their thinking. It means having a planned approach to the future, avoiding ad hoc solutions, but, nevertheless, having the flexibility to adjust to changing circumstances or responding to the take up of any particular strategic option. HR, in particular, should see successful implementation as part of the strategic process: getting things done in the end changes things, having great strategies does not.

Playing a corporate role HR can also assist in ensuring the whole organization pulls together in one direction. Most organizations have centrifugal tendencies that lead to fragmentation because strong-willed individuals are usually appointed to lead business units and they want to achieve success their way. This tendency may be of little concern if the organization operates a decentralized model, where independent businesses are linked together in a light federal structure. It is of greater concern if the sum of the parts is supposed to be more than the whole. HR can play a significant integrative role in helping organizations to combine their efforts so as to realize the benefits of commonality. HR is well placed to do this because it is a function that operates across the organization in a way that is true of few others. It should have a perspective on what should be common to the divisions within the organization, but also what can be different. The recent process changes, investment in technology and introduction of shared services should have sharpened this debate.

Where strategy in decentralized or multidivisional companies is not determined at the top of the organization, but at business unit level, HR has to achieve strategic influence through business partners, not just corporate HR directors. Business partners, like HR directors, must successfully participate in the formal decision-making process, but also look to participate in any informal processes. Alternatively, the corporate strategy may be driven or significantly influenced bottom up. Again the business partner should play a part in both the analysis of the organizational situation and the framing of strategic options. Another variation is for the organization to set a general strategic course at corporate level leaving the business units to implement based on their interpretation of this overall organizational approach. This situation does not deny business partners a strategic role, it just makes it more informal and closer to implementation.

If we have discussed the strategic process, what should be the strategic content? It should reflect the issues we will cover in Chapter 4, but in a general sense it is about fulfilling the organizational purpose or mission. This might mean satisfying or 'delighting' the customer with its products or services. It will require superior performance and productivity, whilst giving due attention to quality. It is likely to include the capacity to grow and generate new ideas. The strategy will have to be underpinned by sound finances and effective and efficient internal processes. The distinctive HR contribution to this aspiration will be in having:

- well-managed planning of workforce resources so that supply and demand are synchronized for now and the future, taking account of current workforce skills and labour market dynamics such as the ageing workforce and changing retirement age
- building people capability to ensure the delivery of the business strategy now and in the future
- a branding of the employment offer so that the organization attracts quality people with the right skills and attributes
- work organization and structure that places people in jobs they can do but with scope for proper development
- performance management and reward processes that focus effort and motivate staff to contribute fully

- learning mechanisms that encourage personal growth and knowledge sharing for business benefit
- ways of retaining staff where desired, but successfully exiting them when not required.

These may seem self-evident points, but too often organizations assume that there is an unlimited supply of skilled and talented staff, trained to meet business requirements immediately. What HR should ensure is that the business strategy takes account of the numbers and skills of the workforce available for immediate use and facilitates the building of capability over the longer term to meet future requirements. This means development initiatives need to be linked to workforce planning. Reward needs to attract, retain and motivate in the context of business priorities. And so on. The key point is that there should be an integrated and holistic approach to people management that flows from the organization's long-term purpose and shorter-term strategies. The different dots of people management activity need to be joined up so they present a coherent picture.

All these HR processes that reflect the employee life cycle have to be done within an overall organizational philosophy that accepts and celebrates difference, that does not permit discrimination, except on the ground of merit.

It is characteristic of strategic HR that people management and its implications for the organization are on the agenda of the top team; that its leaders take notice of the HR director, who is armed with credible information on people management performance; and that decisions taken (and implemented) are influenced by the business impact, thinking over the longer as well as shorter term, and an awareness of what is going on in the external world.

Change management role

As we saw in Chapter 1, HR has always been at the heart of change within organizations. The nature of its participation and the context may have altered but it has long since been accepted as a component of HR's role. But it is easy to gloss over the challenge of managing change in the future.

It is really the complexity, speed and depth of change in large organizations that makes the difference. Business volatility is not new, but its impact is profound on HR. Just take three examples:

- Enron went from being an award-winning, successful business to being one that was broken into bits. Imagine managing change in that arena.
- RBS went from being one of three Scottish banks to being the fifth biggest in the world in five years. Think of the impact on people management policies, practices and processes with that degree of growth.
- T-Mobile was once One2One, owned by Cable and Wireless and Media One, before being bought and renamed by Deutsche Telekom. This meant a major internal and external rebranding exercise that tested employee loyalty.

So business change still takes the usual forms of downsizing, takeover, acquisition, etc., but this can all happen so much more quickly. Shareholder pressure to deliver is more intense and horizons shorter. CEOs – already on short-term, rolling contracts – face dismissal if one of many things go wrong, from inappropriate sexual liaison to the misleading of shareholders. Surely the events that have damaged some of our biggest companies have come from business leaders' response to this relentless pressure to succeed?

And the public sector is far from immune from these pressures. There has always been a need to respond to externally driven change. The UK government has increasingly ratcheted up its demands for both quality and speed of service, often in the context of an increasing volume of activities. It too has reconfigured structures to achieve the best operational fit. Take the examples below:

- The merger between Customs and Excise and the Inland Revenue to produce Her Majesty's Revenue and Customs: an organization that at the merger employed around 100,000 people and raised nearly £380 billion in revenue.
- At the other end of the scale, ambulance services have been required to reach 75 per cent of Category A emergency calls within eight minutes. In 2004/5 it just exceeded this objective, having moved from a position in 2000/01 where only three of the over 30 services were able to reach that performance level. This success has been achieved against an annual rise in demand of about 7 per cent.
- The Gershon review, a government cost-saving initiative, is driving among other things greater efficiency in back office processing by simplification and standardization of policies and processes, and cross-organizational sharing and consolidation.
- The prison service has had to cope with a growth, at peak, of approximately 10,000 in prisoner numbers in the last five years, with only limited expansion in the number of penal institutions and with a cost-control regime in place.

And in a further mimicry of the private sector, public sector CEOs have also faced the sack if performance fails in what the government deems to be an unacceptable manner; this ranges from dead bodies not reaching the mortuary to the mishandling of an industrial dispute.

Those working in a global business world face these same difficulties but also others they would not previously have faced. These may relate to geography: HR staff may be working for bosses that operate transnationally and are located some distance away. The businesses they run are regional or international in nature. National, let alone local, considerations may cut little ice with them. So the managers' frame of reference has altered: their nationality is incidental, not central. It is both harder to influence under these circumstances and to operate. Decisions may need to be implemented across a number of countries. The economic circumstances may be quite different in one country compared with another. There may be an economic imperative to make labour more flexible in Germany that is irrelevant to the USA. Adopting work–life balance measures may be a quite different challenge in Japan to Sweden. In some countries, there may be no trade unions to face or convince of the need to change. In others, there may be formal employee consultation procedures. Opposition to change may come more from threatened local managers than their staff. So the employee relations challenge of operating cross nationally has a variety of dimensions – legal, cultural, organizational and economic.

And this tendency is likely to grow, partly with China and India's entry on the world economic stage as first division players and partly because offshoring and international procurement mean that processes will become ever more global. It is a sobering thought to those living in the advanced economies of the West, where the population is tending to age or shrink in number, that by 2030 half of the global workforce will be living in China or India. As Pam Hurley (Smethurst, 2005a) says: 'A big question for the (UK HR) profession is whether to send the work away or bring people here.'

For senior HR managers this change of context will have a number of implications, some of which are tackled elsewhere in this book – the selection and management of talent, the

> A Shell shop steward used to complain about the impotence of his local site management and how he needed to 'speak to the moguls in The Hague'. Nowadays he would certainly be right about remote decision-making, but the locus might as well be Houston or Singapore, as The Hague.

whole question of organizational governance and the implications for personal relationships between CEO and HR director. But thinking of HR's future effectiveness, operating in this changing environment will place a number of demands upon the function, described below.

Change may be internally or externally driven – e.g. it may be a home-grown restructuring or it may be a response to state regulations on the minimum wage. It may be principally a business-led change (e.g. dealing with an acquisition) or an HR-driven change (e.g. introducing a new reward system). The change programme may be concerned with structures, processes, activities or business strategy.

The origins and nature of the change programme will affect the sort of contribution expected from HR. Thus it could be that it is the professional knowledge and skills that HR has to deploy. Alternatively, the input may be of more concern to project or process management – ensuring resources are available, planning deliverables, consulting stakeholders and communicating.

So, at one level the challenge is to be an effective professional, advising and supporting management, managing certain legal and procedural issues. Siemens Business Services, for example, has frequently to absorb parts of other organizations. This means a lot of consultation and discussion with employee representatives. It involves ensuring that the terms of Transfer of Undertakings regulations are respected. It requires the eventual harmonization of disparate terms and conditions. In other words, HR has to deploy its knowledge, experience and skill to smooth the path of business change. HR will be both a facilitator of change (helping employees adjust through communication and discussion) and an expert on legal matters.

In other situations HR may be even more creative – at designing new structures, systems and policies to respond to new business demands. This might be constructing competency frameworks to respond to new Health and Safety Executive (HSE) requirements; producing a revised sales incentive plan to drive up income; or developing coaching interventions to assist technical professionals move to line manager posts.

At another level, HR might be involved at an earlier point in the change process, participating in the change decision-making process itself rather than effectively implementing a decision already made. This may then develop into securing support for the decision inside and outside the organization, convincing stakeholders of the need for change. Once confirmed, the HR role may be to ensure that the actions agreed upon are carried through by mobilizing resources. HR has then executive authority in the change process.

Finally, HR should have a role in checking progress as the change proceeds and evaluating the degree of success once the change is implemented. If the change is successful, then HR should be working to see how it can be institutionalized and, if appropriate, extended to other areas. If change is not successful, then it needs to understand the cause of failure, both to put things right for now and to learn for the future. Seeing change through is critical. Too many initiatives in the people management arena are started and not properly finished. It is all very well designing new policies or processes, but their value comes from institutionalizing change, be it a new attitude to learning, higher productivity or greater resource flexibility.

Naturally, these levels of involvement are not so clear cut. They may blur in practice. The distinction we draw is between the HR professional (functional advisor, consultant and expert) and strategic change agent (partner, planner and executive). HR should be capable of performing both roles. The weighting between them will depend on circumstances. What HR should ensure is that it is sufficiently respected and its role deemed sufficiently important for it to participate at an early enough stage to choose which is the most appropriate contribution to make – as strategic decision-maker or functional expert. This requires management acknowledgement of the capability of the function and for the importance of people to the organization. It emphasizes that organizations give more attention to cultural change. This is obvious where the objective of the change programme is to effect a reorientation in attitudes or behaviours (say in customer service). It may be less obvious, but is just as vital, if the change concerns other issues because people will react – and often negatively – to structural, role or business changes. Frequently staff reaction is that any change is threatening. As Lynda Gratton (2000) has pointed out, people are different to machines. They have an emotional side and increasingly seek meaning in their work. They are slower to adjust. They do not always like change. This makes both the requirement to try to effect cultural change all the more important (as it will be necessary to sustain any transformation) and the challenge that much harder. This is especially true for organizations with a diverse workforce, those operating in a number of countries or those (such as voluntary or charitable) organizations where change conflicts with strongly held values. HR therefore must ensure that the cultural dimension to change is taken seriously in process terms – communicating, consulting, supporting – so that there is a good chance that the programme will be successfully implemented. Moreover, HR can act as the trusted advisor to the line in gauging employee reaction.

And this is more important than in the past because employee expectations of how change will be managed have grown. Organizations cannot get away with command and control in places where employees are no longer deferential to their leaders. Organizations need to explain and, if possible, convince staff before organizations will get their participation in a change process. As Rick Brown explains, organizations cannot 'buy or bully' their way to success. Organizations have to be much more adaptive, adjusting their approach in the light of employee reaction. This requires a mindset that accepts that 'it is not weak to change your thoughts'. Or, more positively, HR should be aiming, in the words of Dean Royles, 'to create an environment where the individual can release their potential'. Growing the organization's capacity to change is one of HR's important (if most difficult) objectives. Failure to achieve this goal leaves the organization vulnerable to adverse impacts from the external environment – the world may have moved on but the organization has stood still.

HR as professional

We described in Chapter 2 the debate about the extent to which HR would perform a professional, operational role. Some strong supporters of the new HR structure model see a place for deep technical knowledge in centres of expertise, but they think business partners need a stronger business than traditional HR capability. With extensive devolution to the line, this leaves HR's professional input limited to legal compliance and policy design. Others take the view that line managers want more support than that on the more day-to-day aspects of people management, from recruitment through employee relations to disciplinary management.

Our view is that there is a strong argument to say that delivering HR services will remain the core activity to the function. This is not just in the transactional area (administering records, running payroll, etc.), in providing information (via call centres or intranets), in monitoring organizational performance and in an advisory and policy development capacity, but also in designing HR processes and executing people management tasks. For example, HR will continue to establish recruitment processes, design selection methods, run assessment centres and evaluate recruitment performance. HR managers may no longer do the candidate selection (if they ever did), but they may still be heavily involved in the recruitment activity. And if managers want HR to participate in the selection decisions alongside them, what is the problem in them so doing?

There is a danger that the philosophy of strategic HR and of devolution to line management, which is accompanied by putting more distance between the function and employees, together with the marginalization of administrative activities, leaves HR with no contribution to make.

> *There is a crisis of direction (in HR) because of the preoccupation with strategy at the expense of operational personnel work ... Personnel people have a clear role in strategic development and its implementation. Their expertise and their authority in strategic discussions derive from their activity at the operational level. Abandoning operational activity and specialist knowledge is a high risk strategy.*
>
> (Torrington, 1998)

We would argue that these tendencies to devolve, become business centric and minimize transactional work all have their own logic and will affect HR's role to a degree, but this does not mean that HR should only play the role of strategic partner, not least because it overstates the importance of strategy, as described earlier. People management responsibility should be seized by line managers, and HR should, in some organizations or in some situations, back off giving them more scope to manage. But if HR is to be customer-centric, then it needs to respond to customer needs and, if it is to be an effective business partner, this might mean more involvement than the HR model might suggest.

As to employees, if HR is to have an understanding of what motivates them, then the function has to find ways of taking the organizational pulse and getting a feel for the aspirations, frustrations and positive vibes from the workforce. This can be done without intruding on the line manager–employee relationship. Knowing about the external labour market through an active resourcing role allows HR to be able to develop appropriate attraction mechanisms. Getting involved helps it get a feel for the aspirations of those active in the employment market. Improving administrative performance and extricating some HR managers from unnecessary transactional work, does not mean that HR administration is unimportant. Practitioners will tell you, as one American HR manager graphically put it: 'Administration ... doesn't get you anything but a black eye if you screw it up' (quoted in Eisenstat, 1996). It will also deny HR access to the 'higher value-added' activities. E-HR, including both manager self-service and employee self-service, will reduce the number of transactions that will have to be processed by HR, but some will still remain, and these will be the more complex.

We reject the arguments advanced in the Introduction on the impending death of HR, which are based on the view either that if it does not change it will die or that if it does successfully readjust, it will also die but in a different way. Line managers do not have the time or inclination to replace HR's role as policy or process designer. Similarly, they are not going to participate in the political process, lobbying government on employment bills or implementing their enactment. And the recent flood of regulations covering working time, minimum wages, temporary contracts, information and consultation, etc., has kept HR busy enough. As Trevor Bromelow put it in an interview for this book: 'Managers may be ok on the implementation of HR policies. They would not be so good at designing them. They lack the experience, knowledge and networks of the HR community. HR will always have these advantages over them.'

Nor do we accept the suggestion that professionalism is an adolescent phase through which HR is going that will end with its maturity as a strategic player. We do not of course deny the validity of the strategic partner role; rather, we believe it needs to be underpinned by professional HR knowledge and competence. So HR has to 'find the delicate balance between day to day operations and big picture initiatives' (Pfau and Cundiff, 2002).

HR as regulator

We have already said that we believe that HR should not take its need to be customer sensitive to extremes. We do not wholly accept the proposition that 'strategic HR management' is 'to support rather than constrain what the organization is seeking to achieve' (CIPD, 2005c). Most of the time HR is indeed there to support line managers deliver business results. Help with HR administration, advice on policy or the law, and participation in selection processes and similar activities are all designed to make people management more effective and lead to positive outcomes for the organization. The more skilled, experienced and knowledgeable the manager, the less the requirement for HR's involvement. The more people-centric managers are, the more likely they will invest time in getting the best out of their staff. HR policies and procedures should be designed to give managers the appropriate freedom to manage, but in the context of the overall corporate need. Intelligent and supportive managers make this task easy; mavericks are harder to deal with.

And this is where the regulator role comes in. If managers always looked at their needs in the context of the bigger picture, if they were never fallible in their judgements, if they were always well informed of company policies, legal necessities etc., then HR would not need to have this governance role. It is precisely because the world does not run smoothly that HR may have to intervene.

However, the governance role should be carefully defined. Interventions should not be taken lightly, and so should be rare. So what is the basis of HR stepping in? We would argue that HR should do the following:

- Protect the values of the organization. This means that where such principles as diversity, meritocracy, honesty, integrity and so on are threatened, then HR takes action. This might be to challenge performance assessments if they discriminate against women or disciplinary processes appear to be biased against ethnic minorities (an area researched by Rick *et al.*, 2000). HR might intervene if there seems to be an in-group favoured for projects, for overtime or in job selection. It is all about 'giving employees a fair shake' and 'not being abused by the organization' or its agents (the line managers), according to Neil Roden in conversation with the authors. This protective role is all the more important, the less trade unions are available to play this role. Clearly if corruption, cheating or falsification is going on, HR would take steps to stop it. But sometimes the problem is more insidious, where a climate has developed permitting staff to be careless of ethics and principles in what they do. This might require a more systematic change programme, including reaffirmation of the organizational code of conduct. Specific cases of bullying or harassment, where the manager is the accused, will necessitate HR's intervention at the individual level.

- Defend organizational policy. For example, managers might be acting outside the guidelines on pay increases or offering benefits to new recruits that go beyond the rules. But HR should not find itself defending outdated policies, ones that are not well aligned with business requirements or are overly focused on principles of people management good practice without being rooted in business requirements.

- Insist that the organization prepares to meet the people management requirements that emerge from regulations issued by bodies such as the Financial Services Authority, Securities Exchange Commission (especially now under Sarbanes-Oxley rules) or the various Of-bodies. This might include having proper succession planning, workforce planning, remuneration management, etc. The same argument can be advanced if securing and keeping Investors in People membership is seen as a useful badging for external and internal consumption.

- Ensure that undue risks are not taken with respect to employment law. Outright legal non-compliance should be prevented, such as paying below the minimum wage or employing staff without a formal contract. But the law is not always black and white. Take equal pay. Legally, organizations should not discriminate on the grounds of age, gender, disability, ethnicity, etc. However, the law does allow differences between men and women and between ethnic groups, but only if there are 'objective' grounds. Whilst there are indications of what constitutes 'objective' grounds, in any particular case judgement is required. HR should position itself to assist line managers make these judgements. However, there may be situations where HR has to lead the organization to prevent excessive financial exposure. Some of these situations will be clear cut. For example, in one research organization HR discovered that managers were systematically giving higher starting pay to men because they negotiated harder than women. HR was able to reform this practice due to the risk of a severe financial penalty if it did not do so. In other circumstances, the balance between taking one course of action instead of another will be much more even. Paying one occupational group higher salaries than another may rest on remuneration data, but how robust this is may be more debatable. HR has to help the organization weigh up the potential costs and benefits of effective hiring and better retention against the chance of losing a lawsuit.

- Manage other people management risks. There is an increasing liability for people costs associated with risks arising from acts of terrorism or from putting employees in unsafe situations. The 'duty of care' means organizations have to take seriously personal threats from either business practices (such as animal medical research) or employment circumstances (this is especially true for expatriates, whose work may involve dangers to health from violence, epidemics or natural disasters).

The combination of these drivers argues for a more holistic approach to managing people risks and line requirements. It should lead to a more professional response from the HR function in helping the business develop tools and practices both to identify and quantify the risks in the first place, and help mitigate their potential impact.

Within HR itself there is a need for a consistent approach so that the employee proposition is not undermined by different advice being given by different parts of the HR team on the application of fundamental values. Variety of guidance on the operation of HR policies and practices is acceptable, even desirable, but not on the principles of how employees should be treated.

4 *New Content*

Introduction

One of the arguments in this book is that HR may have new roles to play and this means it has new skills to develop, but this is only one aspect of the transformational journey. Another is that HR has to be more effective in new content territories, as in old. HR will still need to develop policies and practices in reward and performance management, in training and development, in recruitment and retention, etc. What it has to do in addition is to look at these areas of professional expertise and recontextualize them. The combination of globalization, tight labour markets, changing employee aspirations, regulation of employment conditions and intensified competition has driven the best in class to be more holistic in their approach to people management and more sophisticated in how they go about their work. But what is changing thinking in the most sophisticated organizations is the evidence linking employee performance to business outcomes. Whether it be under the heading of high performance working, high involvement management, high commitment practices or engagement, there is a volume of evidence that indicates that organizations can succeed better if they give due attention to their employees. Much of this thinking chimes with HRM and with theories on human capital management, the resource-based theory of the firm and the notion of core competencies/capabilities.

We have already discussed the HRM philosophy, and the other three sets of theories have much in common. The resource-based theory of the firm (Barney, 1991) argues that human resources can be a source of competitive advantage because they are rare and difficult to copy. In the knowledge economy this is even more true. Somewhat in the same vein is the notion of core competencies/capabilities. These ideas (led by Prahalad and Hamel, 1990) suggest that companies ought to nurture the competitive advantage they obtain from those things that they have or do that are distinctive. This might include reputation, brand, particular skill or knowledge. Depending on which management guru you read, core competencies may be aligned with the business strategy or may shape it. Either way it should be appropriate to the company's business activity and environment, and should be capable of being sustained.

Of course concepts such as these are closely allied to that of human capital. Human capital is not yet a fully established term in the HR community. There is very loose usage and no agreed definition. The relationship between it and related terms (like intellectual capital, knowledge management, social capital, organizational capital) is not always clear. However, it is a concept that has been around a long time in economics. Economists have used 'human capital' to describe investments, either by individuals or organizations, in knowledge or skills. It is called 'human capital' as an analogy with physical capital: something that can be measurably invested in and from which there may also be a measurable return. The benefits of such investment can be recouped through higher earnings or profitability. Firm-specific human capital needs to be protected, otherwise it may be lost via undesirable wastage.

Human capital seems to have relevance to HR professionals in two ways. You can think of human capital in terms either of the value-added application of the knowledge, skills and competencies of the workforce in some aggregated sense (which may be akin to core competencies) or through the way in which employees are engaged in the success of the organization. Ulrich (1998b), for example, has argued that human capital is a function of the combination of both competency and commitment.

The commitment part of the jigsaw puzzle has moved on in recent years. We now want employees to be engaged, not just committed. The difference between the two is a matter of degree. Some employees can be committed to their employer in a purely transactional way: I'll work for you if you pay me. This is not engagement. Other forms of commitment that relate to job satisfaction and being prepared to go beyond the call of duty are much closer to employee engagement. What they lack is the degree to which employees are aware of organizational purposes and determined to achieve them through active participation (e.g. in encouraging friends to join the organization). It is the striving for success that is characteristic of employee engagement. It will not last, however, if the employer does not reciprocate and encourage that sense of engagement. As in the notion of the psychological contract, employee engagement should be a two-way deal.

So what does this all mean for HR practitioners? Thankfully for them, there is now a substantial body of research on high performance workplaces and HR practices[1] which shows that if the organization can take the human raw material and mould it to the needs of the organization in such a way that it generates a positive response, then substantial benefits will arise. People management practices can produce improvements in productivity, quality, client service, employee retention, attendance, flexibility and business performance benefits through such things as:

- providing employment security, encouraging employee ownership, sharing information with staff, adopting employee-participation practices and changing job design in an involving manner (Pfeffer, 1994; Huselid, 1995; Ostroff, 1995)
- offering an employee involvement approach to total quality management (Lawler *et al.*, 1995)
- giving an opportunity for employee 'voice' (Black and Lynch, 1997)
- allowing decentralized responsibility and problem-solving teams (Kelly and Emison, 1995)
- creating a climate where employees are involved, satisfied and enthusiastic about their work (Harter, 2002)
- introducing gain-sharing (Kaufman, 1992) or profit-sharing schemes (Kruse, 1993)
- ensuring (amongst many other things) that employees are properly selected (Thompson, 2000)
- offering greater opportunities for employees to be directly involved in decisions concerning their work (Gallie *et al.*, 1998)
- investing in training and development (Tsui *et al.*, 1997).

The pattern to this research suggests that organizations need to be effective in recruitment (using appropriate selection mechanisms), training and development (building skills), employee relations (giving employees a chance to express their views), work design (allowing employees

---

1   Rather than give all the references in detail at the back of the book, readers can follow up this research in three places: Barber *et al.*, (1999), Robinson *et al.*, (2004) and Tamkin (2005).

to shape their work as much as possible) and performance management/reward (encouraging good performance through appropriate incentives at individual and team level).

The management characteristics of trust, reciprocity and mutuality are vital, too, in leading to the greater engagement of the workforce. The key influence in this process, according to US (Rucci *et al.*, 1998) and UK research (Barber *et al.*, 1999), is the beneficial effect front-line supervision can have on employee attitudes. This involves managers supporting staff, valuing them as people, giving and receiving information and feedback, and allowing them to grow and develop.

As Figure 4.1 proposes, HR policies and practices should support the relationship between manager and employee. HR should also give attention to the cultural context within which the employment relationship operates. The aim is to generate an environment that fosters a positive attitude in managers and encourages the right sort of behaviours in what they value, support and promote. As we described earlier, cultural change is both difficult and necessary in many organizations.

In considering the HR agenda of the future, it is worth looking at two further pieces of research. The CIPD study *Unlocking the Black Box* (Purcell *et al.*, 2003) usefully describes what HR has to do to lift organizational performance. The authors of the study emphasize that employees need three characteristics:

1. the ability to perform (i.e. the requisite knowledge, skills and attributes)
2. the motivation to perform (i.e. the right disposition)
3. the opportunity to deliver (i.e. the opportunity for their skills to be effectively deployed).

If HR and line managers can meet these objectives then performance benefits will flow. This adds the opportunity dimension to those of competency and commitment. It emphasizes that if organizations are to get value from their employees, they need to provide the means by which they can contribute. The so called '4As model' by Tamkin (2005), shown in Figure 4.2, separates out point three above into two elements. Besides giving *ability* and *attitudes* as necessary components, her approach distinguishes between the developmental and deployment parts of opportunity. In the former, the employer gives employees *access* to work through recruitment and then by way of job structure and design ensures the *application* of this capability.

In many ways the discussion above presents HR with familiar challenges, what may be different is that the function must:

• be more self-conscious in what it does, be clear in why it is undertaking activities

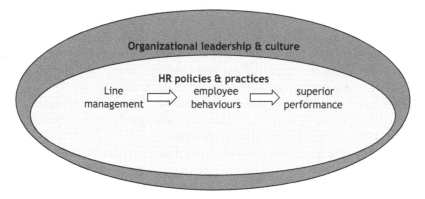

Figure 4.1   An employee engagement model

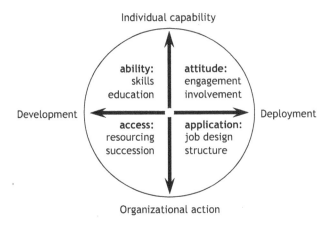

Source: Tamkin (2005)

Figure 4.2   The '4As' model of human capital development

- more effectively link its activities to the aims of the organization
- better combine people management practices together (its own and line management) so that its effects are not dissipated by organizational siloism
- become more knowledgeable on what engages staff, what makes them use their discretionary effort for the good of their employer
- be more creative in offering solutions that will drive higher employee engagement.

HR must exercise care with any best-practice models of people management, of which organizations are so enamoured. In two respects they are inappropriate. Firstly, competitive advantage does not come from 'me-tooism', it comes from being different, being distinct. If the search for top talent is to be effective, organizations need to build a distinctive offering, a particular brand. This comes from identifying the organizational USP, not making a copy of what others do. If it is difficult in the nature of the activity to do things that differently, the search must be on the most productive or efficient way of performing standard tasks. This should offer both 'infrastructure efficiency (need to do things right) and differentiator effectiveness (doing the right things)' (Whittaker and Johns, 2004).

Secondly, best fit must replace best practice in HR thinking. What will ideally suit our business strategy, our organizational requirements? This reinforces the point of requiring a strong link between the business direction and the approach to people management. The danger with best-practice thinking and associated benchmarking processes is that HR imposes solutions on the organization that do not fit its needs. Examples have been seen in performance-related pay and performance management processes, where models are imported from elsewhere because they 'work' in these other environments. This may be done with the best of intentions: the aim may be to deliver good professional practice. The risk is that ideas are uncritically taken up. Either the practices are just not suitable for the organization or they may not have been proved to work. Have they been evaluated over a long enough period to show whether they have met organizational objectives?

There are those that argue the contrary on best practice. For example, Richard McBain (2001) wrote: 'this growing focus on best practices may, it seems, even be replacing the notion of "best fit".' The basis of this argument is the research of Huselid (1995) and others, which shows that there is a 'bundle' of HR practices that can be applied to organizations to drive superior performance. The difficulty, though, with this argument is twofold. Firstly, as we have seen, there is a long list of HR practices – employee involvement, employee financial participation, incentive schemes, skill development, role autonomy, etc. How do we select from the list when it is not clear from the research which of these practices is going to work, and in which circumstances? Knowing the headings does not give you the detail of how best to deploy them. Secondly, are we expected to apply these practices irrespective of context? Individual performance-related pay may work very well in a sales environment, but be completely ineffective in a public sector back office processing unit. Why? Because in sales there are very clear objective targets to meet; whereas in the back office employees do not have individual targets, they have group ones.

The more sophisticated view is that there has to be strategic fit between the business and HR, but there still are a number of best HR practices that should be adopted. The Becker, Huselid and Ulrich HR scorecard (2001) posits that the human capital features of competency and commitment are the product of the implementation of certain ideal HR practices, competencies and systems, all governed by the strategic focus. There is more validity in this approach, depending upon how you specify strategic fit. Some approaches are rather simplistic in distinguishing between say a cost, customer or innovator strategic direction, and are rather deterministic in nature. Organizational strategy is often more complex than this, more multifaceted in nature. Philips, for example, has a business strategy that aims for strong brand management, customer-focused delivery, innovative product/service development and efficiency in processes. In other words, there are elements of all types of strategic direction in the one strategy.

And even taking an idealized approach, there are still the problems with determining which of best practice concepts should be applied and how. Take the reward example again. Best practice suggests that a process involving staff in remuneration design is more likely to achieve successful results than a process that excludes them. However, the principle cannot always be implemented in practice. Staff may not be interested; their representatives may be hostile. It may not always be necessary if employees trust in the integrity and competence of their management. For example, in experiments in team-based pay in the NHS, some employees were prepared to participate in trials because they had faith in management. They did not need formal involvement in the decision-making process (Reilly *et al.*, 2005). The important point here is not to pursue the principle of employee involvement, even if it is best practice, even if it is part of the HR bundle, where such action is likely to be a waste of time or worse. And remember, it is poor implementation that frequently bedevils reward change.

The vehemence with which this point is made stems from experience with organizations that do not use the best practice concept in a sophisticated manner. They have seized upon it either as a substitute for thought (we just have to take it ready-made off the shelf) or through a lack of self-confidence (if others are doing something, it must be right). HR managers might argue that they are pressured into best practice adoption through a shortage of time or because their bosses want reassurance that they are doing the right thing. HR managers need to be able to argue that their choice is appropriate to the needs of their business, without having to show that a competitor has done the same thing. As to time, it is a fair point made by hard-pressed HR managers that they 'do not want to reinvent the wheel'. Borrowing tools and techniques can be helpful, but only as long as they are critically applied. Learning from others is beneficial and the 'not invented here syndrome' can be as unhelpful as the unthinking application of best practice. The mantra should be adaptation, not adoption.

Getting this wrong can endanger the very changes HR wants to see implemented. Eisenstat (1996) quotes the salutary tale of a new HR vice president hired for his track record, coming to a new company with proven programmes. He launched a number of initiatives in performance appraisal and learning, but they had little impact on his new organization, despite their 'technical quality'. Indeed, imposing such ideas as these, rather than responding to the articulated need, can really irritate managers.

In describing the content challenge faced by the HR function, one can look at it from the perspective of employee life-cycle process – attract>deploy>develop>motivate>retain – but we have clustered the key content areas under three headings:

- organizational capability
- organizational effectiveness
- organizational proposition.

As you can see we have stressed the organizational imperatives of the HR agenda. This is because too often the HR effort is disconnected from what the organization needs. It follows professional best practice or, worse, the latest fad. It too often starts with the people management tool (say competency-based pay) not what the problem is.

In our view, organizational capability is about attracting people to the organization and then developing them. In other words, it is about bringing in the raw material and nurturing it so that it is of value to the organization. Thus organizational capability includes talent management and building the stock of human capital. Growing organizational capability offers the chance to produce something that is greater than the sum of the individual parts – 'core' capability. This stock of human capital must then be utilized so that it can deliver results for the organization. This comes under the heading of 'organizational effectiveness'. This provides the infrastructure (including design, systems and processes) and tools within which talent can perform. Deployment of people to the right sort of jobs is critical here. The engagement part of human capital management is covered under the organizational proposition. This ensures that employees are motivated to perform.

In our review of the segments of the content of the HR role, an interesting dilemma emerges when looking at the sequencing of organizational capability, effectiveness and proposition: quite simply, which comes first? Figure 4.3 is a traditional view of human capital development and exploitation in that specification of demand precedes supply. This would

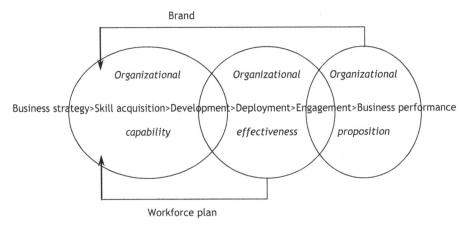

Figure 4.3   A traditional process model of delivering business results through people

apply to organizations with largely homogeneous or commoditized jobs that are relatively easy to fill. In this situation, the role of HR is to assess the demand of the business (usually based on volumes of work and number of heads to produce that volume), look at the organizational capabilities (often a review of skills) of the current stock, work out the gaps and determine the resourcing strategy (e.g. train or recruit) and then generate the employee proposition that supports that strategy.

In the ever-increasing knowledge economy, and especially with tight labour markets, the employee proposition becomes absolutely key for specialist skills and talented staff because there is likely to be fierce competition for them. The order of the sequence may then need to be reversed (see Figure 4.4). The organizational proposition comes first because of the overwhelming need to acquire talent. This puts the emphasis on attraction, but retention is not far behind in importance. Once scarce skills have been found, there is a high premium on keeping them.

The availability in the market of very specialist skills may even affect the business strategy, putting an even greater premium of getting the employee proposition right. As an example within financial services, a team of investment bankers or private equity partners may be recruited, even though their skills and market knowledge may not be primarily in the company's targeted growth in, say, India. The new team may have particular expertise in, say, the acquisition of businesses in China. As a result, the bank's market strategy is expanded based on this broader capability. Interestingly, we are not yet convinced that many HR functions, or certainly business leaders, have understood the necessity of approaching the market by looking at supply before demand.

Another difficulty is that these three themes link and interact. As Figure 4.3 shows, although the process can be viewed sequentially – organizations need to acquire the talent; build capability through increasing the skills of the workforce; deploy and engage them – there are overlaps. The employment brand is something that forms part of the means to attract recruits, but it also forms part of the proposition to existing staff to retain and motivate them. Organizational effectiveness overlaps with capability in that the development of skills leads directly to improved performance. Employee engagement can come from working in well-designed jobs.

We have had to tread a fine line between not getting into too much detail of people management policies and practices, and yet give readers a sense of the sort of areas it will

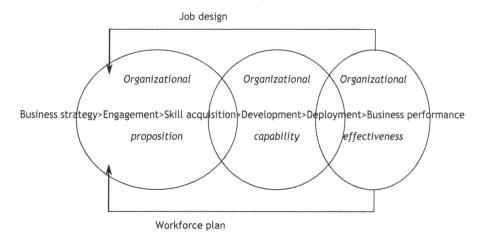

Figure 4.4   A 21st-century process model of delivering business results through people

need to tackle. By not being comprehensive, we are not suggesting that the areas we have omitted are unimportant: far from it. One way of understanding the dynamics of the challenges HR must meet if it is to add value in a significant sense, is to see content and role in combination. Thus the undoubted requirement for operational excellence is part of HR's role as a professional. Some of the work that HR does in employee relations can be seen as it performing its regulatory function. The change management role encompasses vital activities HR undertakes with respect to mergers and acquisitions. Diversity runs as a thread through so much of what HR does. And so on.

Organizational capability

Organizational capability operates at two levels: the individual and organizational. Human capital management can synthesize what needs to be done at the organizational level. Talent management is a convenient shorthand for what organizations must do to build organizational capability both at the individual and corporate level.

TALENT MANAGEMENT

In surveys of key issues talent management is often up there as a critical item. This perception has partly developed because of the shortage of talented people in a tight labour market. Yet it should be recognized that real talent is always in short supply. But it has also developed because, as we argued in the previous section, of the growing recognition of the importance of people to organizational success. McKinsey's original book on the war for talent (Michaels *et al.*, 2001) quotes several examples of organizations that were concerned that talent might inhibit their organizational plans. It also emphasizes the change of context of companies chasing people rather than the opposite. As Shell's HR functional excellence overview says: 'Talent is our legacy. Arguably, it is the most enduring contribution we can make to Shell's sustainability.'

Unpacking the talent shortage argument, what concerns organizations varies greatly. For some it is that they cannot get hold of ready-made executives. Others are looking for those with managerial potential. Another constituency is more bothered about the difficulty of finding particular professionals – radiographers, social workers, reward specialists – or generic skills – project managers, etc. Or organizations might share the Shell perspective that the talent need is ubiquitous. It has been concerned not just with the recruitment and development of graduate entrants, nor only with deep technical specialists, but also with refinery operatives and customer service staff.

If there are different views on who constitutes the talent – is it high fliers alone or the whole workforce? There are also differences about the range of interventions. Is 'talent management' an umbrella term like human capital that sweeps in everything and everybody, or is it narrower, more focused on attraction, retention and career management? We tend to take the latter view. In which case, one suspects that HR has been deeply involved for some time in a number of these issues. Most HR teams will be competent in a range of resourcing techniques. What has changed is that the intensity of effort and the sophistication of method have grown in response to a more competitive market for talent and a more demanding group of employees. The need for organizations to adjust quickly to changing circumstances has also meant that they must respond faster to attract and hold talent. Finally, the talent issue has been on the minds of senior management, concerned about succession and present or future capability.

Organizations that in the past could be relatively ad hoc in their selection or development processes have found that this is no longer tenable. Some organizations that have given responsibility to management, or left the individual wholly responsible, have found themselves with insufficient knowledge of their talent to support the appropriate business strategy. Those that were relatively good at career management have had to up their game. Selection techniques at recruitment have moved well beyond the structured interview to exercises, group work and psychometric testing. Assessment centres are now not only common place at the recruitment stage, but pretty common to manage career advancement, even if they may be called 'development centres'. Organizations can use these methods to link to succession planning so that the right number of executives is in place with the right skills and experience to assume more senior jobs when required to do so. Knowledge of the market is essential to have the right type and quality of resources in short order.

So in the organizations that are most concerned with talent management, there is a desire to better integrate succession planning and development; to diversify the talent pool (not just in terms of gender and ethnicity, but also in balancing internal development and external recruitment); to more explicitly engage individual employees in the process; and to make the whole talent pipeline more structured (effective links between levels) and more dynamic (able to adjust to changing personal or business circumstances). Organizations have found that career intervention through training or planned moves may be necessary to grow people towards their ultimate destination, since leaving it to the vagaries of the internal labour market may be too hit and miss.

These resourcing and career management techniques need to be in the kit bag of any self-respecting specialist in this field, but senior generalist HR managers should be broadly familiar with what can be done (and should not be done) with these techniques. The challenge for HR is to articulate a vision of where it wants to be in talent management, in a way that is consistent with the business strategy, and then implement this goal. The term 'employer of choice' has grown up to put into business-speak what is being attempted in recruitment. It is about formulating and delivering an attractive proposition. Borrowing concepts from marketing, HR is seeking to make a compelling offer to the labour market to draw in quality staff and then ensure that the employment experience and processes live up to the promotion.

Once again it is the marriage of the general and the particular, the theory and the practice, that is the key to success. Moreover, the vision and the delivery should be joined up, not fragmented. Organizations may be top class at recruiting talent, but poor at developing it. They may have excellent graduate programmes, but ones that are accessible only to external recruits, excluding home-grown talent. Some organizations may be elitist in their approach when they should know that the dearth of talent lies in other areas, such as in specialist skills, not just among 'hipos'. Finally, they should evaluate the effectiveness of the whole range of interventions over the longer, not just the shorter, term. So, for example, does the organization know whether individuals reach their expected potential? Do they know whether those recruits whom they have rejected might have been at least as good as those they have accepted?

These points are made against the backdrop of evidence that a number of these requirements are not being met. IES researchers (Barber *et al.*, 2005) were critical of both the exclusivity of graduate recruitment programmes and the weakness of their evaluation. Chris Watkin, Head of Talent Management at Hay, was concerned about how few organizations connect talent management to the business strategy or gave much time to its consideration (Watkin, 2005). More worryingly still, according to a Hay survey, only 10 per cent of organizations have a clear picture of individual capabilities. This suggests that organizations have not moved on much since the turn of the century when McKinseys were reporting that 72 per cent of respondents agreed that talent is critical to their success, but only nine per cent were confident that they were developing a stronger talent pool (Michaels *et al.*, 2001).

What HR must ensure is that their organizations take talent management seriously. They need to get the subject regularly in front of senior managers. The CEO must be encouraged to give leadership to demonstrate the importance of talent. This may require the spending of more money (on development centres, coaching, mentoring, etc.), it will certainly involve spending more time on these issues (in succession planning meetings, attendance at management development events, etc.). It will probably involve the use of his/her own personal capital in persuading colleagues to invest time and energy on talent management. It may require persuading reluctant executives to risk taking an untried colleague because they have potential or releasing a key resource to another job for their development and for wider organizational benefit. It may mean banging heads together to achieve cross–business-unit or cross-functional moves.

HR should be there to encourage the CEO, to facilitate discussions and to design interventions. The role of talent manager has a number of dimensions including:

- building robust profiles of the talent in the respective parts of the organization
- understanding the competition and its core people strengths and gaps
- building processes that feed the talent pool and taking clear accountability for developing the capability in partnership with the business
- developing programmes to build internal talent through training and development.

Moreover, HR should ensure diversity, fairness and consistency in talent management, guiding against the halo or horn effect. It should be the source of good data – on employees, the supply/demand balance, skill gaps and development needs. It should bring an awareness of the external labour market to bear: where are there talent shortages or opportunities. It should bring imaginative ideas on secondments, cross business transfers or expatriate assignments.

HR should be mindful of good practice and what happens elsewhere, but its proposals will work if they resonate with colleagues. One way of making sure that this happens is to solve real business problems. According to Mankins and Steele (2005), shortage or inadequacy of resources is the leading reason why there is a gap between strategy and execution. HR can help the organization by doing the simple, but necessary, task of seeing whether supply will equal demand. This is both ahead of time, through a proper HR planning process, and just in time, in ensuring that there is an awareness of short-term resourcing needs. The Mankins and Steele article approvingly quotes Cisco Systems and the way it ensures that the people and the work match. However, the process described did not feature HR in a lead role. The operations and finance directors were assisting the CEO. HR has to be seen as the function that knows about the workforce as a whole (both numerically and in terms of the skill profile) and at individual level (past track record, work preferences, shortcomings, etc.) – at least for those in selected talent pools. This information needs to be available to the operations director and CEO to compare to work requirements.

You might say that line management should have all this data. It might well have all of it, but only for its sphere of the business and only in terms of recent history. Managers can be surprisingly ignorant of what employees have done in the past, of their skills and experience profiles. At an aggregate level, managers may not be aware of spare resources elsewhere in the organization. Companies such as BT found that in decentralized organizations there was plenty of resourcing inefficiency – recruitment in one unit in ignorance of redundancy in another. Too often business leaders have assumed that they can rely on unlimited resources. They have failed to join up the dots over recruitment and training, deployment on multiple activities and the dynamics of business change. This is why organizations have found themselves short of train drivers, production workers, IT consultants, etc.

And there is a clear prize from getting talent management right. Not only will the organization benefit directly from being able to use skilled, experienced and competent staff, but there are motivational benefits too. Good development leads to greater knowledge and skills, but also to greater individual self-confidence and job satisfaction. This in turn leads to better performance and greater organizational affiliation. Lack of development or blocked development leads to the reverse: 'an emotional cycle of reduced job satisfaction and motivation, reduced organizational commitment and either prolonged frustration or escape' (Hirsh *et al.*, 2005).

HUMAN CAPITAL MANAGEMENT

The research evidence presented earlier supports the argument that increasingly organizations compete more on the basis of their human capital than on their physical assets. This is because it is easier to replicate a product or service: what is much harder to do is to copy intangible assets. Hence the interest in developing or protecting the brand image. Likewise, employees' own knowledge and the organizational culture within which staff operate are almost impossible to imitate fully. And if Western economies are going to be sustained by their intellectual added value, then once more the employees' contribution will be vital.

Their efforts need to be harnessed to other intangible assets of the organization – brands, organizational culture, intellectual property rights, knowledge management systems, supply-chain processes, etc. – if full value is to be derived from their contribution. A key challenge for HR is to develop these employee inputs that help make their organizations effective.

Whichever particular view of human capital you take (and there are many more than are described in this book!), it is obvious that the concept puts people at the heart of the business. Employees contribute hugely to growing organizational capability.

Whilst employee capability and the activities of the HR function are by no means synonymous, HR managers ought to grasp the opportunity presented by human capital ideas. However, it seems that, recently, the concept of human capital has been seized upon by consultants as a new peg upon which to hang profitable products. This includes rebranding HR as human capital and, as explained in the section on monitoring in Chapter 2, proposing a whole number of metrics that seems to recycle old ideas, rather than develop new ones. The risk is that the emphasis will shift to human capital *reporting,* not human capital *management* and give Finance the chance to seize the initiative. 'Organizations must remember that metrics do not in themselves have value; it is the use to which they are put that adds the value' (Reilly 2004b). As Figure 4.5 illustrates, besides measuring and reporting human capital, organizations have to go on to manage human capital. This will demand of HR insights into what makes the organization productive and successful at achieving its core purpose. It will require an understanding of what people management processes and polices help contribute to this situation. For example, it might be necessary to know how best to develop skills, how to promote learning, how to encourage staff to be motivated to take on new tasks, how to get front-line staff to see the value of customer service and so on. This means that organizations

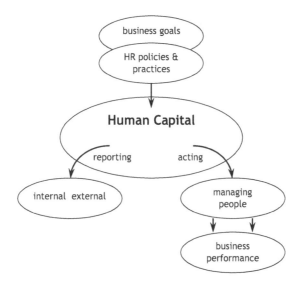

Figure 4.5   Human capital reporting and management

should get into a positive loop of diagnosing the need (not just a current problem but also a future aspiration), identifying the appropriate solution, implementing that solution and evaluating its effectiveness. Through the careful selection of the issue to be tackled HR can build human capital in a purposive way.

To move in this direction HR needs time, space, data and intelligence. It has to get itself the time and space to think about the big picture, to see where the fundamental problems lie (not just the superficial ones), where the future challenges will come from. This is where the data and intelligence come in. Survey results and metrics on organizational health will help give insight, as will facts about the external labour market and extent of competition for labour. Softer intelligence is, however, vital to build up a qualitative picture of the organization. What is bugging people? What is stopping them achieve? What positive signals have they received? And so on.

This discussion emphasizes the importance of getting the business partner role, and the skills that underpin it, right. Business partners are the ones to get the organization to focus on the long term and the strategic. If they successfully achieve this, it is more likely that human capital management thinking and capacity building will occur.

Organizational effectiveness

One American commentator wrote in 1996 that HR's 'traditional mandate has not been to improve organizational effectiveness in the business units, but rather to solve problems' (Eisenstat, 1996). There is though, we believe, a growing consensus that a key role for HR in the future will be to help their organization improve its performance. Some might be surprised to read this: surely all HR teams have tried to do this. The difference may be in the breadth of ambition and business-centric nature of this role. And, as Eisenstat implies, the difference is also in being proactive in leading change, not reactive to problems. In a sense this is a shift from a defensive industrial relations mentality (images of defending the wagon train against attack) that imbued Personnel in the post war period to the more confident can-do attitude to change it has had in more recent years.

How organizations will drive improved organizational performance will vary with the context, but the essentials are the same. HR will need to be constantly upping its game in:

- what forms of structure can organizations use to deliver the most effective results
- how will different parts of the organization be linked to maximize efficiency and effectiveness
- how will relationships with third parties be managed, e.g. with partners, joint ventures
- how best to decide which activities to keep in-house and which to be done externally
- where the best location is for activities to be undertaken
- what sort of processes will lead to efficient delivery
- how are jobs to be designed to deliver optimum performance
- what sort of skills and competencies will be required to perform these jobs, now and in the future
- what the organization demands in terms of resources (by number, skill, type) now and in the future
- how resources can best be deployed to meet fluctuating business needs
- how organizational productivity can be measured and raised.

This is a very broad agenda but it goes to the heart of operationalizing the business strategy. It is the 'how do we get there?' question, once the direction is set. Thus raising productivity requires diagnosis of where the current bottlenecks are located. Specification of the workforce requirement and how it will best be deployed underpins work on job design, resourcing needs and terms and conditions of employment. Is annual hours working the way to meet a variable workload? Is multiskilling cost effective to meet production targets? Would matrix structures help balance corporate and local interests or would it gum up the works?

Structures, processes, job design and skill/number requirements are all included in organizational effectiveness. Clearly organizational effectiveness is closely related to capability (in its utilization of resources) and to the employment proposition (in that improved organizational effectiveness can lead to greater employee engagement). How one pursues this task can result in further engagement (through flexible working arrangements or greater task autonomy) or the opposite (by process engineering that takes no account of human needs or poorly executed outsourcing).

It should also be obvious that this is a very business-oriented agenda. This means getting inside how the business works and being constructively challenging. Questions such as 'Why is overtime required at this level?' or 'What impact will the automation of this process have on workforce numbers and skills?' need to be asked. Have call centre jobs been too narrowly defined and performance managed? The reach of organizational effectiveness goes beyond traditional people management areas such as performance management or training and development. Or at least it subsumes them within it. Managers and employees have to be trained and developed; staff need to be set goals and their contribution assessed; but we have to go further than this to meet the organizational effectiveness challenge. Partly this is a matter of integration, bringing different aspects of people management together. Good HR departments have always striven to have horizontal alignment between their different activities, as well as vertical alignment with the business direction. But organizational effectiveness, described in this way, enters what for many is new territory in the areas such as organizational design, process engineering and supply chain management. What may have been discrete tasks then should be combined into a new whole. Macro-structure questions are linked with micro, processes with skills, attitudes with service decisions. The very nature of such a holistic approach not just cuts across boundaries, but regards silos (be they structural, emotional or intellectual) as a real handicap. This is because over-emphasis on one element can be to the detriment of the whole. The Enron story can in part be understood as a calamitous obsession with talent (Gladwell, 2002). Having talented people is a necessary but not sufficient requirement for success. Staff need to be effectively deployed if they are to contribute successfully. Enron apparently gave too much emphasis to hiring exceptional people and insufficient attention to performance managing them. Organizations that survive and prosper over the long-term know how to get the best from talented people for the benefit of the organization. Organizational effectiveness concerns itself with putting round pegs in round holes with the space for people to develop.

Organizational proposition

The term 'employee proposition' has grown in use in organizations, as the term 'psychological contract' has declined. The reason for this is perhaps that in the oft-quoted war for talent organizations feel they have to attract staff by making a proposition to them and keep them by honouring this deal. As the McKinsey report put it: 'a strong employee value proposition attracts great people like flowers attract bees' (Michaels *et al.*, 2001); though ironically bees will always move away to the next flower! The psychological contract does not have this feel of the organization drawing people to it, rather of establishing the nature of the understanding, once they are employed. This was particularly associated with job security and employability in the weaker labour markets of the early to mid-1990s. In other words, the employee proposition is about attraction and retention, while the psychological contract emphasizes more the retention dimension. The concept of the psychological contract, though, should not be ignored because its violation has significant effects on individuals, leading to psychological withdrawal or even exit from the organization.

A key element in developing an employee proposition is that it communicates what the organization is offering in exchange for the application of their skills, knowledge and attributes. By this means the organization is setting out its stall to the world, describing its brand. Hence we are emphasizing the term 'organizational proposition', not simply employee proposition.

BRANDING

And we have seen much more attention in recent years given to the brand as the external representation of the company, not just for the purposes of product marketing, but also in terms of how the organization is viewed as an employer both by employees and by potential recruits. The employer brand should reflect the vision the company has and be consistent with what the individuals inside the organization perceive the organization to be about. For job applicants the organization must get the attraction components 'all in a row' to deliver an integrated message. Then, on the employee's arrival in the organization, the induction process needs to be effective and the job content as advertised. Individual failure of delivering on the promise will get the organization a poor reputation.

Whilst private sector firms may have been in the vanguard of this move, many public sector organizations have become similarly conscious of the requirement to market themselves, especially where they are in competition for scarce skills.

Trying to develop the employer brand image will be closely linked with the organizational brand. Take, say, Virgin, or the very different John Lewis Partnership – employees will probably have a very clear idea of the sort of organization they are working for. Virgin projects an entrepreneurial image. John Lewis emphasizes that it looks after its staff. Employees may even have chosen to work (or certainly to stay) because they are comfortable with what the brand implies in terms of values and culture. HR should be trying to get a message across to the market that is consistent with the commercial image. And the brand then has to be seen through in practice: the rhetoric needs to be matched by the reality over a period of time. The consistent projection and delivery of the brand is an essential element of how it is received.

> Shell has borrowed thinking from marketing to see people as customers. How can we develop something that they value? We need to find this out by asking them. It will be a case of 'demand pull, not HR push'. We need to recognize as well that not all customers are the same. This means we have to segment our offer to deal with the variety of needs. This approach requires HR to be more 'humble', better at listening than telling.

Care, therefore, needs to be exercised that the brand described is a reflection of what the organization is, not what management wants it to be. Advertising the organization, say, as vibrant and innovatory, might attract the sort of recruits that are wanted, but if the new employees find the organization dull and bureaucratic they will leave. Organizations may have to build the brand slowly and purposefully, reinforcing each step as it moves forward. As Martin and Beaumont (2003) suggest, there is a path that starts with a simple logo that develops into the 'centrepiece' of corporate strategy with HR playing a major role ensuring that the employee perspective is taken into account in the specification of the brand. The end result is that the brand image and the way the organization represents it should coincide. This is especially true of customer-facing organizations where the brand is continually being demonstrated by staff.

Yet, interestingly, a *Personnel Today* survey (2005b) of recruitment managers found that 95 per cent thought that branding was important, only 25 per cent had the responsibility for it. In 41 per cent of cases it was marketing that took charge and in 25 per cent corporate communication was the lead function. These figures are disappointing if they mean that HR is excluded from thinking about the brand. It is important not just to sell products, but also to attract staff and to connect current employees with their employer.

CORPORATE SOCIAL RESPONSIBILITY

A new dimension of branding is corporate social responsibility (CSR). Its growing importance in organizations is a reflection of wider social change. The boundary between what is formally regulated and what are socially expected obligations is a shifting one, as are the interfaces between the responsibilities of government, the citizen and the corporation. In some organizations CSR is merely window dressing, something to put in the annual review to keep the environmentalist lobby happy. In others it has become inextricably bound up with business success, even survival, and much effort goes into spotting trends in the external environment. Take Shell, for example: after its negative publicity over the disposal of Brent Spar and the execution of Ken Saro-Wiwa in Nigeria, it is obvious that how Shell goes about its work has a knock-on effect on its sales and share price. Bad publicity can impact investment decisions. Conflict with pressure groups can even endanger the safety of staff. Shell, for example, in its

HR Excellence overview, called 'Ahead of the Game', puts as one of its seven 'people principles': 'we will contribute to realizing the aspirations of the societies we live in through our work.' As this quotation shows, another motive for corporate social responsibility is simply a belief that organizations need to do some good; plough back time, money or resources into the community. Charitable giving by companies has had a long tradition, especially in the USA, but, as the social conscience of the world can be so quickly mobilized (in relation to climate change, poverty or war), good works need to be projected, not hidden. Organizations want to be known for their corporate social responsibility actions. The Shell Foundation, for example, believes that business can help generate economic growth in developing countries and so works in more than 23 countries helping small businesses through issuing loans of between £50,000 and £500,000. Kurt Hoffman, the foundation's director, emphasizes that it is an independent charity, but describes the organization as being an, 'a benign parasite on the [Shell] group, exploiting not just their money but these business assets' (Smith, 2005).

There are three approaches that HR can adopt to link corporate social responsibility and people management. One is that the whole notion of corporate social responsibility is based on recognizing the stakeholders and taking their needs seriously. This includes employees, their representatives and potential employees, as well as the wider society. Balancing the interests of different stakeholder groups is a task HR is well used to. The second angle is the diversity aspect to corporate social responsibility, and this too is linked to stakeholder management. All sections of the workforce (irrespective of age, ethnicity, gender, disability, etc.) must be brought on board, just as all parts of the wider society should be respected and their ideas listened to. The more the workforce is a mirror image of the external employment community, the easier it will be to promote diversity internally. Thirdly, HR can explicitly use CSR for branding reasons.

If one excludes those companies that cynically exploit the concept, but equally those that support social initiatives for purely altruistic reasons, then those that are left are pragmatically using CSR to support their brand. What organizations are trying to do, in people management terms, is convey to employees that they work for a good organization and are right to stay, and to prospective recruits, that they are a good employer to join. Commercial organizations are similarly encouraging customers to buy their services because they are socially responsible.

If you accept the idea that young people are more interested in environmental and development issues than previously, then a key part of the attraction process is promote the organization so that it is perceived as 'cool' by the applicant's peer group in these respects. This must be especially true of organizations that by virtue of their activities have to work harder to attract good recruits.

The CIPD (2005d) report *Making CSR Happen* gives several different types of examples of organizations taking their wider responsibilities seriously. Duncan Brown (Assistant Director General) commented that the report 'illustrates how closely intertwined HR and corporate social responsibility have become to the business agenda' (Brown, 2005). But giving practical realization to the concept is harder for HR to do. As we saw earlier, HR may have little role to play in brand development and management and, according to a CIPD survey (2003a), only in 19 per cent of organizations does it have responsibility for CSR. This is not necessarily a bad thing. What it does require is for HR to work with other functions, such as public affairs and marketing, and ensure that the recruitment, retention and motivation angle is not neglected. HR has its own campaigning to do in getting the management colleagues to realize (if they do not already) the benefits to be had by consciously recognizing the effect CSR actions can have on the internal and external employment. Employee opinion surveys can be used to register employee concerns or support on CSR matters. These can be used both as a surrogate form of popular opinion polling and as a means of testing whether colleagues will be campaigning on the organization's behalf or rubbishing its behaviour in discussions with friends. Should it be the latter, the organization will have an uphill task in convincing the wider society of the validity of its actions.

One way of drawing attention to this link is by setting relevant goals and monitoring against them. Corus Colors, for example, uses EFQM, which has a social element in the evaluation. Targets include improving stakeholder perception of the company and compliance with brand values. Some HR leaders in the USA are already responding to grassroots' pressure to change specific business practices or changing policy because of environmental concerns (SHRM, 2005).

> Some major US-based organizations indicate that launching programmes that sought to align business objectives with sustainable development principles significantly decreases staff turnover. Sears saw a 20 per cent drop and healthcare company, Novo Nordisk, experienced a 5 per cent reduction (*The Ethical Corporation Magazine*, 'Links between CSR and HR', www.ethicalcorp.com).

Another mechanism is to encourage staff to work in the community on projects at weekends or through short-term secondments. This might include leading fundraising events. At RBS those employees who help local community groups, schools or charities as fundraisers or volunteers can apply for a 'Community Cashback Award' ranging from £100 to £1,000 for their organization. In 2005, RBS gave 7,000 Community Cashback Awards totalling £2.5 million for the schools, charities and local community groups that employees helped. PWC has agreed to match the funds raised by staff who participate in a campaign for VSO. The company also seconds employees to work for VSO. These approaches may well appeal to young people, especially those who want to do something more meaningful for society.

A third approach is to participate in competitions like the *Sunday Times* Top 100 Companies to Work For. This surveys practices against a number headings that show clear links with CSR and HR alike (Barber and Wolfe, 2005). These include:

- fair treatment
- diverse workforce
- good human rights record
- non-excessive pay for directors
- donating resources to the community.

EMPLOYEE ENGAGEMENT

IES research based on workers in the NHS (Robinson *et al.*, 2004) suggests that for employees to be engaged they need, above all else, to feel valued and involved. It seems that the components of this concept are employers getting employees involved in decision-making; allowing staff to give their opinions and the manager listening to their points; developing employees' jobs; and recognizing staff health and well-being. In other sectors and for different occupational groups it seems that, whilst feeling valued and involved is still important, other factors come into play, such as job satisfaction (long recognized as positively impacting upon commitment) and how well the organization functions co-operatively.

Staff who feel engaged are likely to be positive about their manager, their training and development, their career, how their performance is managed, the extent to which they are treated fairly, their pay and benefits, and the quality of communication.

RBS found that the factors affecting employee engagement varied by employee group. Clerical staff were affected by the products they had to sell and their relationships with customers. 'Appointed' staff (i.e. first-line managers) were more turned on by total reward. More senior managers were more likely to be engaged by the way that their work–life balance was treated.

Overall the company identified eight drivers of employee engagement:

1. leadership
2. product brands and reputation
3. the work itself
4. relationships
5. total reward
6. recognition
7. performance and development
8. work–life balance and physical environment.

RBS regularly measures the extent of employee engagement by biographic characteristics (e.g. age, length of service and gender) and by business unit. This shows where engagement is flourishing or not.

Engaged employees are more likely to care about their jobs and their organization, seeking proactively to improve both. They tend to see the bigger picture, putting organizational needs above their own personal needs. They are more likely to stay with their employer and work on developing their skills. Such attitudes and behaviour will lead to positive organizational benefits in terms of important measures of performance such as productivity and creativity.

If this research is right, organizations will have to spend time on a variety of issues. As we continue to emphasize, organizations need to build their line management capability. So much depends on them to show they are interested in their staff, to achieve proper two-way communication, give their subordinates scope to shape their work and so on. It also requires organizations to invest in processes that support the line manager's people management responsibilities. These processes include such things as team briefings, consultation mechanisms, performance feedback, etc. There are obvious challenges too for the HR function in policy design. The RBS list of drivers of engagement points to giving attention to policies on reward, people management, job selection methods, flexible working and non-financial recognition so that they encourage employee feelings of being valued and involved. Finally, there is a sense in which employees like working for well-organized and successful organizations, where people work together towards the common good. This has implications for the structure of the organization, as well as its products and services.

The research on employee commitment, which, as we have said, has a longer track record than does the research on employee engagement, points to a number of other areas that organizations should give attention to if they want responsive employees. These include:

• Developing people's sense of belonging to the organization. Organizations can convey their values and the type of work environment through the recruitment and induction process. Branding should enable the organization to set out its stall in this regard. This sense of being wanted needs to be sustained through the life of the organization. When successful, values and brand are bound together, and this is self-evident to those who work in the organization bringing an emotional attachment to the brand.

- Meeting employee expectations. Failure to do this is one of the reasons for high wastage rates soon after joining, especially where the employee feels the job has been mis-sold. This is closely linked to the point above and, at recruitment stage, can be helped by the use of realistic job previews. Managing expectations, with respect to job content, careers, training, pay, promotion, is not easy, but it addresses a major source of dissatisfaction.
- Relationship building, which is important with managers, as we have discussed, but it is also important with work colleagues. Team building is a way of addressing the employees' need to affiliate and belong, at the same time as harnessing collective effort for the organizational good. Developing wider communities based on common interest of some sort can take this sense of affiliation a step further.
- Demonstrating fairness and justice. How people are treated in everyday affairs and at moments of crisis (e.g. disciplinary matters) is vital to secure their support. This is especially true of change. Work on the 'survivor syndrome', for example, shows that the way redundant staff are treated affects the way the organization is perceived by those that remain. Similarly, procedural justice seems to be more powerful that distributive (i.e. the process of decision-making or how they are treated often influences employees more than the outcome).

Obtaining employee commitment produces a whole range of benefits in terms of employee performance and satisfaction, attendance and retention, and in terms of business outcomes (better sales and return on investment).

Returning to the notion of the psychological contract, if an organization, and by this we really mean the management of the organization, offers, and delivers, on a deal that is based on trust, integrity and sound values, it may obtain high commitment and low turnover from its employees. If the organization behaves in ways that violate the psychological contract then disengagement will result. According to Guest and Conway (2004) the state of the psychological contract is based on fairness, trust and the delivery of the deal. This in itself is affected naturally by the promises made, supervisory leadership (again) and the work environment. HR policies have a more distant influence. If promises are not kept, trust is lost and staff believe they are being unfairly treated, then there will be behavioural and attitudinal consequences. Employees will do the minimum necessary, distract themselves by moaning about their employer, look for other jobs and so on. All the 'going the extra mile' and 'doing something beyond the call of duty' will stop stone dead.

HR's role in the development of employee engagement should be clear from this analysis:

1. Discover what engages employees. Is it the same as described above?
2. Establish whether it varies by employment group or business unit.
3. Identify the areas (parts of the organization or content) where engagement seems weakest.
4. Seek to improve these areas by working with line managers and by looking at whether the people management policies or procedures are to blame.
5. Be explicit about the values of the organization through a statement of intent, as the Ikea boxed example below shows, and, if necessary, support this with programmes that

emphasize trust, honesty, openness, etc.

6. In any event, give particular attention to line management selection, training and support.

7. Celebrate success to help others learn from what has been done well.

8. Review the HR policies and practices to see whether they support or hinder employee engagement.

> Companies like GE and RBS use updated forms of suggestion schemes to drive process change. Rather than following the old-fashioned, ad hoc methods of the past, managers are required to decide whether to implement staff's ideas or not. RBS measures the degree to which such involvement affects the level of employee engagement.

> One of Ikea's ten business objectives is to sustain the company culture, by keeping it a living reality. This means recruiting staff on the alignment between their values and the organization's. It means managing staff in a way consistent with those values. One important element in the business philosophy is that the company seeks to improve the everyday life of not only customers but of staff themselves. This is close to Lynda Gratton's notion that employees are more than organizational assets, they are vital investors in the future of their employing organization.

The above tasks are distinctly easier when the organization is doing well – making profits in the private sector, not under threat in the public sector. Once profits or share price start to dip, or there is a whispering campaign about the future of the organization, it is clearly much harder to keep employees engaged. However, it is even more important to do so because their efforts may well turn the organization around. In these circumstances what is required is leadership from the top. It will not be about financial rewards as the motivational tool – there will not be the money – even if they were appropriate. It will about senior management communicating what needs to be done and mobilizing the organization to do it.

Summary

As we said at the outset of this section, it is the interlinking of organizational practices that will bring the greatest rewards for organizations. This is illustrated by the views of Clutterbuck (quoted in Hirsh *et al.*, 2005). He argues that companies retain their competitive advantage through balancing the 'soft' and 'hard' aspects of people management. This means driving for stretching targets but giving staff a lot of emotional support. To achieve this situation, organizations need managers with the capability to manage in this way, but in a context where organizational goals are well specified and the route to achieve them is clear. As Bartlett and Ghoshal (1992) argued some time ago, the context has shifted in organizations from strategy, structure, systems to 'purposes, processes, people'. Giving staff well-defined targets to aim at has long been recognized as a way of increasing performance. As this research shows, organizational capability and effectiveness can be combined in a way that engages employees.

5 New Relationships

With line management

There is little doubt that, despite reports of difficulties in achieving their goal, HR directors are universally convinced that they are right to devolve people management responsibility to line managers and to continue to devolve as much of what might previously be deemed HR activity as possible. There may be a benefit to HR in this, in that the size of the function can be reduced. There may be a practical gain from faster decision-making more attuned to business needs. But the argument in favour of devolution is also philosophical. In HRM theory, 'business managers [are] responsible for co-ordinating and directing all resources in the business unit in pursuit of bottom line profits' (Legge, 1989). HR directors will tend to agree with Storey: 'if human resources are really critical for business success, then HRM is too important to leave to operational personnel specialists' (Storey, 1995), or with a Marks and Spencer manager: 'It is part of every manager's job to respond to the needs of staff. We do not relegate it to a personnel ghetto' (Keenoy, 1989). HR directors may not like the tone, but they agree with the sentiment. Some HR directors may even find the whole debate strange, or even the term 'devolution' odd, because line managers should have owned these activities all along. Indeed, Neil Roden argues that 'HR is not there to do the line managers' job for them', and has suggested that if managers do not regard people management responsibilities as being of interest that they should be prepared to forego a proportion of their pay! Nevertheless, the fact that these statements have to be made at all implies some resistance from line managers in discharging their people management responsibilities or from HR itself in refusing to let go.

So what should the model ideally be?

One approach, which makes a lot of sense, is that people management policy direction and process design remain with HR, but the practical people management tasks switch for managers to do (if they were not already with the line in the first place). Thus managers recruit, train, performance-manage and reward staff within the context of a set of policies provided by HR. Devolving responsibility of implementation to line managers is beneficial because it locates responsibility at the point where it is most appropriate, that is at the interface between management and the managed. The service profit chain research emphasizes the importance of the line–employee relationship, borne out by survey evidence within RBS that, the closer the decision-making is to the immediate manager, the more engaged are the employees.

This should leave a partnership arrangement, where line knowledge and HR skills dovetail. What does have to be clear is that the relationship between the manager and his/her own staff must be protected. HR would only interfere where this relationship has broken down or if staff are being unreasonably treated.

This approach would be consistent with another way of looking at devolution. As long ago as 1994, Bevan and Hayday advanced the notion that organizations should devolve on the basis of standards and values, not rules and procedures. This would allow line managers their freedom to manage, but with the organization protected against violation of its operating principles, often expressed through a code of conduct. This would allow HR to monitor people management performance without interfering in day-to-day matters. This division of responsibilities fits the message of Figure 4.1: managers get on with people management within a framework supplied by HR.

However, monitoring needs to be done sensitively. If it is heavy handed in its approach then the line will feel that it really is a compliance model by another name. HR should both monitor to learn – i.e. to pick up signals of what is working well and not so well in people management – and monitor to detect any failures to perform to standards and values. If the latter are clear, and HR intervention only relates to them, then its oversight should avoid the accusation that the function is being a 'cop' or corporate enforcer.

As should be evident, we believe that the answer to the devolution question is not about whether HR should entirely devolve or not, but where on the continuum of manager dependence on HR to complete independence should the relationship sit? We do not accept the argument that line managers will entirely displace HR professionals. Alex Wilson, Group HR Director at BT, used the phrase 'going beyond Ulrich' in a *People Management* interview to advance this argument (Wilson, 2003). He talked about line managers taking on most of the functions previously undertaken by HR staff. He made the comparison with sports commentators at the BBC – no longer are they professional media people, they have been replaced by ex-sportsmen or women. He has the evidence to support his case in athletics, but the argument is less true for football. In athletics past competitors have replaced professional commentators. In football, professional broadcasters give the commentary and the former players give the summary. This approach recognizes the relative broadcasting skills of the parties.

The conclusion we would draw from this analogy is that the professional sportsperson brings knowledge of the subject; the media-trained professional brings broadcasting expertise. The same distinction is true between the line and HR. The ideal situation is to have both knowledge and expertise either in one individual or in a team. Individual athletics commentators may have both knowledge and media expertise. In football commentary the blend of technical content knowledge and process expertise is achieved through a team, bringing together the capabilities of professional commentator and former players.

This example suggests that in some circumstances HR can work best in partnership with the line. In other cases, HR is in a subordinate role, and sometimes HR takes the lead. Results from the CIPD survey (2003a) reported earlier suggest that this largely is what is happening. On some issues the line or HR is in charge; on others it is shared. Which model should apply will depend on managerial knowledge, skills and time, and it will vary with the activity. HR skills are more in demand on some subjects than others, but there is not a fixed line on devolution rigidly applied to organizations, or even within organizations. HR must be flexible enough to adapt to the legitimate needs of its customers. This should not be a reflection just of managers' skills or the work environment, but also of the business context. Support for the line will clearly need to be stepped up from steady state conditions during, say, a redundancy exercise. And there are also practical considerations. HR might lead, for example, on employee relations because much of the activity is conducted on a collective basis.

It is clear from the research that managers value HR expertise, but at times of their choosing. They want HR's help when they are handling a hard case or intractable problem; when there are legal or HR technical issues to consider. This might lead some to conclude that the line/HR relationship should best be set up on a commercial basis: if the line wants and is prepared to pay for a service, then it should have it. We would not support such an approach on two counts. Firstly, there are some tasks that are fundamental to the nature of staff management that cannot be abrogated. Managers have to set objectives, give feedback, recognize effort, etc. These tasks cannot be subcontracted to HR. But on other topics, like the role of HR in recruitment and reward, there may be more of a legitimate discussion. Secondly, as we said in the section on HR as regulator, the function should have the right of intervention when this is necessary for business good. So a commercial arrangement would have to apply, if at all, to specific activities, not across the board.

We are also clear that it makes no sense for HR to simply pass the administrative or operational parcel to line management. Overall organizational efficiency is not advanced by simply transferring a task from HR to the line without there being an underlying rationale. And this rationale may be understood differently between HR and its customers, differently between business units and even differently within the same business unit. So there is need to have the debate with the line on where devolution should begin and end, but within a context of the mandatory people responsibilities of line management.

As Figure 5.1 suggests, HR can be very efficient by divesting itself of as many people management tasks as it can. This may, however, be at the cost, not only of line satisfaction, but also of people management effectiveness. Managers' response to taking on more people management tasks (especially time-consuming, administrative ones) may be to spend even less time dealing with employees. At one company this point emerged during a focus group. Employees complained that their managers spent all their time in their offices doing paperwork, not out on the shop floor talking to staff. Conversely, line managers may be very happy with limited devolution, but at the cost of HR's effectiveness. This may occur if HR spends its time sorting out the line's day-to-day people problems with little space left for higher-value-added activities. The aim, of course, is to get the optimum balance between efficiency and effectiveness, and between HR and line satisfaction. We would emphasize, though, that where the optimal position sits will vary across and between organizations.

Indeed, the employee may perhaps be the most disadvantaged if the point of equilibrium between HR and the line is not correctly positioned. If the managers feel weighed down by HR bureaucracy and think they have little scope to make decisions, employees may suffer because of the line's state of disempowerment; for example, managers might rail against the performance appraisal process rather than giving time to the individual. At the other end

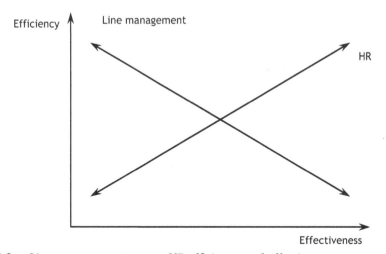

Figure 5.1   Line management versus HR efficiency and effectiveness

of the spectrum, if HR devolves to the point of being invisible, employees may resent their absence at critical moments such as when the employment relationship is in difficulties.

With senior management

HR needs the support of the top team if it is going to be effective. An unsympathetic CEO can be a major block on getting people management issues properly on the agenda. If the HR director is low in the pecking order, well behind the chief financial officer or chief information officer, the same result will occur. So HR as a function and the HR director as a person need to be respected by the board, executive committee, etc. Senior management needs to both understand and support what HR is doing. At one level this is commitment to the HR operating model (devolution, shared services, strategic partnerships, etc.) and at another a recognition of how vital employees can be to the success of the enterprise. Senior managers need to understand what HR is trying to do and back it up with words and deeds. In an interview with the authors, Trevor Bromelow described how keen his colleagues in Siemens Business Services are to support HR with the resources necessary for the task. This is not through an abdication of their people management responsibility but through a recognition of the importance of people to the success of the company.

Much of what HR needs to do is to build personal relationships with key senior managers. These relationships will no doubt in part depend on personal chemistry, but they will be underpinned by acknowledgement of the competence of the HR director and of the function s/he leads. Thus success has to be delivered at every level in HR function, but especially in the business partner role because of the frequent contact with business leaders. Confidence in the integrity of HR by the leadership is also vital. Management must be able to trust the function. Again at a personal level, senior managers need to be able to share confidences, test out ideas in a safe environment and so on. Indeed, HR can be effective as a coach as well as a mentor. The benefits of being a coach work both ways. Senior managers benefit from HR's advice and guidance: not only do these provide an opportunity for HR business partners to demonstrate their engagement with the business, they also help build greater awareness of organizational issues.

At an organizational level, if HR is the guardian of organizational values, then managers must believe that HR is reliable and trustworthy. HR also needs to demonstrate that it is knowledgeable about the people management state of play – the organizational health and emerging issues. Senior management, more than the devolution theory might suggest, looks to HR for counsel, and even action, on employee matters.

And of course, HR directors and business partners play a professional role in relationship to business unit top teams. This means involvement in succession planning (internal and external appointments), remuneration and development. Having this role gives HR legitimate interest in enquiring about how top managers are performing, and discovering about training or experiential needs.

Success at the personal and professional level will provide important support for HR. Delegated authority to tackle issues will give permission and, even, encouragement to HR to intervene and challenge. Giving profile to people management issues by setting aside proper amounts of time on the business agenda sends a signal to executive or board colleagues. Senior management can back or oppose risk taking by HR. It can certainly discourage it by punishing 'failure'. So, allowing calculated risk taking may be part of a cultural shift that encourages purposeful creativity, where HR facilitates change.

HR for its part can push 'to raise the standards of strategic thinking for the management team' (Ulrich and Brockbank, 2005). Obviously this thinking especially relates to people management, but it can be also in terms of encouraging awareness of external issues and debate about resource management and its effectiveness. There is no reason why HR cannot challenge organizational productivity or the flexibility with which resources are deployed. This is when HR truly demonstrates its business interest.

With employees

A key aspect of HR's USP must be that it understands employees – what causes them to join the organization, to stay with it, to come to work and be productive. It should understand what makes people tick, what motivates them and what irritates them. This means that HR must be capable of judging the state of employees' opinions, reporting them to management colleagues and reflecting them in people management policy. This does not make HR responsible for the management of employees. That still rests with line managers. Nor does it support, as we have already argued, Ulrich's 'employee champion' description of part of HR's role. His more recent (Ulrich and Brockbank, 2005) 'employee advocate,' there to 'represent' employees, is in our view not much better. Indeed, Schuler as long ago as 1990 (quoted in Buyens and de Vos, 2001), talked of the shift in the HR role from being an employee advocate to being part of the management team. And that is the point: HR cannot champion, advocate, represent or even sponsor employees whilst it is a part of the management team, especially since the prime responsibility for engaging with employees rests with line managers. Indeed, according to CIPD research (2003a) only 6 per cent of survey respondents want to play the role of employee champion.

However, as we described in Chapter 2, there has been a tendency for HR to put a greater distance between itself and employees, for the reasons listed there. And this worries some practitioners, especially the many as we shall see (page 174) that joined HR to be in contact with people. It also worries those that continue to believe that HR should campaign on behalf of the employees.

We do not accept that HR should be a branch of the trade union or a home for those who want to have lots of people contact. But, even if we reject the 'employee champion' concept as a general principle, Ulrich is right to continue to raise this issue, whatever HR managers in the CIPD survey might have meant to say, since it does capture an aspect of HR's role in certain circumstances. Organizations need to be concerned with employee well-being. A recent North American survey reported that nearly two thirds of respondent organizations have a 'wellness' programme and nearly half claimed that it improved employee health, morale and absenteeism (*IPMA News, 2006*). Most organizations seemed to be offering wellness education through books, newsletters and seminars. Some organizations provided various forms of health screening and assessment. There is similar evidence that organizations in the UK, in the public and private sectors, are offering fitness programmes, giving up smoking campaigns, gyms, free fruit (a meeting-room alternative to coffee and biscuits), and such like.

There will be times when HR should act to defend employee interests. This may be through the regulatory role we described above. Employees should have the opportunity to raise issues with a third party if they are suffering at the hands of the line manager. Clearly harassment and bullying would fall into this category, but there may be instances where managers put unacceptable pressure on staff (e.g. to work voluntary overtime) or act in an unreasonable way (e.g. to deny a request for leave). It might be argued that employees should go to their bosses' boss, but that may not be possible. What HR might be performing is a mediation or conciliation role, seeking to find agreement between competing views for the good of the organization, be they disputes between the line and employees, or between managers themselves. It should be emphasized though that this sort of intervention should be exceptional. As one HR manager put it to us, 'we don't want to get involved in the bickering that can go on between managers and staff'.

Of course there are formal processes for dealing with matters of dispute, and HR should ensure that they are seen as legitimate by both managers and employees. It is important that all stakeholders see that grievance and appeal processes fulfil a vital function in the organization. They allow individuals to vent their frustration and dissatisfaction. Neil Roden takes the view that these procedures are not to be managed to protect managers or management. If there are legitimate issues they should be surfaced and dealt with. He points out that about twice a year appeals reach Fred Goodwin, RBS's CEO. These appeals are treated very seriously, and if management is in the wrong 'it should own up to its mistakes'.

If performing this role sounds like either acting as employee advocate or as a welfare worker, it is not. This is hard-headed business. Employees will not perform if they have grievances against their line manager, cannot trust their behaviour or judgement. Remember the research, described on page 65, that demonstrates the link between line manager and employee in the service-profit chain, and the positive results it can generate. HR has to be in the position to act *for* the organization in dealing with problem cases. Just as it would assist managers in tackling the poor performance of their subordinates, so HR would investigate whether managers are failing in their duties.

> Alan Warner acknowledges that, whilst line managers should be the first port of call for any problems, employees must feel that there is an alternative route to dealing with their concerns, if need be. The circumstances where this might occur include harassment, bullying, discrimination, corruption, etc. Indeed, at Hertfordshire County Council it seems that it is for helping with whistleblowing cases that staff seek out HR, rather than for dealing with more day-to-day troubles where line managers provide the help. None the less, HR can be in competition with the employee's trade union over which will be seen as the best interlocutor.

So how does HR go about this twin track role with respect to employees: being there as a listening ear in case there are legitimate grievances to investigate and taking the temperature of the workforce in terms of morale and disposition to perform? Though these activities are linked, HR should not base its views on organizational health on the problem cases. It would be like a GP commenting on the health of the community based on those coming into surgery.

There have to be multiple sources of information:

- Regular employee opinion surveys, well designed and properly analysed.
- Periodic 'intention to leave' surveys testing on strength of retention.
- Exit interviews on why individuals are leaving, together with questionnaires on why employees joined.
- Focus-group inputs to HR policy reviews.

- Intranet chatrooms, allowing staff to give their views. (These need to be treated with care as they can be abused by the disaffected to sound off.)
- Blogs (such as those being used at Cadbury Schweppes by graduate recruits to describe their early experiences with the company).
- Information from third party providers such as those running EAP helplines or counselling services.
- Customer opinion surveys on HR processes.
- Feedback on the introduction of HR policies.
- Content of discussions at consultative fora.
- Soundings taken with managers, especially from employee briefing sessions.
- Issues logged by the HR call centre.
- Number and nature of grievances put into formal procedure.
- Analysis of e-mails sent in to a service centre on problems with interpretation of HR policies or procedures.

This long list of sources of information is to provide HR with quantitative and qualitative, general and specific material. The trick is then to build a representative picture of what is going on, how well people are being managed and whether people management policies are effective. If there is no trade union present (or it is unrepresentative of the workforce), then these sources of information are even more invaluable. Where trade unions are effectively representing employee opinion, their contributions should be added to the list. Staff surveys can supplement inputs. They have a number of purposes and these include giving chance for employees collectively to voice their dissatisfaction with the organization and/or its people management policies and practices.

> Alan Warner achieves this through a form of triangulation, as shown in Figure 5.2. He checks out whether the information gleaned from line managers is consistent with his and his colleagues' experiences with staff and the results from employee attitude surveys. He then sees whether 'it all adds up'. If it does, it gives him confidence in reporting to the board; if it does not give a consistent picture, it causes him to find out why.

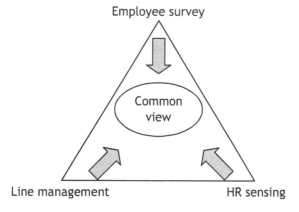

Figure 5.2   Developing insight into employee opinion at Hertfordshire County Council

The 'representative' nature of the feedback can be hard to establish if you suffer from professional focus-group attendees and survey-form completers. The great unheard mass of employees may watch from the sidelines, not participating. Yet, if employees can see value in filling in a questionnaire, attending a meeting and giving a view, then they will participate. Nationwide Building Society, for example, raised its response rate in its attitude survey to 90 per cent through taking the results seriously. It acted upon the messages it received. Such action sends a powerful signal to employees that it is worth the effort to contribute.

Another strand of HR activity is for HR to influence the way in which managers manage their staff. Thus HR should be encouraging line managers to 'blur conventional [management] prerogatives' (Keenoy, 1989) to allow scope for employee involvement and space for employees to act. In practical terms, this might be supporting the consultation of staff if changes are afoot. It should be arguing for the maximum disclosure of information to keep staff aware of business developments. It should be encouraging the granting of greater role autonomy and work discretion, subject to maintaining operational integrity. At the individual level, HR might be encouraging an appropriate work–life balance or participation in development processes.

All this is being done for good business reasons. There may be times when such an approach will seem over-optimistic, even foolhardy, but in the end it should deliver benefits. As the research on high performance working demonstrates, these efforts will bear fruit in terms of greater commitment and engagement.

In trying to understand employee opinions and attitudes, HR must recognize the changing nature of the workforce. It never was as homogeneous as it was presented as being, with the male breadwinner going home to a wife and two kids. But it is certainly even more diverse now. Less than half the UK workforce works full time on regular contracts with a fixed pattern of hours. We referred earlier to the feminization of the workplace, with nearly half of employees being women, over 40 per cent of whom work part time, and there is the growing issue of ethnic diversity (whilst only 10 per cent of the workforce are from minority ethnic backgrounds, they have a younger age profile). There is also the impact of migrant workers – small numbers, but increasingly important in some cities and sectors. Finally, there is the vital question of age. The expectation is that employees will have to stay in employment for longer than in the recent past. Some employers (especially in retail, such as B&Q) have seized the opportunity to hire the older worker in the belief (borne out it seems by experience) that they will attend work more and deliver greater productivity than their younger colleagues, and that their 'grey hair' can offer more reassuring customer service.

And research is confirming that the various generations of workers approach work in different ways. A US study (Radcliffe Public Policy Center, 2000), for example, found that pay declined in importance with age, whilst work–life balance moved in the opposite direction. More surprisingly, the average scores given on the importance of work–life balance and challenging work were 50 per cent greater than 'earning a high salary'. This reinforces the point made earlier on the shifting priorities of workers as affluence grows. Another survey (Age Wave and The Concours Group, 2005) came to similar conclusions about pay, but felt that age was less critical in determining attitudes to work. Nevertheless, it reported that many of the youngest workers were 'uncommitted to their work', whereas older workers were 'blossoming, showing a can-do attitude'.

But even if American attitudes to employment are replicated in the UK, it should be realized that views will be affected by the type of employment and economic status. Work from the Institute of Public Policy Research in the late 1990s showed the importance of money to 18–29-year-olds in lower-paid jobs, especially to males. If you do not have a decent and secure income, then money will play a bigger part in your attitude to your job. Thus opportunities for bonuses or overtime may be more motivational, time out for development of less interest. It may be a more transactional relationship with the employer. Young women in this age and income bracket are already concerned with flexible working and work–life balance, perhaps because they already have responsibility for children or expect to have it soon.

The views of graduates emerging onto the labour market are different from those of their predecessors of 20 years ago. Not only are they a much bigger group, they are a more diverse in terms of age, gender and, to a lesser extent, background. What they want from work and at work is different. Some from the top universities may well be in demand from the blue chip employers. Others are more dependent on the state of the labour market – whether their particular skills are in demand or not. There is much less likelihood than in the past that either group is likely to move from university straight into their career job for life. They are more likely to experiment first, seeking interesting and challenging work, and opportunities for training and development.

The lesson from diversity should surely be that people management policy and practice should adjust accordingly. It should allow differences where they are justified and do not imperil HR principles. Work flexibility is a good example. People's needs vary greatly with their personal circumstances and preferences. To attract, retain and get the best from them, in a tight labour market, organizations must be seen to be responding. This means offering a variety of types of contract and working arrangements that, whilst not inhibiting production or service, benefit employees. This balancing the interests of employer and employee may be an anathema to those line managers from the command and control tradition. They might simply find it difficult to manage difference. They might see it as 'marshmallow management', far too soft and insubstantial. HR itself can aid and abet this tendency by enforcing the dead hand of precedent. Or, HR can facilitate 'mutual flexibility' by getting managers to see the advantages of taking account of employees' wishes whilst ensuring the business does not suffer (Reilly, 2000a).

The introduction of flexible working hours at a major holiday company's call centre:

- extended sales centre opening hours
- cut customer complaints by 19 per cent
- saw an extra 12,538 calls dealt with in a month (compared with the same month in the previous year).

The message from this section is therefore that HR will not be advocating the views of employees, it will be listening to employees and encouraging managers to listen. It will be recognizing that the message may be complex, that different groups will have different expectations and ambitions. HR will ensure that the employee's voice is heard, even if it is decided (and HR will be part of that decision-making process) not to accept what the employee says. The knowledge, though, of where employees are coming from should positively impact upon the process of framing policies and implementing decisions. It should affect the nature and extent of communication. The very fact of listening will also have beneficial effects on employee morale and motivation. Failure to listen will lead both to employee disengagement and, in a tight labour market, to problems of retention. Getting a name as a poor employer will also hinder attraction.

6 *New Structures and Roles*

In Chapter 2 we described what is becoming the standard model for HR organization, namely the combination of shared services, business partner and centres of expertise with a corporate centre. However, as the box examples below indicate, some organizations have rejected this sort of approach. There have been criticisms levelled against all parts of the new model, but in particular against shared services and business partners, for very different reasons. In this section we will advance our support for the model, but indicate where it might be modified to make it more effective.

> Penny Davis at T-Mobile has doubts about the 'new' HR model. She is concerned that consultants and academics are overselling its benefits. Organizations are too ready to follow the latest fad. She questions how deliverable is the business partner concept: OK in theory, but the ideal of strategic contributor is hard to realize in practice. She worries that 'shared services' is really 'centralization' by another name, likely to last until the pendulum swings back to decentralization. Most critically, she asks, is this a change something customers support? Is this what the businesses really want? And can you really use structural change to alter the behaviour of HR people to fit HR's ideal model?

> Canon Europe organizes itself on a country-by-country basis. It does not have a shared services centre. Instead, in each country there is a full HR team from HR director through HR business partners and specialists to administrators (Pickard, 2004b).

Shared services centres

HR shared services may not be favoured because of:

- Size – a segmented approach to HR services may not be appropriate where there is a small HR function.
- Location – the shared services concept may not offer economies of scale in a single location, but it may also be too challenging where business activities are spread widely, especially across small units.
- Philosophy – organizations may prefer an integrated approach to policy development and service delivery. Or, more radically, some HR professionals object to the domination of shared services by a management agenda driven by cost saving achieved through economies of scale and standardization of service.

• Recognizing difference – in large diversified organizations, some business leaders may feel that a central shared services function will not be able to appreciate the need for difference from the standard core process to meet their distinctive circumstances.

It is certainly true that the shared services model is inappropriate where the size and nature of the organization do not offer benefits in cost saving, rather add complexity through the segmentation of service delivery. It is also a valid criticism that some organizations have treated shared services only in terms of a cost-saving device, and that this has been achieved through centralization and standardization of activities. There is little sense of customers choosing their services. This can be especially jarring to those parts of the organization that are separated out as independent business streams and might expect to have a different approach to HR. In large financial service companies, the investment banking/financial markets might be such a group.

However, opponents of shared services do have to recognize the effects of technological change in data management and information services. The e-HR revolution is not yet complete. When it is, it will have transformed the way much business is conducted. The fact that a dispersed population can now be serviced from a common, remote centre, that a single intranet and helpline can deal with over 80 per cent of customer enquiries and that a line manager or employee can access and alter records, or process data, has permitted a whole new service delivery methodology to be used.

Nevertheless, it should be acknowledged that there is a real tension in the model between offering customers a 'vanilla' service where they get a common product which delivers efficiency, and a customized service where there is differentiation to suit customer need. Clearly, the latter puts the client in the driving seat, but is more expensive.

Of course this does not have to be an all-or-nothing decision between standardization and customization. As Figure 6.1 shows, centralization brings economies of scale and cost reduction, but tends to be remote from the customer. By contrast, decentralization offers greater flexibility to meet customer requirements, but at a higher cost. Hybrid structures seem

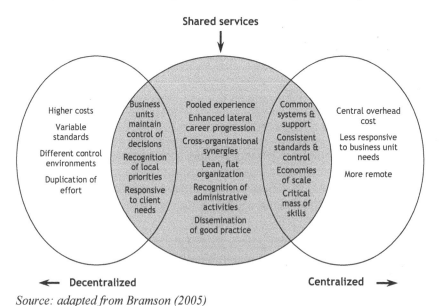

Source: adapted from Bramson (2005)

Figure 6.1   The benefits and disbenefits of different organizational models

to have the best of both worlds. Properly organized, they offer decentralized decision-making where it is most necessary – at business unit level – and centralized activities where cost savings can best be achieved, e.g. with respect to administration. The new HR operating model achieves this through the centralizing nature of shared service centres and centres of expertise providing common administration and advice. Business partners can deliver what individual operating units want. Sydney Lentz (1996) found, in his study of shared services, that the successful organizations: 'Managed to integrate the competitive features of customer focus and flexibility with the equally competitive features of economies of scale.' To achieve these gains organizations need to introduce proper *shared* services that deliver benefits to customers, but in both an efficient and consistent manner. HR can control standards yet offer service.

There are then choices to be made on the degree to which shared services is extended across the organization both in terms of its geographical reach and service content. The box below illustrates how different companies have approached this issue.

> RBS's HR shared services model is in its fourth incarnation. It started out in 1998 servicing 16,000 employees and 7,000 pensioners in a largely UK retail bank environment. It now offers a wider and deeper range of services to over 115,000 employees and 70,000 pensioners across a broader geographic and business spread, reflecting the company's success. This has involved the integration and standardization of 15 payroll/records systems for 100 separate strategic business units. But not all parts of the group are in the single model. European and Asian businesses, where there is currently insufficient scale (below approximately 5,000 employees), do not form part of the shared services operation. The business case to move is not strong enough relative to other investments the bank can make. Citizens Bank, RBS's US company, has its own, separate shared services unit with only moderate sharing of experience and knowledge with the group, and limited adherence required to group policies and procedures. This shared services model was built on the back of that company's own acquisitions, rather than from a group directive.
>
> Thus RBS does not currently operate a single global template that must be adhered to anywhere in the world. This approach differs from other large organizations, such as Unilever and Citigroup, where there is one model, without exceptions. The business case for a single model is that the overall savings made from commonality outweigh the absence of savings, or indeed extra costs, in certain parts of the company.

Multinational companies and early adherents to the model, in particular, are taking advantage of new technology to broaden and deepen their shared services operation on a global scale. This may be a matter of applying shared services to a wider geography, covering a wider range of business units, giving less freedom to opt in or opt out in the shared services ambit. For example, Shell is moving to greater scope for shared services through increased standardization of HR policies and practices across the globe. It is giving businesses less discretion in choosing whether to use Shell People Services (its shared services operation). This development is seen as necessary where, as Rick Brown put it when we interviewed him, 'the customer has gone global'. Managers ask: 'Why are HR processes different in Asia to those in South America?' Standardization in this case meets the customer need.

Further development in shared services is coming from cross-functional offerings. These are built on common technology platforms as offered by SAP or Peoplesoft/Oracle. They handle processes from HR, Finance, Logistics or IT. Companies like Procter & Gamble are exploring the benefits of single-line process models. Take the induction process as an example. This can combine both the HR elements (e.g. contract, role profile, personal details, etc.) and those elements which are the responsibility of other functions, for instance furniture, PC and associated IT information, and phone and financial requirements. From the perspective of the new recruit (or their manager), the advantages of an integrated approach are obvious.

Extending the reach of shared services through greater consolidation will last so long as it is aligned with the business organization. This is critical because imposing a standardized approach will meet opposition. There will be business units that will claim they have specific needs. Those operating companies that reflect geographical boundaries may assert that a common approach to services is impossible with different legal systems and cultures. They will have a point unless there is something else pulling operating companies together, like an integrated management structure. There will also be different responses from different areas of HR. For example, Philips found that it was easier to standardize resourcing processes than learning and development. There may be special pleading from parts of HR, but their views could reflect real differences in what makes sense in the local context. For example, common records administration may work everywhere, whereas a call centre may not.

Neil Roden believes that many companies will have to be careful with standardization, and be respectful of culture, history and context. It may be right for companies like Shell, with a long record of integration of HR policies and practices. It will be more difficult where autonomy has successfully flourished and there is no business pressure for consolidation, rather the reverse: individual business units may reflect independently successful brands. Indeed, in highly centralized firms that do not give scope to business units to adjust to their own particular circumstances, much frustration is produced at the front line at the lack of autonomy. What we would wish to avoid are violent swings of the pendulum back and forth between centralization and decentralization. Rather the aim should be prescribed commonality on some matters and business unit freedom to adapt on others. This might be a distinction between policy and application: the former is common, the process to achieve the latter is local. The adage 'think global, act local' might be an appropriate way for multinationals to manage on the centralization continuum. It might be a tight/loose formulation that gives local discretion where it is due, but allows the benefit of economies of scale and meets the need for corporate consistency where necessary.

The balance between the two – common or customized – should therefore depend on how homogeneous or heterogeneous the business operation is. To illustrate the point, an undifferentiated HR service can be more effectively delivered to a company with a chain of retail units than to a multidivisional company that has a mixture of large and small business units with different employment profiles (size, skills, grade, etc.).

And the model can be adjusted so that different parts of the organization can elect to use some services and not others. This is already happening in some mature shared services operations that are starting to add back in some levels of service differentiation to business units where it is genuinely needed to meet real business-driven requirements. As the Powergen example shows, an organization can achieve economies of scale where appropriate (especially with payroll and HRIS and/or a common information service), but give choice where it matters to customers (e.g. in advice services, training and development or recruitment activities).

Some organizations may not have adopted all (or even any) of the features of the new HR model because of their size or shape (preventing economies of scale) or because they cannot afford the cost. Whatever the objections, shared services are here to stay in larger, more

> Powergen faced the issue of standardization versus customization head on. The company distinguished between those services which are common, as determined by corporate fiat (payroll and records), from those which are optional (recruitment, relocation etc.), where the business unit can take the corporate service, do it themselves or buy from elsewhere (Reilly, 2000b).

complex organizations. For people like Richie Furlong, shared services will develop further because 'that will be where all the professional HR expertise will reside'. The efficiency gains achieved through consolidation of services will be too good to miss. A reasonable return on their investment through improving their delivery infrastructure is almost guaranteed.

The degree to which this model lasts depends upon how well its proponents recognize the limits of standardization and consolidation in their particular context. Imposing a one-size-fits-all shared services model is a mistake in the long term if it is out of line with the business model. It can perhaps offer short-term cost saving, but customers will eventually revolt against that degree of standardization.

Another inhibition to the growth of the shared service centre is that its size may dominate the HR function. This is especially true if centres of expertise and consultancy roles are included within its purview. Too big a shared service operation may be difficult to manage effectively, may marginalize business partners and may inhibit creativity.

Corporate centre

There is no ideal design for the HR corporate centre. It will be affected by the size and complexity of the organization, and its operating model – decentralized or centralized. There are, however, in our view a number of key tasks that it should perform, as set out below. Some are internal governance functions for HR itself; some for the organization as a whole and some as the professionals for the population they service. Activities might include:

- setting out the HR strategy and integrating the organizational strategy
- operating as the guardian of the HR operating model
- performing the role as budget holder and resource allocator for the function
- acting, as the board/executive committee's principal agent, as guardian of the organization's values and principles
- upholding those values and principles in its regulator or governance role
- performing the role as conciliator (or even arbiter) in disputes between different arms of the HR function
- servicing the senior executive population in terms of recruitment, reward, succession planning, etc.

We would regard policy formulation as an optional extra. The corporate centre may develop policies in some detail (or leave this to the centre of expertise) or it may simply give a broad indication of the shape of policy, following on from the HR strategy. Similarly, it may be the corporate centre which provides the direction of management development for the organization or it may be the training and development centre of expertise which does so.

What is in our opinion critical is that the corporate centre is given sufficient resources and a clear enough mandate to do its job. There is a tendency to cut the corporate office, simply because it is seen as an overhead. We have seen examples of the corporate centre pared down for presentational or ideological reasons so it is unable to perform its tasks. And we have seen the HR corporate team so neutered that it cannot undertake its governance function.

Centres of expertise

Organizations need growing expertise through deeper specialization because their work is becoming more sophisticated and complex. Ways of motivating staff are receiving greater attention through financial and non-financial means. Application is spreading across the whole organization, but differences of treatment are being used to reflect the different types of employee – from those in call centres to knowledge workers. Resourcing is a tougher activity for fast-moving organizations. Getting in the right people, deploying them to meet business needs, flexing them to respond to changing circumstances and exiting them when required is especially problematic in tight labour markets. Organizations have to sell the proposition to the employees and then deliver on the promise if they are to keep them engaged and at work. Techniques in training and development, like coaching, mentoring and action learning, increasingly require specific knowledge, skills and experience.

Jobs in the centres of expertise may appear to be more straightforward to design because they seem familiar, but that does not mean there are not important decisions to take:

- What specific work areas should be contained within the centres of expertise – reward/ performance, training and development, recruitment/resourcing, employee relations, etc.?
- Should the centres of expertise have a policy-making role or is that taken on by the corporate centre?
- Are centres of expertise responsible for implementation of policy? If not, who is? The business partners?
- Can centres of expertise successfully combine a regulatory role regarding people management policy as well as being an advisory body to business partners?
- Do centres of expertise mainly advise other HR colleagues (business partners or shared services centre colleagues) or do they have direct contact with line managers?
- Is their role primarily reactive or proactive?

Trevor Bromelow sees Siemens UK's centre of competence as being an important source of creativity, a generator of ideas, as 'agents provocateurs'. They are to act as 'think tanks' to their HR colleagues. In Shell the emphasis is on deep knowledge, skills, experience. In their conception, the centres of expertise house experts of worldwide standing who can be effective globally. A number of these positions have been deliberately filled from outside the company to bring in fresh thinking and to obtain the sort of experience built up from doing a variety of jobs. Other organizations position the centres of expertise more in relation to their problem-solving role, dealing with issues escalated from the shared services centre.

We do not favour any particular model, but we believe there are certain characteristics of an effective centre of expertise. In all cases there is a need for the following:

- Having the right number of expertise hubs. There is a balance to be struck between greater efficiency and greater effectiveness. The former imperative demands few hubs, to ensure they are busy, but risks expertise being diluted; the latter requires much more segmentation with the twin dangers of becoming too specialized and underworked. Thought also should be given as to where to locate expertise in the newer or less standard areas of HR – brand management, CSR, OD, organizational effectiveness.

- Ensuring that they add value as they are supposed to, not by involving themselves in low-level work or by overengineering what they design to justify their existence.
- Having both a policy hat and a problem-solving role. Again the important message is to get balance. Getting too engaged in implementation will cut across the business partner role; being remote from execution leads to poor policy formulation. Acting as the expert tier in the escalation ladder keeps those in the centre well grounded, but if they spend all their time on operational queries, the policy side will get neglected.
- Employing people with real knowledge, skills and experience in their area of expertise is of course vital. Having outsiders in these roles has obvious advantages in bringing learning from elsewhere (indeed they may be one of the best slots for external recruits), but this should be balanced by those with insider knowledge who are aware of organizational history and culture.
- Employing staff too with more than just content expertise. They need, in the complex operating model we are describing, to have good interpersonal and excellent communication skills.

Consultancy/project pool

There is a lot of sense in having a consultancy or project pool. It allows:

- business partners to stick to their strategic role
- a diagnostic input that can be separate and independent of the business partner – i.e. it can be used as a second opinion
- additional resources to be provided to business partners or the centre of expertise, which they can call upon if there are needs that require resources over more than the short term
- greater resourcing flexibility in that the consultants can be deployed as and when required
- the building up of technical skill and experience (if organized by subject area) that offers a career development link to the centre of expertise or the building up of business knowledge (if organized by business unit) that offers a career development path to the business partner role.

It is useful in the consultancy pool to have a variety of backgrounds so that any project is resourced with the appropriate skills and experience. A mix of reasonable specialist skills in training/development, change management (including restructuring), communications, reward, employee relations and employment law is a good basis.

To avoid unnecessary work generation, it is important that there is a proper resource allocation model based on an appropriate prioritization mechanism, as used by companies like British Airways, Absa and Coca Cola. This means that only those projects that will deliver real value to the organization have resources committed to them.

Coca-Cola Enterprises uses a 'sieve' that selects out HR projects that satisfy five criteria:

- contributes to business performance
- promotes early delivery of business benefits
- maximizes employee engagement
- improves or simplifies people management activities
- supports legal or regulatory compliance.

(Brocket, 2004) Reproduced with permission. www.melcrum.com. E-mail: info@melcrum.com

Business partner role

The business partner role is *de rigeur* at present. Every self-respecting organization needs to have business partners. (Adverts for business partners grew by 30 per cent in 2004, according to *People Management*.) Every self-respecting consultancy, trying to improve the HR function, will offer advice on establishing the role and training to operationalize it. Yet, it is not so obvious that we are always talking about the same job. The salary range on offer in adverts suggests that there is divergence of view on the nature of the role and who should fill it. In some organizations all that appears to be taking place is a rebranding exercise. You take an HR advisor to a business unit and call them a business partner. The tasks they perform and how they perform them will be no different from the past; whereas, in other organizations there is a real shift in content and expectations. The worst of all worlds is to incur the additional cost of employing expensive business partners without getting the benefit.

The difference between the two sets of circumstance (rebadging or redesign) may be a reflection of what degree of wider change there has been. The true business partner role is likely to be found where the rest of the function has been reformed. Where shared services centres and centres of expertise have been established, business partners are more likely to play the 'proper' role.

So what are the characteristics of a 'true' business partner. There are several components to it. It is self-evident that the role should be business aligned, i.e. that its tasks should flow from the needs of the organization. It should also be obvious from the title that the occupier of the position should work in partnership with their other business colleagues. The aim of partnership with the line is for HR to help their colleagues focus attention on the key people management activities. Much has been made of business partners as strategic contributors and indeed it is important that they do concern themselves with long-term and fundamental issues, but we would stick by our view that the 'strategic' has to be interpreted broadly so that it covers conception and delivery. And this should be connected to a human capital model of how employees can be managed most effectively to deliver value to the organization.

Andrew Mayo talks of the primary duty of the business partner to work with managers to build a framework of measures that will help them manage their human capital better (Mayo, 2005). It is certainly vital that business partners should build the evidence to inform their decision-making, but measurement should not be interpreted as providing a battery of statistics that managers are asked to wade through. Rather, HR should be bringing together information from multiple sources and multiple perspectives to identify what the issues are, recognizing differences by employee group, as well as similarities, as in the triangulation method reported earlier.

In order to perform the business partner role, the individual will at times be an analyst, facilitator, a critical friend, a project manager and consultant. S/he will have to be business aware, but also professionally capable. Some tasks will require generic management skills (e.g. in effecting change), whilst others will require HR expertise (e.g. in implementing a new appraisal process).

This description suggests to us that in general the business partner role should be performed by those with HR experience. It is after all an *HR* business partner role. There will be talented individuals who can come from elsewhere who can do parts of the job exceedingly well, and better perhaps than their HR equivalents. These elements of the role will be those where knowledge of the operation is vital (e.g. some aspects of resourcing and career management) and/or where the tasks require the generic skills. However, HR business partners are in essentially generalist roles. They must bring a broad basis of people management knowledge to bear in order to influence the strategic direction of the business unit. There may be particular business units where the balance is more in favour of operational knowledge where non HR people are more likely to flourish. One can think of jobs in research and development where getting to understand organizational needs is easier for those with a technical background. By comparison, those business units with a higher element of labour relations would benefit from extensive industrial relations experience. It is also the case that, where centres of expertise are well developed, the business partners can draw the technical, professional input from them. This is probably true, but still the business partner must have a 'feel' for people management issues. S/he must be able to make connections between business issues and the corpus of HR knowledge.

The other matter of debate is whether the business partner role is equivalent to that of an internal consultant. It is likely that at times the business partner will be asked to analyse and advise managers in their part of the organization, but we do not see this job as being at its core a consultancy role. Consultants are distinguishable from partners because they advise; they do not take the ultimate decisions. If, as they should be, the business partners are sitting at the same management table as colleagues from production, marketing, finance, etc., they take decisions collectively. Within that forum, the HR business partner may give their opinion on an issue. Their advice might be rejected but they are still party to that decision and are expected to defend it to staff or contribute to its implementation. There will also be occasions where colleagues will defer to the business partner's greater knowledge or expertise on people management matters, and even a few situations where the business partner insists on a particular outcome in playing the 'regulator' role. This might be to do with legal or organizational compliance. What we would not want to see is the business partner behaving like a consultant offering a 'take it or leave it' view and walking away from the implications of the decision taken.

Nor can the role be seen as the manager of a series of disconnected projects. Business partners may at times lead projects, but these should have been generated out of the business team's decision-making process, unless they are participating in corporate projects. They are not primarily project managers. They will oversee, lead or contribute to projects just in the same way as other business leaders.

So what would success for business partners look like?

- Adding useful value to the business at a strategic level, especially covering the people management content we described above.

- Challenging the organizational status quo to improve business performance, particularly where employees have a contribution to make.
- Facilitating discussion of the management team on big ticket items relating to people management, and ensuring that, where necessary, change is successfully implemented.
- Anticipating issues before they arise be they on the external horizon (e.g. upcoming legislation) or occurring internally (e.g. a resource shortfall) and proposing solutions tailored to business need.
- Ensuring that the right resources are in place to meet current business needs and work with colleagues to identify future requirements.
- Helping formulate the employment brand and managing its deployment in the particular business unit.
- Working together with line colleagues to build employee engagement and social capital.
- Hitting the organizational 'hot spots' (Kenton and Yarnell, 2005). This means addressing real business problems that need an HR intervention, not pursuing HR best practice for the sake of it. Offering creative, but practical, ideas to long standing or complex problems.
- Diagnosing shortcomings in people management processes, for example, from analysing data from staff surveys, from issues raised with contact centres and from management information – absence, resignation, overtime statistics.
- Managing risk by ensuring the organization is properly legally compliant in what it does whilst, at the same time, not allowing fear of potential legal comeback to prevent the proper conduct of business.
- Acting as a trusted sounding board on tricky management or delicate personal issues.
- Coaching or mentoring management colleagues, especially those new to senior management.
- Improving management perception of the utility and credibility of business partners themselves.
- Seeking the means to increase the quality and effectiveness of people management throughout the organization by integrating the contribution of the various players.

This is a long list and organizations might sensibly focus. Some ask their business partners to concentrate on performance and development issues; others see the role more in process terms as a facilitator and coach to their business colleagues; a third group gives more emphasis to business partners acting as commissioners of services and projects, as the people that link line management to the rest of HR.

But, as Figure 6.2 shows, if HR business partners are to be effective whatever the role emphasis, they have to be attuned both to business requirements and to demonstrate professional capability. Having the first without the second begs the question of whether this is an HR job at all. Having the latter without the former leads to HR solving its own problems – what we have called 'hobbyism'.

In our view, there are arguments both ways on reporting lines. Should business partners report to business unit directors or HR directors? The risk of going native is greater where business unit heads are their managers, and of HR hobbyism where business partners remain part of HR. But whichever way the organization has its prime reporting lines, there will be dotted lines to the other party. A matrix structure is inevitable. Good quality business partners can operate well whichever way the matrix is set up. Poor business partners will fail even in well-designed structures. In the end, success comes not from the precise structural definition,

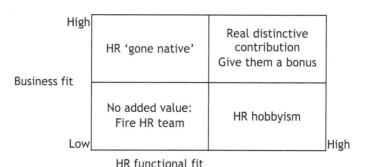

Figure 6.2 Getting the right professional/business mix

but from the people and from the culture. If the right people are not in place, HR directors will choose to have business partners reporting to them where they can control HR activities and address the fear that the business partners will fail to resist line pressure for local interpretation and practice. If HR directors have more confidence in their colleagues, line reporting has the benefit of emphasizing customer responsiveness.

Culture is important because it will affect how client managers see their priorities. In very decentralized organizations, satisfying individual business unit need is the key to personal success. The business partner might not be bothered about the HR director's injunctions to follow corporate policies. In highly centralized firms, on the other hand, business partners will need to satisfy their corporate bosses. The second approach is more likely to apply at present. Introducing the new HR model has for some organizations been a real opportunity to reverse earlier decentralization and the fragmented organization of 'baronies' (to use the pejorative term applied within some companies) that it created. 'The goal is to ensure greater strategic control from the centre and greater consistency and uniformity of approaches among business units' (Connolly *et al.*, 1997). Shell's current approach to standardization, described earlier, is driven by a wish to reverse the development of a business silo mentality.

Certainly, in the new model, business partners will have to operate as brokers between business units and HR services – be they from the corporate centre, shared services centre or centre of expertise. They will avoid getting drawn into discussions between shared services and line managers on transactional matters, but they may be involved in monitoring service performance. With respect to both the centre of expertise and corporate centre, business partners are likely to deter managers from getting into direct discussion on matters of HR policy. Their role is to act as a conduit between the HR policy-setting process and its interpretation and application in the business unit context. This can mean seeking business unit management views on emerging policy ideas and gaining their buy in to agreed changes. This may mean translating the management views into a form understandable by HR policy-makers, but also demystifying the jargon of HR for the line.

7 *To Make or Buy*

One of the critical decisions for HR directors is how much HR activity is done in-house and how much by third parties. How are these decisions typically made? In Reilly and Tamkin (1997)'s review of outsourcing, they distinguished between organizations that chose to outsource on the basis of three differing models:

- the rational strategic
- the ad hoc pragmatic
- the ideological purposive.

Simply put, the rational strategic process is based on 'a well considered, rational analysis of their business position' – 'long-term in focus and strategic in intent'. The ideological purposive might be chosen on the basis of core/periphery or a 'transaction cost economics' analysis, or an understanding of the organization's 'core competencies'. The ad hoc pragmatic decision-making is characterized by responding to 'immediate business strategies and needs', rather than any kind of master plan. The ideological purposive model is, as the name suggests, driven by a philosophical view in favour of outsourcing, often because of perceived benefits in terms of market exposure, organizational flexibility and management focus. Organizations might choose to outsource as part of a process of organizational transformation, in order to change employee attitudes to work. Such cultural change programmes may be underpinned by a belief that those exposed to the rigours of the market are, by definition, more productive.

Illustration of these different models can be seen in how various organizations have approached outsourcing. Take BP for example. BP has a long history of outsourcing, including a major contracting-out of IT operations in the 1990s. This seems to stem from a philosophical predisposition to externalize service delivery wherever possible. It believes that its Exult deal was necessary in order to bring standardization to its plethora of policies (as well as to fund technological innovation) and that outsourcing drives change through commercial imperatives. Geoff White, Surrey County Council's Head of HR, takes the argument a step further. 'Outsourcing is the ultimate solution because HR still contains too many non-core elements' (Pickard, 2005b). These can be 'delivered by others more cheaply, more efficiently, more effectively and probably more appropriately'. Here the philosophical argument in favour of outsourcing comes through strongly in the desire to see HR as 'a philosophy, not a department'.

By contrast Shell's argument is different. It has achieved standardization and e-HR through in-house management. Its decision thus far not to outsource significant numbers of activities seems to stem from fears over a loss of organizational learning and of a shared corporate vision. This is close to the Lynda Gratton view that one of the ways to avoid fragmentation in the HR function is through 'intellectual integration through the creation of a shared knowledge base' (2003). There is integration also through shared loyalty to a common cause that also argues against outsourcing. Dave Thomas, Head of HR Shared Services for Orange, said his company had decided not to outsource the activity 'because its brand was strong and staff were proud of the organization' (Pickard, 2005b).

Essex County Council appears to straddle these positions. Their move to outsourcing seems to be about concentrating resources on core or vital tasks. Lorraine Pitt, Head of HR at Essex, expressed their reasoning thus: 'We wanted to free up HR staff to work at a more strategic level, providing added value,' (Clake and Robinson, 2005). However, outsourcing has been progressive, rather than a step change. It has extended external supply from an initial base. Lorraine Pitt is mindful of the risks of going too far: 'You need to be careful that the delivery of HR services by your outsourced supplier does not get disconnected from your internal HR strategy and direction' (Scott-Jackson *et al.*, 2005).

Then there are the pragmatists. Neil Roden would count as one. His view on outsourcing is that if it were in the shareholders' cost interest to outsource, he would do it, providing that he could also guarantee an increase in service for his internal stakeholders. He does not accept either of the main arguments given to externalize, namely cost reduction on its own or because the activity is 'hard' to perform. Whilst certain forms of outsourcing might give quicker access to technology which improves the customer experience (such as self-service or online delivery of information), the potential risk of change could outweigh any gain in cost reduction given RBS's considerable efforts in system/process integration over the last six years. The doubts he might have that cost savings can be made with the level of quality maintained, are similar to those expressed at Absa. The bank felt that by becoming more efficient they had taken out all the cost they could. Where, Absa asked, would the supplier get their profit (Reilly, 2004a)? This mixture of leaving a supplier to manage uncertainty and to make a profit comes across in the case of Marconi. When it hit a major financial crisis in 2002, Kath Lowey, Head of HR in the UK, said that: 'There was no way an outsourcing provider could have taken on the business, delivered the technology to underpin the processes and remained profitable' (Clake and Robinson, 2005).

Thus organizations may be inclined to accept or reject outsourcing because of an explicit or implicit organizational philosophy, from a well-considered cost/benefit analysis or a reaction to a specific set of events – e.g. short-term cost pressures. This last category is the most likely to be swayed by current mood music. At present, organizations seem to be under a lot of pressure to consider outsourcing from the press, conferences and consultants. It is presented as the progressive thing to do.

In our view organizations need to be very careful before rushing into outsourcing significant parts of the HR function without sufficient analysis, lest the organization exchanges one set of problems for another set. This is especially true if the activity to be outsourced is a significant chunk of the HR function. It is one thing choosing to have a payroll delivered by a cheaper supplier or to have counselling services undertaken by experts in their field, who offer an objective, even-handed service; it is quite another to contract out the whole shared services operation, let alone advisory services or strategic input. Outsourcing specific activities may reduce costs, improve quality or obtain access to specific skills, but it should not be seen as some sort of wand which, through a quick wave, can magically transform the HR function. Simply outsourcing to reduce HR headcount may be a shortsighted means to transfer costs from the fixed to the variable column, especially if the outsourcing deal commits the organization to ten years' worth of expenditure.

Although economies of scale can be obtained through outsourcing, there are potential problems that come in the wake of this decision even for transactional activities. Organizations find that changes in policy or procedures that need technological modification can cost a lot of money. This has led some organizations to steer clear even of payroll outsourcing, especially if they have complex pay systems. Similarly, extracting data from an outsourced HRIS can be difficult if bespoke reports are required. This can make data-led reviews slow and expensive.

So organizations should be rational and strategic, deciding on a case-by-case cost/benefit basis, conducting the analysis over the long-term as well as the short-term, making sure that non-financial considerations are given as much emphasis as financial ones. This might suggest a progressive move in the direction of outsourcing rather than a sudden shift. This allows the market to be tested and providers given a chance to show their worth. Choosing largely on cost grounds (it cannot be exclusively) makes most sense when the activity is a commodity in the market. In other words, there is healthy competition that keeps the price down, and product variation is limited. Even here, however, organizations need to tread carefully. Experience in the US healthcare market suggests that if competition gets too tough then providers find that their offer becomes unviable or even more standardized (SHRM, 2002). In the UK the suggestion has been made that lack of profit in delivering transactional services is causing suppliers to push up the value chain, not least because what organizations want for their money is increasing. The expectations of purchasers have gone up as an understanding of what they require has grown. The arguments to outsource then become more complex.

Non-financial issues are more important the more you move away from simple, commoditized, transactional services. When organizations are dealing with such things as strategy, engagement with employees, organizational effectiveness, etc., they should be emphasizing their distinctiveness from, not similarity with, the competition. If HR does not maintain its grip on these subjects, not only is it weakening the employment proposition, it is endangering itself. Larry Hochman expressed this point clearly: 'What gives HR its relevance is capitalizing, attracting, retaining and organizing talent. Never contract these out if you want HR to be relevant in the future' (Dempsey, 2005).

What might be the non-financial issues that need to be considered before outsourcing?

- Clearly there is the matter of *quality*, and the linked case of expertise. Organizations will rightly turn to external providers where they think a better service will be offered. And not 'better' because the organization cannot properly get its act together; no, better because the supplier has *skills, processes and/or technology* that the organization does not possess and where it would be uneconomic to hold them internally. The required skills might be found in aspects of recruitment selection (e.g. psychometric testing), training (e.g. in specialist subjects) or welfare (e.g. health screening). Access to particular software and processes has driven the outsourcing of benefits administration in the UK, and, more particularly, in the USA, where benefits provision is more important and complicated.
- Another consideration is *complexity*. Powergen rejected outsourcing its payroll in 1999 because it was concerned that its complex systems would make it hard to obtain an effective service from an external supplier at a reasonable price. BP brought its pensions administration back in-house after mergers and acquisitions had left it with more than 30 schemes to support. The company decided in 2003 that these complicated arrangements were better managed internally. So where activities are very specialized, it makes little sense for a vendor to hire in an organization to do tasks if the vendor also has to train the organization to perform them. If there is much flexibility required in service provision, because activities change in the light of business circumstances, then the outsourcing solution may not only be costly, as the contractor may charge for every change, but also of questionable quality if the supplier is less knowledgeable than the client.

- *Skill development and career issues* might be a third issue to review, being closely allied to the point about retaining knowledge, skills and experience within the organization. If the organization's aim is to build up internal capability for long-term resourcing advantages, it should carefully judge where outsourcing might hinder that development. By contrast, some tasks are so specialized that there are career management reasons to externalize them. Medical services is a good example. Few organizations can offer proper career development to doctors, nurses, therapists, etc.; certainly not anything that can adequately compete with employment in the health sector itself.
- Then there is the matter of *connecting with stakeholders*. Organizations need to consider how dealing with a third-party organization will be received by users. Where the activity is mundane this might not matter. Where the supplier offers professionalism or independence (e.g. in counselling, relocation or medical services), using another organization may be very positively received. Well-managed outsourcing arrangements, where the join between vendor and customer is seamless, can mitigate problems of perception. Yet there will be circumstances where the organization loses the opportunity to connect with stakeholders because there is a middleman in the way. More specifically, recruits may be put off by the fact that they have little chance to meet their future employer until late in the recruitment process. Employees may be frustrated that they are getting an unsympathetic hearing from somebody other than their own employer. From the organization's perspective, it is denied the full range of opportunities to communicate directly with its employees. Instead, it has to rely on its contractor to act as its agent.
- In some contracts *conflicts of interest* can arise. How does the client respond to the supplier's proposal for investment in services, if it is the supplier that will benefit commercially from the decision to invest? This is much harder to manage if there is limited internal capacity to make judgements on the quality of the proposal. The higher up the value chain outsourcing moves, the more critical are these decisions, but the more internal resource is depleted. And remember that for the contractor these are core commercial matters; they are not incidental to the business. One HR manager leading the outsourced team told us that he spends 40 per cent of his time on contract management matters. Is an equivalent resource being offered by the client?

In circumstances where outsourcing might have its downsides, as well as upsides, organizations ought to give serious consideration to the alternatives. One variation is to set up an in-house service provider separate from the internal customer (also known as *insourcing*) that mirrors outsourcing, but keeps the service in-house. Many shared services centres have been set up along these lines. For example, the MOD has set up a separate agency to deliver a substantial range of HR services (the People, Pay and Pensions Agency or PPPA) and Defra intends also to create an agency. This approach has the advantage of identifying clearly how much the service costs. Moreover, through service-level agreements (SLAs), a more precise specification of what is expected of the provider by the user is defined. And, if SLAs are used with formal charges attached, the real demand for services is more clearly established. Users pay for the services they consume. Insourcing is in other words a move from *soft contracting*, where controls are informal and social, to *hard contracting*, where controls are formal and explicit, without having to go external. They bring a potentially useful commercial thinking to providing HR services, so long as the internal contracting notions are not taken to extremes by applying overly complex rules to the purchaser–provider relationship that require costly administrative support.

Another means of getting economies of scale is through cross-organization sharing of services. Companies such as Shell and RBS can obtain economies of scale internally, which can save money or fund technological improvement, in a way that smaller organizations cannot so easily generate. Cross-company sharing, outside an outsourcing arrangement, has been floated as an idea in the private sector, but not taken up, no doubt because of commercial difficulties. In the public sector (and possibly voluntary sector) cross-company sharing is more doable and might become more common, particularly as the Gershon review, with its motto 'simplify, standardize, shrink and *share*', encourages such thinking. Over the years, there have been experiments of cross-Trust sharing in the health service, which have not always been successful. One serious problem has been the lack of single point of accountability and differences of view among participants over the services provided and the costs charged. Many of these experiments are more like one organization 'hosting' the services for others, rather than a genuine sharing of common resources.

Local government also has been talking about sharing services. Success to date has been found in one authority hosting a service for others. The pressure to do more is there, but there are concerns about political commitment, particularly if different parties are in power in the local authorities involved. In areas such as recruitment, there are also examples of co-operative working across sectors, such as NHS and local government organizations advertising vacancies together.

Selling services externally is another means of covering the costs of internal provision. IBM has been doing this for a few years in the USA. BT had the same idea, but gave up and outsourced its HR administration instead. Siemens set up a commercial outsourcing operation that also serviced its internal HR transactional activities. For the time being it has suspended its commercial HR operation. PPPA, the MOD's new shared services agency, has the aspiration to offer services to other public sector bodies. Whilst the idea of harnessing expertise and capacity so that they can be utilized for the benefit of others is an attractive idea, in practice it seems difficult to do unless there is long-term commitment of resources.

Offshoring

Our view on offshoring is the same as on outsourcing, except more so: proceed cautiously. As we suggested earlier, offshoring is only likely to be contemplated where there are cost advantages. Organizations need to be certain that these really will apply and there is not any hidden financial exposure. However, it is certain that, despite the negative publicity, the benefits of wage arbitrage (i.e. the differential between sender and receiver of work) will encourage a continuing interest in offshoring. If India is no longer suitable, then organizations will go further east. Government inducements will play a part in which country to select, but, for multinationals, the location of existing operations should be more of a factor. It is much less risky keeping the work in-house and associated with an established operation in a low-cost environment than giving it to a third party where there is no local representation. That is why it is more straightforward for Standard Chartered to set up a service centre in India than it would be for AN Other Ltd of Birmingham.

Ensuring quality standards are maintained is also not that simple, though easier if the work is kept in-house. It is also not so difficult if the work is routine and uncomplicated, like records and administrative management. Organizations should be mindful of their internal customer opinion. Managers and employees may find it hard to deal with a distant call centre, especially if there are language barriers or cultural insensitivities. Mind you, what will be acceptable will depend upon what customers have previously been used to. A fast, efficient, 24/7 service, despite its limitations, may be a vast improvement on a slow intermittent service within the UK. For some organizations, exploiting time zone differences can be helpful in speeding up service.

In addition, offshoring will only work if attention is given to managing the risks of separation and instability – political, environmental, social and so on. Work can be done on the former to try to ensure that the offshore entity feels part of a single operation. Some of the wage benefit can be spent on training and integration activities. It is much harder to deal with matters outside the organization's control – the government, the environment or society. An evaluation of these issues needs to be at the forefront of the decision-making on whether to offshore or not, and the choice of location, if the organization proceeds. Contingency plans should be in place which acknowledge that things can go quickly wrong, and are harder to put right at a distance.

8 *New Skills*

In order to function appropriately in new and changing business models, HR teams and individuals are likely to need significant skill development in order to develop appropriate competencies. This view was confirmed by 80 per cent of respondents to a CIPD survey (2003a).

In this section we look first at more generic questions of the skills and competencies that HR professionals will be required to have, before moving to those that apply to specific roles. We have, for simplicity's sake, grouped the latter into those relevant business partners and the rest.

Looking at HR practitioners' own views on this subject, there are various sources to draw upon. The CIPD survey (2003a) asked respondents to identify the skills, attributes and competencies that they felt would be most important in changing organizational models, along with which of these they feel currently pose the greatest challenge to the HR community. Key areas of challenge were reported as influencing/political skills (by some distance the most important and challenging), strategic thinking, and ability to deliver on target. A third of respondents picked out business knowledge as important and challenging.

In another CIPD (2005b) survey respondents were asked about a range of factors that might be important to them when pursuing an HR career. Business awareness and strategic thinking were seen as being far more important now than previously, as were awareness of information technology, financial literacy and numeracy. Future skill requirements were less clear in people's minds. Academic and vocational qualifications were seen as having less importance over time, while strategic thinking and consultancy skills were seen as increasing in importance. Personal drive also featured as important to career development.

The UK civil service has produced a 'capability framework' that sets out four areas of competence:

- knowing the business
- personal credibility
- acts as a change agent
- HR mastery.

This is a mixture of a role and competency description, but it emphasizes the professional and business focus of the function, and the importance of the personal characteristics in achieving role objectives.

Looking at US research on new HR skills, SHRM's (2004) investigation based on case studies came up with five categories of skill requirements:

1. business
2. leadership
3. consulting
4. technological

5. global awareness.

There is no doubt that HR has to be more aware of the business of which it is part, if it is to be effective. As Richie Furlong describes it: 'You'll get no credit for your HR experience, only credit for what you've achieved, and this is your track record for dealing with issues in a business literate way.' So HR staff must be business savvy, able to speak the language of business through understanding how it operates. This relates to the importance of confidence and personal credibility. HR has got be able to represent itself as able to tackle problems and be seen to be adding to shareholder value or organizational effectiveness. It has to deliver its promises, not just articulate what the difficulties are. The trick is to combine a strong business perspective with an awareness of how softer skills can be deployed to bring the best out of employees.

> The HR function in a law firm is taking the view that, in addition to gaining functional credibility, individuals also need to build their own personal credibility in order to be able to demonstrate the value that HR can bring. This means having people in the HR function who have the same personal attributes and are of the same calibre as their internal clients – bright and articulate – and able to debate the issues (Tamkin *et al.*, 2006).

As to leadership skills, in one way leadership should be expected at all levels in the HR team. In their own right, every individual should display such qualities. Naturally, though, those in management roles will be required to offer leadership in greater measure. This point especially applies to some key positions – obviously the HR director, the business partners (because of their pivotal role), and the manager of the shared services operation (because of the taxing performance challenge they face in balancing cost and efficiency in service delivery) and, in some models, the functional leadership which the top expert offers. Strategic thinking is also likely to be important in all these roles.

The consultancy skill requirement identified by SHRM is closely connected to the influencing skills needs described in the CIPD (2005b) survey. It is interesting that the latter also refers to political skills. We emphasized their importance in the context of making a strategic contribution to the running of the organization. Especially where people management responsibilities are extensively devolved, HR will have to be able to persuade line managers to adopt appropriate people management practices.

Technological awareness is of growing importance as e-HR becomes more pervasive. There has been a tendency for HR managers to be somewhat technophobic. The comment has been made to us by a management consultancy that HR directors are insufficiently knowledgeable about IT and the possibilities it offers. This in their view can lead to outsourcing through ignorance. This might be a generational matter: the new breed of HR professionals is more likely to be both more familiar and more at ease with technology. Knowledge of what technology can do leads to the production of more sophisticated management information on which better-quality decisions can be made.

The relevance of 'global awareness' will naturally vary from organization to organization. For those that have to manage cross-nationally, there are particular skills that are needed. Cultural sensitivity is clearly vital, but how this will be deployed will depend on the operating model of the firm, as we discussed earlier. In most, though, there may be tension between the local and global perspectives. This is especially true in people management because there are differences in attitude and context that do not apply to Finance and IT. So the skill for the HR professional is to navigate the rapids, avoiding the global rocks and local crocodiles.

> RBS is aiming to grow its business into China, but it suffers from the perception by some of being parochial and Scottish. (The truth is different.) HR, recognizing the stretch from 'normal' operations, has instigated three levels of culture training: awareness, acclimatization and expatriation. This is aimed at those involved in the China deal so that they can better appreciate the nature of the cultural differences involved in doing business in China.

In describing the new skills, we concentrate on those for business partners because this is where there is greatest change and challenge. We then consider any specific issues for the other roles.

Business partner skills

Business partners obviously form the bulk of those working in a close relationship with managers, but there are also those in the corporate centre, including the HR director him/ herself, who may need the same skill set.

At a generic level business partners will need a number of competencies:

- communicating
- facilitating
- coaching
- influencing
- interpersonal
- negotiating.

However, they will have to be deployed in a particular context. This includes operating as a broker of HR services in the matrix structure, described earlier. This will test negotiation skills, and political skills will again be demanded: balancing corporate and local needs, satisfying both to the extent that is possible. Given, too, that business partners will be part of a team, relationship building is important. They may have to act as a coach to senior management, not just in advice and guidance on people practices, but also on a one-to-one basis, providing feedback and support. HR also has to have the ability to influence without formal authority. In Neil Roden's words, HR leaders need to be 'street smart'. They may well not be as professionally knowledgeable as more junior colleagues or certainly those in the centre of expertise. They may not be in as much control of resources as past HR managers, but they must know how to influence the top team. And, as we pointed out earlier, business partners will need to be aware of the power dynamics. They will have to be capable of mobilizing those in favour of their views and dealing with those against. So business partners will require well-honed political antennae, able to pick up signals of support or opposition. They will know the method to choose to achieve their objectives. This will be true not just in relation to dealing with business colleagues directly, but also in the interrelationship between HR and business management.

None of these competencies should be new to HR managers, but, because business partners are supposed to operate in a strategic manner, they will have to demonstrate a high level of ability. What, according to some of our respondents, may be more challenging to business partners is to use effectively the data emerging from improved management information systems. They will have to be sufficiently numerate to understand what can be done with statistics (and their limitations). They will have to be good at diagnosis: spotting trends, seeing issues from a variety of sources, making connections in a broader integrative way. By that we suggest examining whether the organization is growing human capital by improving the skills and engagement of staff or allowing it to depreciate. They will have to connect the data to their employment model of what drives high performance through people. Good analysis then needs to be turned into action.

The intellectual capability required can by summarized by the acronym used for many years by Shell: HAIR. Individuals will need the qualities of a Helicopter (able to survey the problem from a distance, yet dive into the detail if necessary), the ability to Analyse, a sense of Imagination (to be creative in solutions) and a sense of Reality (so that good ideas are well grounded in what will work in practice).

All of this takes place in a business context. So, knowledge and understanding of the fundamentals of the business is vital. This is likely to mean being at ease with financial, marketing, sales and production terminology and issues. Problems will have to be discussed in the language of business, not in HR-speak. The latter can put off line colleagues with its particular terminology. And this should be tailored to the particular audience. Some managers want hard, precise, data-driven arguments. Others want to be convinced at the intellectual level. But both want their problems solved in business not HR terms.

This requires an awareness of business context. Do they know enough about the activities of the business unit of which they are part to make a full contribution? How many business partners can answer questions such as:

1. What is the business unit strategy over the short and medium term?
2. How does the company derive its income and make a profit?
3. What are the sources of cost, especially those relating to payroll?
4. What are the sources of value that emanate from employees?
5. What are the strengths and weaknesses of the competition in their sector?
6. What is the capability of the competition compared to their own organization in terms of talent, organization, working practices, etc.?
7. What are the expectations of customers, shareholders and other key stakeholders of the company? What processes does the company have in place to identify these, especially relating to employees?

(In a non-commercial organization, these questions could be appropriately modified.)

Business partners should be able to answer most of these questions, and ones like it, so that they can show that they are on top of their brief, fully conversant with the business context within which they are operating. They need to demonstrate that they are seeking the information to answer the questions through internal meetings with business leaders and external discussions with with key opinion formers or players in their industry, e.g. talent head hunters, sector specialists (e.g. Gartner in IT).

Then there are some personal attributes that will affect their success. Most are common to other senior managers – resilience, courage, achievement, orientation. These strengths turn the good ideas into fact. They are the delivery part of the equation (one too often neglected in the past). The CIPD consortium project on HR in the public sector concluded that 'HR needs to get out more' (CIPD, 2005c). This is true in the sense that HR might in the past have been too concerned with policy design and not enough with implementation. It is even more true for business partners, stripped of any responsibility for transactional matters, they must engage with stakeholders in order to know what is going on in the business.

Of particular importance for HR staff is the development of personal credibility. Building personal credibility is essential in the business partner's ability to challenge or influence. Its reported absence has rightly led Ulrich (1998a) to talk about the requirement of 'HR with attitude'. Trevor Bromelow of Siemens describes this as having the 'grit and determination and the confidence to say to line managers "we have the evidence that people can make the difference to business success"'. This can partly be achieved through HR business partners having the right attributes and disposition, and partly through getting customers to see that HR can help them in transformational, not just transactional, areas.

Many of the qualities required of business partners are special to them, or are characteristics required to a greater degree. More than other professionals, they have to be chameleons. They have to adapt to the preferences of business leaders. At times they will have to move between being sympathetic to the needs of employees and then to the requirements of the business. They need to deliver a strategic contribution, but, as we have argued, they should be effective implementers of change.

Skills for other roles

We described in our earlier book (Reilly and Williams, 2003) the particular skill requirements for those working in shared services centre, either in call centres or records offices. We gave insufficient attention, however, to shared services centre managers. They will need all the generic managerial skills, but there are two areas where they require particular competencies. The first is that they must operate in matrix fashion, not only pulling together the disparate parts of their own operation, but linking it to the other parts of HR. Three obvious interfaces are with business partners and their line customers, centres of expertise if they are the next escalation level up the enquiry chain and the corporate centre, since the service centre has to deliver in a manner that supports the organization's strategy. So all the skills of brokering, influencing, negotiating and communicating will be especially necessary.

The second competency areas relates to the fact that these jobs are to varying degrees commercial. Where there is substantial outsourcing, contract and third-party relationship management will be necessary. Where there is an internal market and services are charged out, the shared services centre manager will need to be able to price the work and manage costs against it. Even without a charging system, but with SLAs in place, there will be an important customer management task. And in all circumstances where the work is retained in-house, resource management capability will be essential. Managers, especially those responsible for a consultancy pool, must ensure the match of numbers and skills to requirement, both short term and long term.

The professional experts working in the centres of expertise will obviously need deep subject knowledge, skills and experience. In particular, they should be outward looking as well as internally focused. They must be well informed of the external environment, in terms both of emerging good practice and research, and of broader social and demographic change. They should be capable of analysing this material so as to assist in policy formulation. Intellectual rigour is required, but also pragmatic realization of what policy is deliverable. Sensitivity to current needs must be balanced by a recognition that policies and procedures must be capable of adapting to changed circumstances. This means that HR must know its business and the needs of its customers. And, as we remarked earlier, these experts need high-level interpersonal and communication skills.

Those working in the corporate centre on HR strategy should be aware of this information and be able to draw attention to any problems with a mismatch between external developments and organizational positioning. Through this external sensing it can help the organization avoid the business strategy *drifting* away from the world outside (Johnson, 1987).

Again, the ability to diagnose problems, separating symptoms from causes, should allow HR to identify the organizational ills and find the means to tackle the difficulties. Here HR can be an innovator, not just dealing with current problems, but anticipating new ones through spotting trends and moving the organization forward.

The boxed example shows that these analytical and implementation skills apply to consultants, as well as to experts. With consultants the relative emphasis is more on delivery of the right solution. This gives even greater emphasis to project management capability, especially experience in risk management and dependency planning.

RBS's consultancy approach illustrates the range of skills required:

1. diagnosing the problem
2. generating options
3. choosing the right solution
4. effectively implementing the solution
5. evaluating the results.

We return later in the book to some of the deeper challenges (in Chapter 15) and potential solutions (Chapter 16) to building the skills that we have highlighted here that are required for HR to be successful in future.

9 *New Technology*

Despite the reservations expressed about e-HR, which we will discuss later, e-HR can support a number of the positive developments for HR described in this book. These include:

- recruitment branding – using the internet to attract the growing body of job seekers that expect to use well designed tools
- devolution – facilitating management decision-making
- database management – organizations go to recruits rather than the reverse, optimizing the deployment of the internal resource
- cost saving for HR – significantly reducing administrative work and having standard processes to operate
- cost saving for the organization – by reducing paperwork and unnecessary face-to-face meetings
- speed and quality of people management delivery – using fewer links in the process chain
- better management information – producing quality and integrated data
- self-reliance – encouraging managers and employee to find information and deal with processes without involving HR
- transparency and knowledge – reducing ignorance of HR policy and practice and making it easier to understand.

To achieve these benefits organizations should provide themselves with:

- a basic integrated records and payroll system that provides decent management information
- a dedicated section of the organizational intranet that provides comprehensive information on HR policy and procedures, written in a way that is easily understood by line and employee colleagues
- sufficient manager and employee self-service to remove HR from being the proverbial post box and allow forms/documents to be completed and authorized without their having to pass through HR's hands
- an appropriate number of applications to genuinely gain efficiency and effectiveness, such as online payroll and e-recruitment.

New HRIS systems are providing data in a way not seen before. This gives HR better information to steer people management approaches. For example, organizations can get better data on:

- absence frequencies and patterns by individual, section, gender, etc.
- wastage rates, by gender, occupation, section, length of service and reason for leaving
- take-up of share options, sharesave or flexible benefit options, or other benefits, by employee characteristics

- use of temporary staff across the organization by reason for use
- skill profiles by individual, team, business unit
- distribution of performance bonuses by gender, ethnic group or section.

This sort of data from an HRIS can be powerfully combined with data from other sources, especially employee views obtained from opinion surveys. This allows data items to be linked, such as wastage rates by job satisfaction or performance bonus by views on performance-related pay. Joined-up statistics offer the chance of proper human capital measurement, which allows organizations to construct and test models of what engages (and disengages) staff.

The boxed examples show what can be done with corporate intranets in terms of communication and standardization. Well designed, they offer simplicity and openness in place of the opaqueness and complexity of previous HR policy materials. The better the quality of the intranet, the fewer the calls on HR staff to deal with queries. This means both a saving in costly resources and also an improvement in customer satisfaction. When the text is written for employees and managers, not for HR, a customer service ethos is also apparent. Moreover, a greater transparency of HR policy is thereby demonstrated for the benefit of employees and managers alike. A perspective of trying to achieve user friendliness is also indicative of a more customer-centric approach.

The downside of standardization of processes and the use of a single intranet to convey the message is that it may not work well in a diverse organization. Imposing a single approach to policies, practices and procedures may be damaging. Certainly, this was a criticism made of the consequences of BP outsourcing its administrative activities. As we described earlier,

---

Shell in the UK used to have written policies on terms and conditions which were centrally produced, but operationalized by each business unit. In 2004 Shell decided to bring all relevant documents together so that there was standardization of material, in a common format that would be used by all the Shell mainstream businesses for their 'core' HR information. In addition, the aim was to move away from a situation where the output was very technical and did not address questions that were raised by employees or line managers in an easy manner.

The decision was made to achieve these objectives by editing the material so that it could be put on the company intranet, as shown in Figure 9.1, accessible by HR staff, managers and employees alike. The intended style was one of information sharing, not selling, and was intended to be understood by the whole workforce. A new categorization was used that aligned with Shell People Services (the shared services operation), e.g. 'myCompensation'.

HM Revenue and Customs (HMRC) is conducting a similar exercise, but in the context of merging two established civil service departments. It too has been keen to find an approach that is line manager and employee friendly. Like Shell, it is using the corporate intranet to provide policy and practice information and guidance. The content is organized on a subject-based taxonomy, but with a strong emphasis on finding material via a search engine. So getting the 'metadata' right is imperative. Three levels of guidance have been written: for managers, for staff and for HR practitioners. Often there are overlaps, but this is accepted. Everyone has access to all three levels.

All draft material, once signed off by the HR policyholder, is user tested.

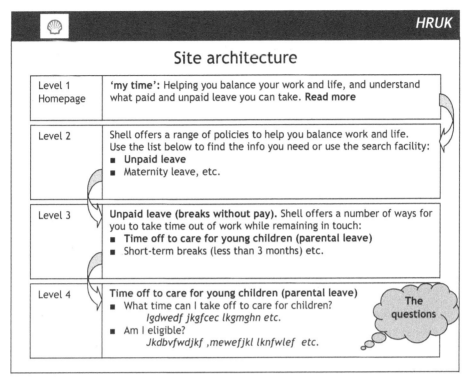

Source: Shell International

Figure 9.1   An illustration of an intranet page from Shell

the e-enabled HR delivery mechanism required commonality. This meant changing policies and procedures to meet a single template. Managers, especially at manufacturing locations, objected (Higginbottom, 2001). Similarly, there have been complaints at a government department introducing ERP (Enterprise Resource Planning) that the tail is wagging the dog because HR policies and practices have to conform to the system requirements, not the other way round.

Manager self-service has made devolution of tasks from HR to the line much easier. It has reduced the volume of transactions to be processed. Line managers may have become more self-sufficient over people management matters and less reliant on HR support for administrative matters, or even more operational decisions. Thus, managers can not only process overtime claims directly, without reference to HR, they can process changes to employees' base pay on their own authority. These tasks could have been done manually by managers, but self-service gives an impetus to transfer work from HR in a way that is more likely to be acceptable to managers. In this way, devolution and automation can go hand in hand. Better management information from the HRIS may allow managers to make these decisions. Adjusting base pay is facilitated by the ability to produce a report on salaries of the team against market norms. Previously, such a report would have to have been commissioned through HR and any pay adjustments approved by it.

Reducing ignorance can be achieved, not only by using intranets, but also through 'hardwiring' policies into manager self-service processes, so that the information is readily available. For example, if a line manager does not know the overtime rates and would have had to check first before entering into a form for submission, e-HR can build in the rates automatically together with any counter-signature facility. Not only does it remove activity from HR, it can speed up the process for the line.

In the same way, employee self-service has supported self-reliance in employees. They no longer need to depend on HR (or indeed their managers) for some forms of information or action. They can access policy information from their desktop. They can update their records. In simple systems, this might mean changing their home address. In more sophisticated systems, staff might add new skills they acquire to a skill database.

> At Aegon UK, the driver for manager self-service is the improvement of processes. Employee self-service is also concerned with getting employees to take more responsibility for themselves. This means not only keeping their personal data up to date, but also ensuring that their performance objectives are agreed and lodged or that their training plan is in place and is executed. The aim is to shift the manager from a controlling role to one of coaching. Better management information from better records systems enables managers to use time freed up from administrative tasks to engage more in performance enhancement.

Manager self-service and employee self-service can therefore deliver efficiency and effectiveness gains for HR. They have allowed HR to cut numbers in the function and freed up the time of the remainder to undertake 'higher value-added' tasks. The American Cedar Workforce Technologies 2003 survey (www.thecedargroup.com) claims an average of a 37 per cent reduction in HR staffing through the introduction of just self-service, or 'direct access' as they call it. Cycle times in HR processes were reported cut on average by 62 per cent and cost per HR transaction was down by 43 per cent. Indeed, Connolly *et al.*, (1997) argues, as more and more routine people management activities are automated out (or done by line management), there is a shift in HR role from 'case' management to organization-wide management. This adjustment separates out the more day-to-day activities from the strategic, long-term ones.

These efficiency gains can extend beyond HR to the organization as a whole. Removing paper from simple processes, such as overtime inputs and promotions, in a large organization like RBS can take out over two million pieces of paper annually. Online learning in RBS can reduce property requirements for face-to-face events and materials costs by around 40 per cent.

To make this sort of scale of saving in numbers, materials and paper, HR may have to force the issue. Some organizations have issued a cut-off date after which they will not handle paper transactions. Other organizations have controlled spending on travel or accommodation, to limit face-to-face meetings and training events, encouraging teleconferencing and e-learning solutions. Companies have also used incentives to develop employee self-service through individual prizes (e.g. entry into a holiday draw) or collective recognition (e.g. a reward for the top response among business divisions). Name and shame methods or league tables are another method of promoting self-service, but are more aimed at the laggards than leaders.

Where self-service is seen to ease existing work for employees or managers (reducing effort or time on tiresome tasks) or allowing new actions to be performed, then systems will be welcomed, along with the cost savings. The right sort of architecture has to be put in place. And 'right' should not be defined simply in terms of technically correct. 'Right' means fit for the specific purpose in the light of customer skills and preferences. If they are poorly designed, self-service systems will frustrate and irritate. In particular, organizations need to ensure that enough processes are e-enabled for users to familiarize themselves with them (occasional use limits learning), and that they are intuitive to work with. Where customers see that tedious tasks have been made easier then they will respond positively to self-service.

Decisions on what e-applications to purchase are harder. Some sound appealing but do not necessarily deliver all that much. Performance management online, for example, allows appraisal forms to be completed and transferred electronically. It has the advantage of removing from line managers excuses about cumbersome forms and it allows easier data analysis, but it has little impact on the quality of the appraisal discussion. Skill databases sound attractive until organizations consider how much time will be required to set up and run them. We have seen the collection of competency data merely to populate a newly acquired records system. Little thought was given to how this would be used, let alone maintained. And, although e-learning has some advantages, it is not without its critics. Reservations have been expressed about inappropriate choice of subject matter for electronic media; inadequate support for learners and poor evaluation of learning outcomes.

There may, however, be more mileage still in e-recruitment. As the e-generation comes of age, organizations will have to adapt. The new techno-literate employee will want and expect a quality technology infrastructure. These individuals will be drawn to organizations that offer an attractive face through a good internet. Failure to provide this will drive away many potential recruits. E-recruitment is becoming increasingly popular for all parties. Employers save on cost, HR can use sophisticated selection techniques, employees get convenience, line managers get better candidate tracking, and everyone can benefit from a faster recruitment processes. The average job posting online costs around £250 compared to £5,000 for a ¼ page in a national newspaper (Elkington, 2005). Standard Chartered cut the cost of recruitment from £6,500 per graduate head recruited via the paper system to £2,000 via a 100 per cent online system.

> It might come as a surprise to learn that an organization like Hertfordshire County Council is attracting 70 per cent of its applicants via their internet site and over 60 per cent apply online. The council has teamed up with Manpower to develop its e-recruitment service. Manpower has provided the technology and expertise that are not available to the council. It has set up the website, and manages the enquiries, deals with vacancies and provides the first sift in selection. All temps are hired via Manpower. This has simplified processes, significantly cut costs and positioned Hertfordshire County Council as an employer in tune with the e-generation. Alan Warner believes that competitive advantage in recruitment will come from database management. Those organizations which can match people to vacancies through their database of CVs will win over those who have to pay the price (in time and money) of using the traditional advertising route to go to market.

With all these forms of e-enablement, organizations should be very clear on the purpose and cautious about the benefits that really will be delivered. For example, it has been argued (by Pollard and Willison, 2005) that e-learning needs to offer learners quality content, a degree of control over their experience, feedback on progress, time and space to learn, and human interaction. This last critical point can be met by organizations 'blending online activities with traditional and accepted forms of learning; and by providing access to appropriate experts and fellow learners'. Skills databases, completed by staff, should have a clear purpose, be kept simple so that they are easy to maintain and should deliver an obvious benefit to users, making them worth completing (Hirsh and Reilly, 1998).

What this description of e-HR should have made plain is that care should be exercised before investing in e-HR, especially in some of the more sophisticated devices. As a manager from a hi-tech company herself said to us, there is a real 'risk that technology will be seen as the solution to all HR ills'. Or, as the reviewers of e-learning put it, this is 'not a quick fix but instead needs careful implementation to reach its potential' (Pollard and Willison 2005). If organizations are not careful, technology may end up driving people management practices. Instead, investment decisions should be taken by looking at costs and benefits over the medium term, not just the short term. Technology has to be business driven to satisfy business requirements. Ease of use by HR, managers and employees is critical to the acceptance of new technology and its widespread take-up. Which form of e-enablement the organization chooses should be a function of what it needs to meet business requirements and what will work in particular cultures. A manufacturing company with a large blue collar workforce with limited computer access will have less need of IT applications than a high technology firm.

Thought specifically needs to be given to the balance between the electronic and personal. 'Not every part of HR is suitable for e-enablement.' E-HR should aid 'efficiency in areas that are suitable to be carried out electronically, not replace face to face contact which is an essential part of HR': so states the about-to-be published e-standards for local government. As the boxed example shows, even in a high-technology firm, there are limits to what is acceptable in electronic communication.

> Hewlett Packard had to put back in place human contact after objections from line managers to having to deal with HR only through electronic means in disciplinary cases. A telephone line was reintroduced alongside the self-service option. HP's assumption had been that, with a technically literate workforce, access to their networks from anywhere in the company and the fact that as an IT company it should have demonstrably good e-HR, managers did not need human intervention.

Organizations should not be overambitious in what they try to do. There are too many stories of organizations that have been unrealistic about what can be delivered and by when. They then make the mistake of cutting resources on the back of technology that does not come onstream at the time that was expected. Other organizations have suffered from over-expectation in terms of the speed and nature of technological improvement. If organizations move too fast, ahead of the culture, there may be duplication of service — electronic and personal – as BP found (Higginbottom, 2001). There may be flaws in the system design, or, more likely, in the way the system was set up. Again, if staff numbers are cut on the assumption that the technology will be effective, and it is not, the quality of the service deteriorates. This gives critics of e-HR a field day.

As an HR manager at a media company said, organizations should be 'realistically sceptical' about how fast technology will work and deliver intended results (Reilly and Williams, 2003). As a CIPD survey (2003a) found, implementation of e-HR is not that straightforward. A third of survey respondents failed to cut costs and a similar proportion had difficulties delivering the desired service improvements. Problems apply as much to outsourced provision as to in-house. The latter may suffer because internal IT support is limited by a shortage of resource, expertise or priority. It may be that computer salespeople have pushed the organization to unsuitable technology. Outsourcing shifts the risk, but adds another link in the delivery chain.

Choice of application will also need to be governed by the organization's existing infrastructure. Any new applications should be able to hook up with the current kit. Not only is customization expensive, it can also jeopardize ultimate effectiveness. And upgrading the technology should be possible without enormous amounts of time and money being expended.

So the benefits of e-HR are clear, the ways of acquiring them are well documented and HR should not be afraid of arguing the business case for investment in new technology where the gains can be demonstrated. None the less, HR should implement change carefully and cautiously and with the users' perspective in mind. This does not necessarily mean moving at the pace of the slowest customer, but it does suggest going with the grain of what is acceptable, rather than pushing the organization too hard in the forms of e-enablement it adopts. These comments may apply to the HR function itself. HR staff may be reluctant to let go to allow managers and employees more control over people management information.

10 *New Approach to Monitoring and Evaluation*

In terms of measurement and monitoring we suggest organizations make a clear distinction between, on the one hand, people management and HR performance measures and, on the other, between those that relate to efficiency and those that relate to effectiveness.

People management measures

The sort of people management *efficiency* measures we have in mind include:

- spans of management control
- payroll cost per full time equivalent (FTE) employee
- profit per FTE
- income per FTE
- number of process transactions/calls/units of output per FTE in operational teams
- payroll cost against budget/target or headcount against 'establishment'/target.

People management efficiency measures are clearly important, as they should relate to the efficiency of the organization itself. A number of the measures listed look at how well structures and processes are working. Others look at the cost of people inputs.

People management *effectiveness* measures should, if properly structured, by contrast encompass a description of human capital, over both the short and the long term. As we described earlier, human capital reporting is a hot topic in the UK at present. It might have remained a subject for MBA studies but for the Kingsmill report. Yet the risk is that HR misses the boat on leading developments in this field. This may be because human capital itself is not taken seriously, because it is left to Finance to account for the value of employees or because the emphasis is on reporting human capital, especially if it is undertaken out of compliance, not because it is useful to do. Consequently, human capital reporting may be limited in scope and relevance to people management. So HR may fail to understand the importance of human capital or may be too afraid of putting its head above the parapet to advocate something novel or challenging. It might be too scary either to advance a view on what model of people management delivers superior performance or to identify deficiencies in human capital formation. It may be seen as too difficult to think of what is it with respect to employees that generates human capital and by the same token restricts its development. It may be safer to produce rather dull statistics on the number of people employed or the training cost per head, especially if there is neither the data nor the diagnostic skill to produce more enlightening information. As was feared as long ago as 1989 by Michael Armstrong (Cunningham and Hyman, 1999) and again in 2003 by Richard Donkin of the *Financial Times* (Donkin, 2003), the accountancy profession may be in the van of measuring and assessing the value of all resources, including human.

Human capital measurement and reporting has value in that it can provide HR with a number of opportunities:

- It causes management to think about human capital and how it is best represented.
- It may be the means by which HR gets people management issues heard in the boardroom or executive committee.
- In trying to account for the value of human capital, the emphasis is on finding agreed ways of measuring this asset. This can place human capital reporting alongside financial reporting.
- Depending upon how it is constructed, human capital may be used to link employee and business performance.
- It might be useful in deciding where and when investment in people management would be justified or, conversely, where action to improve it would be necessary.
- It can stimulate further enquiry or challenge if it reveals something distinctive (positive or negative) in part of the organization's management of people.

There is, however, a problem if meaningless statistics are produced. Generating useless information may confuse more than it enlightens. The greater risk still is if commentators, governments or investors start to make inappropriate comparisons. Comparing, say, retention rates across sectoral boundaries is obviously pointless. But even within sectors there can be significant differences based on different resourcing strategies or approaches to work structure. Ill-informed benchmarking may be positively dangerous if investors drive organizations to ill-founded solutions, especially ones that reflect a me-too attitude, rather than establishing a USP. This is the antithesis of the resource-based view of the firm. Here, difference gives competitive advantage. It follows that standardized reporting is as unhelpful as standardized practice.

But not only should organizations guard against misunderstanding and misuse of the information reported, they should equally recognize the limitations of the sort of data that is likely to feature in human capital reporting. Showing that there is a connection between employee engagement and business performance is very important, but it still begs the question about what employee behaviours and attitudes underpin the engagement. And reporting after all is only reporting. Its real use is if it generates action. This is not necessarily straightforward. What interventions can an organization make that generate the responses which organizations wish to see? As we said on page 66, it is the 'bundle' of HR practices that positively stimulate employees, rather than the discrete elements. This makes it hard to select the right measure to assess and the right action to take.

We believe organizations should develop their own HR practices to suit their own business needs. It therefore follows that organizations should develop measures that monitor the right sort of human capital elements that fit their size, sector, stage of development, organizational structure and business strategy. We would, however, suggest to organizations that they emphasize those elements of people management practice that link to human capital. Thus, they should be looking at people management performance in the broadest sense to see whether organization is building future capability, and this is, as we have said, some combination of competence and commitment or engagement. The capability that is being examined should connect to how the organization creates value or meets its organizational purpose, and how effectively it is performing against such goals. Organizations should be examining the following sort of measures:

- degree of employee engagement by occupational group, linked to performance
- take-up of any share-related offer, by time in post
- extent to which knowledge is shared – areas of good and bad practice
- proportion of employees fully skilled to meet their current job
- number of skill areas where there is competitive advantage
- effectiveness of organizational structure as measured by whether roles are clear and distinct but sufficient collaboration is obtained
- proportion of staff who can fully describe their and their unit's work objectives and targets
- number and distribution of staff failing to meet performance standards
- ability to change/innovate
- percentage of managerial staff with potential for further promotion.

Clearly there would need to be care to protect confidentiality in external reporting, but this should be possible. This approach is preferable to producing figures which are suitable for HR planning (workforce size, age profile, etc.) and necessary for managing resources, but which say little worthwhile about human capital. Having a complement of 1,000 staff with an even age distribution is all very well, but if they are demotivated, ill-trained or poorly led, they are not of much use. 'Value' or 'asset' is the key word in human capital, not 'quantum'.

A key challenge for HR is to offer a small number of meaningful measures that really do drive business performance, and can be demonstrated as doing so. Otherwise, if management is bombarded with measures of performance, it will continue to ask HR 'So what?' questions. What is the purpose of the data? What does it say about business improvement?

Nationwide's 'dashboard', as shown in the boxed text below, concentrates on the areas where employee engagement makes a difference to business results. This is the sort of analysis that does put HR in the forefront of human capital measurement.

Nationwide Building Society has proved to its satisfaction that the service-profit chain works. In analysing what leads to employee commitment, it has identified five key factors:

1. length of service
2. coaching
3. resource management
4. pay
5. values.

Within the retail division, work areas are judged on their performance on these key commitment drivers (through their opinion survey) and on their outcomes in terms of employee retention and customer commitment. A traffic-light system highlights areas of concern.

In constructing a measurement framework we favour a combination of lag and lead measures. The lag measures are as expected: i.e. wastage rates, training provision, absence statistics, productivity, etc. What might be less common are the lead measures. They can provide management with vital data to help predict trends, as opposed to review past behaviour, and then take appropriate decisions. This might mean taking evasive action to prevent undesirable outcomes (e.g. a cycle of poor recruitment selection leading to high levels of early wastage) or enhancing policies that are leading to positive results (e.g. extending an offer of flexible working because of signs of increased employee engagement). The orientation is thus 'Where do we want to be?' rather than 'Where are we now?' It avoids driving by looking at the road ahead through the rear-view mirror. Checking periodically what is behind you is important, but the focus should be on what is coming up next.

Some organizations, such as RBS, have invested heavily in creating predictive processes to highlight people management trends in areas such as employee engagement, as well as models which look at the trends in outputs measures and forecast these forward. Other organizations successfully use organizational capability models that look at skills across an organization and highlight to management where, under certain scenarios, gaps and strengths will emerge. Intention-to-leave surveys are another predictive mechanism used by some organizations.

To take absence data as an example of constructing a lead measure. They can be viewed purely as an inefficiency cost, and left at that. Or HR can tie absence into a measure of productivity. It can show the impact of absence on output. More powerfully still, HR can produce scenarios of what output would look like under different absence levels. This would show the extent of the gain that can be made if attendance is improved. In organizations that do not control absence well, this could demonstrate that some investment in management effort might be worth it in terms of the improvement. The return on this investment might be better than other, more time-consuming activities, such as quality circles. Time could reasonably be spent finding out the causes of absence. If, say, most relates to stress, then steps might be taken to do with job design, workloads or management that would be worthwhile. The cost of an employee assistance programme could be funded out of savings on absence.

HR measures

To date, too many HR measures focus on financial measures of HR cost or input measures of process efficiency, rather than a broader range of indicators of performance. These may be of interest to the finance director, and not necessarily for the right reasons, but they offer too narrow a perspective on what HR should be doing. Again we favour a balanced approach that takes account of efficiency and effectiveness, and recognizes that the value provided can be directly for shareholders, employees or line customers.

Organizations should measure the following:

- Cost/efficiency – of course this is important and will include HR staff-to-employee ratios, HR cost-to-employee ratios and derivatives thereof. Process efficiency metrics also come under this heading, including number of people hand-offs in key processes.
- Client service – the views and opinions of the service that HR provides across the three customer groups, i.e. to senior management, to line management and to employees.
- Functional positioning – using activity analysis to see where the quantum of HR resource is being spent to check whether this is where the function wants to be.
- Strategic alignment – to what extent are the policies and practices designed by HR meeting organizational objectives?

Clearly, the first measure is self-evidently about efficiency and the last two are about effectiveness. Customers can report on either measure or both. Robust, structured and relatively frequent recording and reporting of these key performance areas will allow the HR function to draw good conclusions as to how it adds value in its organization.

Comparing the organization's HR cost, measured through the ratio of HR staff to total employees, or its derivatives (HR administrative cost: FTE, HR administrative staff numbers: total headcount) has its benefits in giving HR an idea of where it stands relative to other firms. Whilst crude, comparing ratios is far better than no comparison at all. It can be a useful wake-up call, a challenge to organizational assumptions. If the organization has one HR head for every 50 staff and a similar one has one for every 250, it is not unreasonable to ask why. But that is the difficulty. Comparing ratios highlights a difference, no more than that. What it does not say is how effective the HR team is. The organization may have a 'creditable' 1:100 ratio, but the HR service may be poor. Alternatively, the organization might have a 1:50 ratio that is regarded as highly inefficient, but the HR division is doing a great job.

Moreover, organizations should take note of the caveats we made regarding benchmarking on page 126. In particular, where the ratio might mislead is that organizations do not necessarily have the same model of HR delivery, or, if they do, they might be at different points in development. Outsourcing, degree of line devolution, intensity of training and development, ease of recruitment and retention will all affect the degree of HR input. The inclusion of unrelated HR activities (e.g. catering, HSE, etc.) in the HR organization muddies the water still further. Some of these differences may be characteristic of the sector (e.g. training spend or turnover), but some are organizationally specific. Some differences are the result of geographical spread or business structure. Moreover, the data collection upon which judgements are made is not always robust. The devil is certainly in the detail.

Organizations should use benchmarking more as a guide to how it has moved on its transformational journey rather than as a means to determine its end point. As such it may have a place, but it should not be a substitute for thinking. For some the e-HR investment may be worth it, in taking out HR resources against the financial investment in technology. For others, the spend cannot be justified. Each organization needs to define its own objectives to meet its own needs. As we emphasized earlier, the organization can see the investment in people management as a source of competitive advantage, and HR is part of the contribution to that.

These points are especially important because large swathes of the public sector in the UK are currently benchmarking their HR functions, many with each other in response to the Gershon review's drive for increased efficiency, especially in the back office function. And ratios are forming part of this debate. If the measure is used in isolation, it is not only a very blunt instrument for driving out HR costs, but also, if implemented badly, can result in the entire HR function losing its perceived value to the organization. There are particular concerns about making comparisons with the private sector. Public sector organizations often have public responsibilities that are not present for commercial firms – reporting, transparency, open systems, model employer, etc. So 'worse' ratios can be for good reasons.

HR should continue to track its performance on process issues, partly to ensure that SLAs are being met, but partly to see whether improvements are possible. To get at how to do this, process analysis can be usefully employed. This describes the chain of tasks, from one end of the process to the other end, the links between the activities, the inputs and outputs. What this may show is overly engineered processes with too many handoffs. Using the consultant-type 'brown paper' method can produce helpful process maps. Red flags are used to identify points in the process where things are going wrong. There is duplication (such as number of times a new address has to be keyed into an organizational system – often seen when the HR and payroll systems are not linked), error (such as overpayment of staff) or breakdown (such as actions that are not generated at all because the process map has not recognized the requirement). Green flags are used as a way of creating opportunities for change within processes that are currently all right but could be improved. An example would be to create a single leaver statement to cover all relevant parties rather than generate individual advice slips for the pensions function, the benefits provider, the IT function, the security function and so on. Dissecting processes in this way enables informed re-engineering to take place.

Regarding client services, many organizations test customer satisfaction with the services provided. This is done through the reaction to a service delivered at point of use (e.g. a training course) or more generally through customer surveys on the quality, timeliness and cost of the service. Random phone calls are sometimes used to probe in more depth, but in general it is the user friendliness and efficiency that are checked, not effectiveness. A more challenging set of questions might include:

- Do business partners sufficiently understand the business they are supporting?
- Do they promote people issues in business meetings?
- Do those offering people management advice do this competently?
- Are they effective in the way that they challenge?
- Are HR staff properly aware of legal issues and balance risk and compliance?
- Do business partners anticipate organizational problems, or are they reactive?
- Does corporate HR develop an HR strategy that fits business needs?

And so on. In other words, customers can be asked to judge HR on the easy process questions, but they can also be asked to evaluate the extent to which HR is living up to its promise to be competent, professional and business aware.

> The NHS has developed a series of questions to ask the views of top managers on HR positioning and capability. This tests how supportive they are of HR management and understand the role it can play in their organization. It thus asks whether they believe HR's role is 'to help modernize services' or 'to influence the management of change'. It focuses especially on how geared up the HR function is to deliver a proactive agenda: 'the HR department understands and speaks the business/service language of the organization' or 'from experience the calibre of HR staff is high'. Similar questions have been designed for line managers and the HR function itself.
>
> The Michigan Department of Civil Service not only uses quality assurance software for recording calls into their service centre, but also, once the call is complete, sends a questionnaire on service satisfaction to every customer. The response rate is high and a remarkable 97 per cent satisfaction rate is obtained (IPMA, 2005.)
>
> WMC Resources Ltd has a standard annual customer survey of HR performance, but it adds three other less common metrics: frequency of meetings with key clients, level of unsolicited mail from customers and number of requests for new services (www.iqpc.com).

This leads to activity analysis. If an organization wants to understand whether its HR function is spending the right amount of time on the right issues, this is the best way to measure it. Organizations can get some indication of how well balanced their HR function is by looking at the ratio of back office staff to front office staff. This gives an idea of the extent of transactional versus transformational focus, or between the inward- and outward-facing parts of HR. Activity analysis allows a more in-depth look. Some organizations have used the occasional activity analysis for a specific task; whilst others, seeking a more active management of the HR resource, have implemented a time-based activity capture system. This requires HR employees to record the distribution of their time on a continuous basis. Some HR leaders avoid activity analysis, citing either concerns over accuracy (because HR employees will fill in what they think is the right answer) or that it would appear to be too much like 'big brother', sending the wrong message to the HR team. It can seem to be overly bureaucratic and resource hungry. Whilst there is some validity to these points, they are more a matter of implementation that can be dealt with in well-planned and well-designed exercises.

A good activity review will look at the HR function across three levels: strategic themes, process or activities, and tasks. The first may help identify the HR function's progress in the amount of time spent in, say, advising senior management on compensation or training solutions rather than on administration. Or more accurately, this form of assessment can determine whether the key roles are being fulfilled in the way intended. The proportion of business partners' time spent on administrative issues is an important measure of success, but it will also be instructive to learn what fraction of the experts' time is taken up with referrals from the shared service centre – too high a proportion may suggest that either the lower escalation tiers are not screening out enough or that HR policies are overly complex, making it difficult for call centre staff to deal with enough questions themselves. Useful learning can be obtained as to where individual casework is being dealt with.

Task analysis can be very granular (as many as 400 tasks could be evident) and may break down an activity such as recruitment into as many as 15–20 different steps – from identifying a resource requirement to amount of time spent generating the new hire contract.

To illustrate the benefits of activity analysis, take performance management. RBS undertook such a project in 1998. It showed that HR spent 3 per cent of its time, headcount and budget simply chasing, collecting and filing appraisal forms. This was double the amount spent on dealing with any performance issues that arose. Reversing these proportions and giving proper attention to under-performance would surely offer better business benefits.

> The NHS has an activity analysis tool that looks how HR's time is spent under 15 work headings. These are a mixture of content areas (e.g. workforce planning) and broader business objectives (e.g. cost control). It helpfully asks the split of time between line managers and HR, and challenges whether the time distribution and allocation is right.
>
> Aegon UK is building a balanced scorecard to measure HR's performance, but starting with process metrics and customer service. This is partly because the data is easy to acquire and is easily understood. It is also a reflection of getting the basics right before moving on to more sophisticated monitoring. It also allows HR staff to get a better appreciation of the cost of HR activity. For example, understanding cost to hire permits a better appreciation of effort versus reward, and allows a better evaluation of the different mechanisms of success. Once the process measures are 'internalized' it will move on to deeper measures.

As to strategic alignment, it is sobering to report that when David Guest looked at evidence of the extent to which there was an effective model linking people management and organizational performance, he found only 1 per cent of survey respondents reported having three quarters of high-performance work practices in place (Guest, 2000). A survey of HR directors found that 94 per cent of them agreed that that it was important to measure strategic HR, but only

40 per cent thought it possible to do so (Cabrera and Cabrera, 2003). As one might expect, organizations in the Cabreras' study looked carefully at HR efficiency, but were particularly weak on the 'interconnections between HR practices and organizational capabilities', and even more so on the impact of HR 'on key business outcomes'. Moreover, Robert Taylor said, on the basis of his input into the ESRC Research programme: 'Most workplaces do not pursue HR management techniques, according to managers' (Taylor, 2003).

By contrast, in a CIPD survey (2003a), 59 per cent of respondents claimed that the performance of HR was judged on the basis of business outcomes. What one does not know is what form this took. Was it that individual HR policies were tested on their impact on the business performance (rare in our experience) or, in a more general sense, that people management indicators were heading in the right direction, e.g. on absence, retention, etc.?

In this context, we should consider Becker, Huselid and Ulrich (2001)'s proposal (referred to earlier) for an HR scorecard that aims to link the performance of the HR function with measures of human capital development. Strategic focus was combined with not only certain ideal HR practices (in reward, communication, selection, work design, etc.), but also functional HR competencies and systems, to drive key deliverables such as workforce knowledge, 'mindset' and behaviour.

The model is very demanding in terms of data requirements and it is questionable how widely it is used in its full form, given how limited strategic measurement appears to be. This suggests that effort should be expended on having the right people management practices in the first place before turning to sophisticated HR measurement systems.

What should be possible is for HR policies to be looked at in terms of how they facilitate the people management enablers described earlier. So, for example, do reward and performance management systems help raise satisfaction? Does access to education help increase useable skills? Do flexible benefits packages assist recruitment and retention? The more statistically sophisticated organizations can use techniques such as predictive validity (measuring the impact of a people management practice) or marginal utility analysis (the financial gain to be achieved from a people management intervention).

If organizations do not get past the cost/efficiency measures they are vulnerable to an external review. If an external consultancy is ever asked to consider HR's performance it will do so on all four dimensions listed (people management and HR, efficiency and effectiveness), and in turn benchmark the data. HR may find itself in the position of having to defend itself against figures showing inadequate customer satisfaction or a poor distribution of time. So it is critical that HR looks at all the areas.

Using the data

Of course much of the measurement data we have described should have been available through management information systems before, and, in many well-run organizations, it was. However, it is equally fair to say that other large organizations have struggled to get decent workforce statistics because of poor technology. This is evidenced by the companies that made a living by selling software that allowed organizations to count the number of their employees! Now there should be no excuse for failing to invest in HRIS.

What is required though is a change in the attitude of the HR community at all levels. Business partners should, for example, as we have said, use data not just to inform but to challenge. It means saying to line colleagues: 'Why is that your section has a higher proportion of temporary staff than others?' 'Why do you think that so few of your team has taken up the latest share-save offer?' 'How can you explain the high percentage of staff in your department who resign because of limited development opportunities?' This means making managers aware of the cost of, say, using agency staff, uncertificated absence or unnecessary wastage. But, more subtly, what do the statistics tell the organization about the relationship between managers and those they manage? Is a lack of staff engagement shown up in the low take-up of share-save schemes or in the low scores in the employee attitude survey? Are the differences in wastage rates between sections explained by apparent differences in management style, as indicated by the explanations for resignation? They should be using the data to improve organizational performance by understanding what the statistics tell the organization regarding employee behaviour or management (in)action, and, where appropriate, about the connection between them. Interpretation and insight into business performance should lead to the proposal of well-judged solutions. In this task business partners should draw to management attention the issues of particular business importance.

For those capturing and entering the data they must realize the importance of what they are doing. This is more complicated if data capture is devolved to line managers. They will then have to be involved, as well as their HR colleagues. But the message to all those with this task is that the data will be actively used. In the past GIGO (garbage in, garbage out) did not matter if nobody looked at the material. Now, accuracy and completeness are vital. To illustrate this point, IES has undertaken a number of personnel data reviews to give the organization a pen picture of its workforce. Beyond the obvious data characteristics (age and gender) and those required for payroll (wage rate and working hours), these reviews were seriously hampered by poor-quality data. It was usually impossible to give an accurate statement on the qualification levels of employees. Descriptions on the distribution of ethnic minorities was always incomplete. But worse were the occasions where it was impossible to provide the sort of information that the organization needed to steer people management policy and practice. For example, one company with a fancy HRIS had 49 reasons for leaving codes so that it could track the causes of wastage. The most populated code was 'miscellaneous'. This was probably partly a failure of data capture (the right questions were not being asked, perhaps because they were not being asked in the right way), but it was also laziness on the part of data entry (what does it matter what code I put in?).

So this is a question of sensitivity to data – understanding its importance and being able to interpret it in a meaningful way that it useful to the business.

Monitoring/reporting

As we have emphasized, we favour a balanced approach to measurement. The reports provided from such a methodology should lead to an integrated set of results that offers a holistic review of people management and HR activity. They should look at the effectiveness and efficiency of people management and HR practices now and for the future.

In recent years, HR has added measures of employee engagement to business scorecards. This has the advantage of making the people element in the model more forward looking and profound than some of the uninteresting statistics that previously occupied this spot. As the Corus example below shows, this means that people management can more effectively be linked to business performance and a proper human capital measurement system can be created.

> Corus Colors (part of the steel company) has used the EFQM model to look at its business performance. It has separate headings for people results, business results, and customer and society results. This is against a set of ambitions 'to champion innovation, to stimulate success all around us, to create value in a worldwide market and to develop our abilities together.' As can be seen, there are number of people measures closely linked to business objectives. One specific measure used is to look at a 'people satisfaction index'. A traffic light system tracks performance against specific targets.

As there is a lot of material on HR's efficiency that can be reported, one way of controlling data overload is by distinguishing between that which needs to be given to customers and that which is required to manage HR. It should be remembered that, measuring service levels is as much a management tool as a client service tool. SLAs should cover *key* volume trends and productivity levels and potential areas for improvement.

> BAE Systems initially had over 400 process measures to judge the performance of Xchanging, its outsourced service provider. It realized that focus was lost in this way.

There are different views on the benefits of having formal SLAs with a monetary element, compared with informal systems. Supporters of SLAs argue that formalizing and defining the services offered and their quality standards has helped remove ambiguities in what is expected. Having a monetary value attached means that the discussion over service provision is taken seriously. It generates a more commercial attitude in HR and gives staff real targets to aim at. Reporting is then also taken more seriously.

The alternative view is that the monitoring process generates such activity that the point of the exercise, the substantive content of the work, takes second place to the process of measuring it. More fundamentally, there are those who argue that SLAs encourage the master/servant role relationship; that professional standards suffer to meet targets.

There is some truth in both arguments. Monitoring and reporting can become an industry in itself if one is not too careful. So care needs to be taken in setting up an SLA to get the level of detail right: sufficient to track performance, but not overly burdensome. And SLAs should concentrate on those areas of HR activity (the transactional) which lend themselves to this sort of monitoring and where rightly the customer should set the standards. After all there will always be a trade-off between cost and service, and the business needs to make its preferences known. This is better done through a formal process than through some kind of covert rationing. SLAs should not get involved in those areas, such as advice or consultancy, where the nature of the task, and its purpose, is less clear cut.

This approach suggests that particular care needs to be exercised over improvement targets. Business as usual targets should be straightforward and regularly communicated. Improvement metrics, if they relate to service levels, should also be included, but only by exception. Reporting should only take place when progress slips. The benefit of such an approach is that it reinforces that standards need to be maintained, but gives emphasis to where discretionary effort should be directed. Reporting should not be for its own sake, but to generate action where required. This means not getting stuck with reporting arrangements that have lost their value. They should be periodically reviewed to see whether they are still relevant.

One danger which this discussion raises and which should be avoided is the possibility that measurement could distort service provision. If organizations are not careful, HR staff focus on those aspects of the work for which there are targets and against which their performance is appraised and evaluated. As the boxed example shows, this can lead to the so-called 'displacement' effect. Only that which 'gets measured, gets done' and other areas get ignored.

> An international company found that its reward system was driving the wrong behaviours in its HR shared services centre. Reward was based on customer metrics: the happier the customer, the bigger the payout to the service centre staff. This had the effect of staff going overboard helping customers, even to the point of violating their own procedures. For example, payroll adjustments were made manually after payroll deadlines. This meant that subsequent adjustments had to be made involving extra work and with the risk of errors.

Evaluation and audit

Part of any HR monitoring should also look at the validity of HR policies and procedures to see how they contribute to the development of people management. One piece of research, albeit from a while ago, produced the startling statistic that only 8 per cent of organizations evaluate HR activities (quoted in Cabrera and Cabrera, 2003). Our sense is that this is still true. Too few HR initiatives are properly evaluated. At worst this is because before there is a chance for evaluation, the organization has moved on and introduced something new again. On other occasions, the difficulty in evaluation stems from not getting good baseline data. It makes it hard then to describe the benefits of any new approach.

The absence of evidence damages the credibility of the function. It cannot specify return on investment, be it in quantitative or qualitative terms. This shows it up as a poor relation to other functions, especially Finance. It makes it harder to persuade executives to spend money in the people management area, if they have doubts on whether the money will be well spent.

So, to develop a climate where evaluation will be effective, organizations should:

1. specify the objectives of the programme, policy, etc. (in quantitative terms as far as possible)
2. explicitly define the current status in the same terms
3. review change after a reasonable period, sufficient for change to be apparent but not so far into the future that the learning will be lost
4. if necessary, re-review the programme to see whether further change has occurred.

Take the introduction of an HR graduate recruitment programme as an example. The aim is to increase the number of graduate entrants (say from five to ten) and their quality (assessed as all being of middle management potential at least), and to achieve a better retention rate (from a loss rate of 15 per cent per annum to 7.5 per cent). The current system is ad hoc, with no formal quality standards.

After one year, the review can show the numbers recruited, the wastage rate and, harder to do but just as important, indications of the potential of the new recruits. Further reviews after three and five years can help consolidate perceptions on the quality of the resources that have been hired.

This evaluation could be strengthened by using qualitative data on the recruits' view of the recruitment, induction and development processes. Those line managing them could also have their opinions sought. Internal benchmarking with the graduate schemes of other functions could indicate the relative success of the HR approach and some external benchmarking could look at how in particular wastage rates compare.

Of course, the results may not all be positive. Rates of refused offers may show up problems at the recruitment stage that question the attractiveness of the offer. Is it the job, the salary or the prospects that is the source of this dissatisfaction? Follow-up interviews and benchmarking salaries can throw light on this. Patterns of attrition and interviews with leavers may suggest that the problem occurs post recruitment, possibly suggesting that induction or development processes are at fault.

We would not regard the above as rocket science, but what stops HR from routinely carrying out such an audit? Is it the fear of finding failure? Lack of data? An inability or reluctance to learn? Or because life moves on at such a pace that there is no time to stop and reflect?

This is where evaluation should be institutionalized. Any change proposal should have not only a justification for the investment of time and money, but also an evaluation plan that specifies the data needed, where it will be collected from, who is responsible and what the time frame is. In other words, evaluation should be built into project planning as a matter of course.

Audits may be undertaken as another form of evaluation, either forming part of a structured approach or being conducted in a more ad hoc manner. The former may be organized against a timetable on an organizational structure basis (i.e. locations or business units are seen in turn) or a subject basis. Audits are useful for examining activities that are less susceptible to formal evaluation. Thus, auditing could be used to see how well devolution is working, and the extent to which business units adhere to corporate policies or to legal requirements. The same methodology can be used, taking advantage of published data, but may be extended by holding interviews with key persons, running focus groups or commissioning bespoke surveys. Audits can indicate how well the HR function is operating or identify areas for change and improvement. It is particularly important to test how well the new operating model is working. Have costs been saved as planned? Has customer satisfaction with the service risen? Are SLA targets being consistently met?

The results may not all be as expected. Initially costs may fall, but they then may rise again if customers demand better service standards that add back activities which were previously dispensed with. Investment may also be required to get the standard of business partner that the organization requires – higher quality will come at a higher price. A step change in service delivery may produce a positive customer reaction, but further approbation may be hard to win. Similarly, if processes are consistently hitting the mark, then the room for improvement may be limited. This does not mean that the model is failing. It does mean that HR may need to be creative in searching for new areas to add value.

3 Impediments to Success ... and Some Solutions

Introduction

In Part 2 of this book we set out a view of what HR might look like in the future if it is to be effective in its ambition to offer an important and strategic contribution, but to respond to this call HR has a number of challenges to meet. These will be described in this third part of the book. They centre on:

- positioning of the function, especially in its relationships to stakeholders
- the operating model, its structures and roles, designed to provide customer service
- the capability of the HR function to deliver on its promise, including the skills and development required.

11 *The Challenge of Positioning*

It is a paradox that, as we described in the Introduction, HR remains anxious as to its role and perceived worth at a time when people management should be of increasing importance to organizations. It has been for a while a primary source of competitive advantage in a knowledge economy. There is generally a tight labour market, where attracting and retaining skills is often a major difficulty. The debate on human capital should lead to not just more reporting of employment issues, but also to increasingly more sophisticated descriptions of the contribution people make to business success. These developments should encourage CEOs to drive for greater performance from their HR functions to realize the benefits to be had from employee engagement.

Yet, despite the function's aspirations, in some organizations HR is far from being regarded as a strategic contributor. It is still seen, fairly or otherwise, as not up to the mark. Many of HR's difficulties with its positioning stem from how it is perceived by, and relates to, its stakeholders. HR is a victim of its history. As we set out in Chapter 1, HR has had an evolving role in organizations, moving from welfare through a strong interest in industrial relations to a broader remit in helping to secure high performance or organizational effectiveness. However, not all HR's stakeholders recognize or want this move. In part this may be HR's own fault. It has wanted to transform itself, but has lacked the will or capacity to change. Inadequate performance by the function, especially with respect to its slow and cumbersome processes, has handicapped its ability to claim work which is higher value added. These process problems can in part be attributed to poor technology, but much of it has to do, as we have described, with poor attitudes and staffing, and with insufficient attention being given to customer needs. The function has in the past been unduly introverted, lacking in self-confidence and inadequately business aware.

These deficiencies have endangered HR's credibility. This is what produces the cynical remarks in some organizations about HR's ineffectiveness and attitude. Some line customers see HR as only offering 'tea and sympathy'. Others resent what they see as HR's unwarranted interference in what they want to do, driven by ignorance of the business pressures, leading one practitioner to say that a small minority of managers want to 'spit on us'.

But even if HR has got its basics right, it still has challenges to face with respect to its relationship with senior management, line management and employees.

...in the eyes of senior management

Whilst, clearly, there are some very keen supporters of HR in the boardrooms of the UK, there are also those who have little time for the function. They give it a low priority or treat it with disdain, even dismissal. A CIPD survey found most CEOs gave a low score to performance of their HR department (Guest, 2000). This does not necessarily mean that they are not interested in people management, but they either think that this is largely a matter for line management or have lost faith in the ability of HR to deliver what they want. In these circumstances, HR will be bypassed, as reportedly happened in the mid-1990s in the USA (Brenner, 1996). HR people lacked credibility in the eyes of CEOs who sought instead the advice of third-party consultants. HR's lack of business awareness and experience was the cause of its marginalization.

> In one public sector organization the retiring HR director was replaced by an internal colleague who double-hatted on an interim basis. A newly appointed CEO had had a 'bad experience' with HR, and, as a consequence, was not prepared to risk a permanent appointment until he could trust that the interim could deliver.
>
> In another public sector organization the HR director 'moved on'. He was not replaced at board level, but at the level below. The head of HR then reported to the general affairs director. This situation pertained until a further reorganization settled the status of HR.

The consequence in some organizations is that HR is merely seen as a cost, not as a value creator. The dreaded ratio (be it of HR cost to overall employment cost or, more usually, HR numbers to employee numbers) is then wheeled out. A kind of virility test follows: how much can the organization cut HR staffing to improve the ratio – 1:100 is not enough, how about 1:200? Ratios of course do have their place in both sizing and monitoring workforce numbers. The problem is that the ratio becomes the point of the debate without reference to what the function is achieving or indeed what its customers want it to achieve. This is exemplified in one multinational company, where local management was worrying that HR had insufficient resources to deliver against agreed plans whilst, simultaneously, group management was driving a cost review aimed at 'improving' the HR ratio.

Though the effect may be the same, there is another group of senior managers who seek to limit HR's influence not because of its lack of competence, but because of the fear that HR will act as a brake on management's desire to manage. They want 'to put HR back in the box' as one interviewee explained it. HR's role is simply to deliver management's wishes. Far from being a partner in business, HR is merely the servant. This reinforces the position that HR found itself in during the downsizing of the 1990s: 'Salving company consciences with generous redundancy payments and the use of outplacement' (Guest, 1994). The function took the flak from line managers and employees, but had little influence over the decisions that led to the cuts. The power remained with senior management; HR was confined to administration and, at best, execution of senior management decisions.

Such executives do not see employees as assets to be nurtured. Whether these managers would be persuaded by evidence that employees can generate value and that HR can facilitate this process is a moot point. A CIPD survey of 462 CEOs found that most CEOs accepted that there was a link between HR practices and business performance, but only 10 per cent put people as a top priority ahead of Finance or Marketing (Guest, 2000). So, whether or not senior executives see employees as a cost or a potential asset may not matter in practical terms, if it does not affect their actions with regard to people management. This view is backed by Guest and Conway in other research. They discovered that senior managers admitted to not supporting the psychological contract despite realizing the negative consequences this would have on staff (Guest and Conway, 2002). Knowing what the consequences of their actions would be did not change the way they behaved.

This attitude is also consistent with the tendency amongst some senior management to accept the benefits of organizational change, especially if it reduces cost, without committing themselves to the consequences. They themselves may not take on their people management responsibilities. The consequences of this attitude may range from their dragging HR into issues they should be capable of sorting out themselves, to failing to conduct performance appraisals. They may talk a good talk, but not deliver. This is important because it sets the tone for the organization. More junior managers may conclude that they can get away with not doing appraisals if their bosses do not do them. A serious consequence of this attitude for HR is that it makes it all the harder for the new HR model to work. Flooding business partners with information of dubious relevance, whilst appearing to be helpful, is one way that has been used to limit their effectiveness. Nor will business partners be strategic if they spend their time on transactional issues for the top team. Advising on the range of colours of the company car scheme is not what they are paid to do. An example of this situation observed by one of the authors was an HR director being summoned out of a meeting on an important change project in order to advise the CEO on the salary of one of his subordinates! This CEO had supported some radical restructuring of HR, but the change of approach had clearly not been internalized.

Devolution difficulties

These problems are further compounded if devolution of people management activities is not working. As we have reported, HR has been for some time been trying to redefine its role vis-à-vis line management. There has been a steady transfer of responsibilities from HR to line management, though not so far or as fast as some would have liked.

You could dismiss the research reported in the section on relationships with line managers in Chapter 2 as merely a feature of the 1990s that has subsequently been dealt with, but there is continuing evidence of HR's resistance to push devolution aggressively. HR departments continue to find it hard to let go because of a strong ethic of helpfulness, as the BBC example described in the box below shows. HR frequently does not trust the interest and competence of managers to successfully handle their people management responsibilities. Thus HR staff are still only too keen to help and involve themselves in matters that should rest with the line.

> A key plank in the forthcoming transformation of HR at the BBC is the idea that the line will contract in advance what services it wants. Stephen Dando explicitly wants to get away from what he calls the 'Heinz 57 varieties' of HR provision: managers constantly demanding more services and BBC People providing them in a multitude of ways (Griffiths, 2005).

At times, this enthusiasm to help is misplaced, even self-justificatory. On other occasions, HR is responding to line pressure to assist. Carol Wright, a former HR manager from financial services, said: 'Mr and Mrs line manager often do not want strategic help, they want quick, practical solutions.' Their issues are short-term and tactical; their awareness of people management options is limited. These attitudes may challenge the 'devolution' deal. Managers may genuinely feel overwhelmed by their workload, and may feel overly exposed to take responsibility for matters outwith their skills. As an illustration of line managers' reluctance to grasp the nettle, even where clearly they should be making decisions, an IRS survey found that 90 per cent of HR respondents reported manager unwillingness to take an active role in absence management because of a perceived lack of competence (Industrial Relations Services, 2003).

As for involving managers in HR policy formulation, most managers do not give inputs even when asked, according to Carol Wright: 'Managers are not good at offering suitable solutions to people management problems. Their proposals for change are unsophisticated, simplistic or naïve. Too often they give ill thought through, knee jerk reactions that give insufficient attention to the consequences of their proposals.' For example, faced with a resignation, managers only want to use money to solve the problem – give them a bonus! Managers frequently lack a sense of the bigger picture. And a CIPD (2005a) survey suggests that managers are insufficiently asked about policy development. It reported that less than half of respondent HR teams consulted managers in the development of the organization's reward strategy.

The lack of humanism in line managers' actions is also still apparent. Samantha Lynch in her research on retail found that, 'even where "soft", high-commitment HR policies were in place, they were not always implemented in the stores (by line managers)' (Lynch, 2003) and, in the City, Augar and Palmer (2003) found that many managers felt 'pressurised and unhappy' because of their employers' negative 'attitude to human capital'. Whittaker and Marchington (2003) observed that 'even the best intentioned managers are likely to cave in' if the goals they are set 'run counter to the high road principles espoused in mission statements and by Chief Executives'.

Other research (Renwick, 2003; Hirsh et al., 2005) has suggested that managers are taking their staff development responsibilities more seriously than in the past, but either there is still a large minority that do not, and fail to give employees support in their development efforts, or have difficulties in properly discharging their people management functions. Barriers to effective staff development remain, related to selection (managers who do not want to manage people), role design (too wide spans of control and geographic distance), pressures from above (unrealistic targets), inflexible HR policies (e.g. relating to promotion and job descriptions) and lack of discretion (the disempowerment of staff).

And, in discussions for this book, practitioners still talk of the limitations of people management skills. One interviewee told us that he thought line managers' capacity to cope with devolved people management capabilities had not developed as fast as HR's capacity to devolve. Another described how some managers are so driven to meet targets that they trample over people. They do not see a link between people and performance, but equally they are not encouraged to do so. Senior management frequently says one thing and does another. It gives the impression of agreeing with the notion of engaging staff, but its actions belie this. Senior management leaves middle managers as 'the meat in the sandwich'. These managers are told they have to achieve their targets as the primary goal, but at same time they must not upset the staff.

Another problem with HR's positioning, which has still not sorted out everywhere, concerns HR's governance role in relation to the line. Ensuring that managers exercise their right to manage in the 'right way' has made devolution more problematic for HR managers. How do they give the line greater authority for people management and yet ensure they exercise their responsibilities in a manner that avoids harming the organization overall? The ambiguity of HR's position is apparent. It seeks to facilitate change, and perform the role of advisor to the line manager, but yet it finds it difficult to stop adopting a policing role.

Whittaker and Marchington (2003) describe HR as being 'caught in a cleft stick, criticized for being too interventionist and remote'.

Naturally, the governance role is less problematic if devolution is working. Failing devolution prevents the HR function adjusting its role from tactical, short-term firefighting to something longer term and more strategic – as the Compaq example in the box below shows. HR does not want to find itself 'following behind line managers clearing up their mess', as Dean Royles graphically put it. 'Clearing up' may come in the form of employment tribunals, higher wastage or employee relations problems.

> Compaq had a policy of devolving HR activities to line managers. This had not proved to be wholly successful because many managers were not sufficiently trained or skilled to fulfil the role they were asked to cover. The result was that senior HR staff found themselves drawn into dealing with employee problems raised by the staff themselves. This meant that HR was distracted from its aim to be more involved in bigger people management issues (Incomes Data Services, 2001).

Getting devolution done in the 'right way' also extends to people management processes. HR might legitimately want to ensure that they are done to a standard. Yet devolution makes it harder to undertake quality control. For example, change management and OD initiatives may be being done in a substandard or inappropriate ways. This is especially so if those undertaking this work lack the skills necessary to perform the tasks. As some practitioners have experienced, HR works in a field where everyone is an expert and solutions are merely common sense. Will those doing OD and change management listen to what HR has to say, assuming it has the capability with respect to, if not the responsibility for, these areas of work?

Relationship to employees

One important issue in the positioning of HR is what is its relationship to employees. As we have described, in adjusting its role, the function has altered its purpose and means of interaction with staff. HR now wants to be closely aligned with the business. This has meant in many organizations that the focus has shifted from advocating, representing or championing employees to ensuring that business imperatives are being realized. In turn, this has caused some in the profession to object that employees are being ignored in the process As an HR manager in the service sector put it: 'In the rush to become business partners we forgot the employee champion role.' In extreme cases this has almost meant that employees have become just one more stakeholder group to be managed. This tendency has been reinforced by devolution: line managers are responsible for employees, not HR. The function has withdrawn from welfare or basic people management activities in favour of the line manager. HR is concerned with policy development, not application. Although there may be contact between HR and employees over administrative matters, even this is in decline. The advent of call centres, intranets and shared services centres has minimized interaction between HR and staff. Employee self-service means that many transactional tasks have been automated, reducing the requirement for contact with HR administration at all.

The result of these three developments (refocusing the function, devolution and e-HR) is that for many employees HR is seen as remote and irrelevant. This feeling of distance strikes some in HR as much as employees. 'We lost that human contact: we were at the end of a telephone. We weren't allowed to go out and see people any more or give advice face-to-face ... We are losing what HR's all about,' said one HR practitioner (Francis and Keegan, 2005). And the accusation from employees that HR is management's 'poodle' has also grown in strength, as HR has become more business aligned, especially where line managers are quick to blame HR for policies or decisions that have been ill received by employees.

If devolution is not working, HR's physical and structural withdrawal may lead employees to feel cut adrift. If for reasons of time, skill or inclination, managers are failing to discharge their people management responsibilities, to whom do employees turn? Not easily to HR if it is either reluctant to interfere in matters for which managers are accountable or not set up to do so. In circumstances where staff doubt managers' interest or capability, they may miss the independent professionalism of HR staff or simply their presence as a listening post.

This may be particularly true where trade unions or other collective representative structures are either absent or ineffective. In these circumstances the employees' collective 'voice' may not be heard. Issues that cut across employee groups may not be properly dealt with, creating the potential for resentment and frustration. Individual line managers may not be able to help with organization-wide issues and are likely to look to HR for leadership. If HR is too preoccupied with its strategic contribution to offer this leadership, problems may build to a critical level.

So, the challenge is, with ever less reason for contact, in what way does HR understand the views and aspirations of employees so that they can be accounted for in people management policies and practices? How does it do this in a manner that does not tread on the toes of line managers who, all are agreed, have the primary responsibility for people management?

12 *Solutions to Positioning Challenges*

HR teams may be at different points on their journey towards offering a higher-value-added contribution. This will reflect the culture and nature of their organizations within which they work, but also the competence of the HR function. If HR's repositioning aspiration is frustrated because it is regarded as providing a slow, cumbersome or bureaucratic service, then the solution to overcome these negative perceptions is obvious: get the basics right and do them well, and then offer a more sophisticated proposition to the organization. In this respect Ulrich is quite right: administrative excellence precedes, not follows, the reorientation to making a strategic contribution. This means achieving the process improvements we described in Chapter 2. HR processes need to be streamlined and automated where possible. They should be simple to manage and capable of delivering a quality outcome. Moving in this direction will stem the negative comments. Demonstrable competence will lead to respect and provide opportunities for higher-level inputs. Attention should then turn to having the right structures, delivery mechanisms and skills to meet the higher-level ambitions.

There is almost a hierarchy of people management needs that have in turn to be satisfied. This is an argument for incremental progress, building on each successive step before moving up the contribution ladder. Demonstrable competence and capability in doing the basics well through modernization of administration and processes satisfies a hygiene requirement before expecting any invitation to engage at the next level of contribution and certainly before full participation at top table can be achieved.

> Royal Mail has been working on line perceptions of HR. Previously the function was seen as slow and bureaucratic, but offering helpful support. Now, according to Francis Bird, HR Strategy And Operations Director, 'the business is beginning to change its view of HR' through establishing different mutual expectations. This has altered their view of what HR is and can do as a function.' Operational managers are 'starting to own people decisions'.

With respect to senior management

To tackle senior management perceptions of the role of HR, there are three approaches we will describe:

- demonstrating the effectiveness of HR in its existing areas of competence
- building personal relationships
- institutionalizing people management as important to business success.

HR can start to shift the attitudes of senior colleagues by ensuring administrative excellence. Next, it can show it is giving high-quality advice to line managers by generating positive feedback that is picked up by their bosses as much as by HR. Designing policies which demonstrably fit the business need will also engender respect from senior management. There is scope for greater influence by showing HR's capability in strategic implementation. As we reported earlier, HR may too often be 'downstream' of the main decision-making, but at least HR is involved in the strategic process. In this situation, HR may not be acting as a strategic partner, but it offers the possibility of being a strategic player. This provides a platform for further advance. Having successfully delivered change, HR can use its greater credibility in the eyes of senior management to acquire more influence. For example, at Onetel the HR director was given the lead in the offshoring of their customer service operation. This was partly due to the importance of the employee element in the change process, but it was also because the HR director was a respected, senior manager, seen as capable of delivering a difficult project.

Another solution to the exclusion from strategic decision processes that may make the vital difference is to develop personal relationships. But this approach is double edged. The HR director can try to become the key sounding board of the CEO, acting as a confidante to what is often an exposed and lonely position. S/he can act as a coach too, giving private help to deal with any professional, but personal, difficulties. Richie Furlong, for example, described the importance of the relationship between CEO and HR directors in the Unilever of the 1980s. By this means HR directors can gradually get their voice heard. The problem is that these days CEOs do not always stay in post that long. The comings and goings of CEOs make it much harder for such relationships to be established or, if they do develop, the HR director is more exposed. If the CEO goes down, do they take their HR director with them? The answer is more likely to be yes if the HR director is closely associated with the old regime. Increasingly, CEOs are akin to football managers and HR directors to one of the team of coaches. Failure to deliver success quickly results in the sack for the manager and the staff. When a new appointment is made, in comes a fresh manager with their team of trusted advisors. So the HR director must guard against this possibility by broadening out their networks and power base.

Moreover, to move beyond being dependent on the personal chemistry of individual relationships, HR must institutionalize the importance of people management. This means getting the management of the organization to accept the real importance of employees in achieving business success. This makes the human capital debate so critical. If proper models of human capital are created and reported, then there is a chance that people management will move to centre stage. This means ensuring that human capital measures are prominent in the discussion of business performance and that the growth of workforce skills and capability is given due attention. Shell has done this through including people management (along with cost, portfolio and customers) as one of the elements of operating company review by senior management. Mechanisms such as this, if they also review levels of employee engagement, can get across that business success is built as much on capturing the hearts and minds of employees, not just in getting structures, systems and processes right.

With line manager devolution

How does HR respond to these problems of:

- HR's own ambivalence to devolution?
- Recalcitrant managers, uninterested in people management?
- Managers disengaged from people management policy-making?

- Contradictory (or even negative messages) managers get from their bosses on the importance of people management?
- Uncertainty about HR's governance function?

We will take these points in turn, grouping our solutions under the following headings:

- HR's facilitation of devolution.
- Equipping line managers to succeed.
- Developing a partnership on people management.
- Institutionalizing the importance of people management.
- Getting HR's governance role right.

We will then conclude this section with some suggested actions for addressing the devolution question.

HR'S FACILITATION OF DEVOLUTION

The first requirement for devolution to work is to ensure that line managers are doing their job, not allowing HR to take the job away from them because they will not do it. This is a common frustration for HR leaders. Some HR colleagues are only too keen to help line managers. They derive satisfaction from being needed. New-style HR tries to limit the chance by constructing HR roles so that they force HR staff to give managers the space to operate, but to be available if necessary. This can be done through a combination of segmenting the HR service so that help is provided in an organized way; providing only long-distance help; specifying job descriptions appropriately; contracting more explicitly with the line what HR will do (as we reported earlier the BBC is doing); limiting the number of job holders to restrict what they can do outside the specified remit; and selecting the right sort of people for HR posts and training them so that they realize the boundaries of their role and can, in the most sensitive way possible, discourage over-dependence from the line. Alan Warner tries to encourage his HR colleagues to let 'managers have first crack at any problems', by not being overly helpful in intervening too early or thoroughly. Whether intentionally or not, HR can disempower managers from finding their own solutions. Moreover, HR should be truly sensitive to line needs, being properly responsive to their problems, not imposing ill-fitting solutions.

Process improvement can also help. Duplication of activities can be stopped, unnecessary links in the chain removed and tasks speeded up. E-HR should facilitate line actions in the people management field, be it through manager self-service, the organizational intranet or through improved management information. Line managers should feel less that tasks are being dumped on them. This should demonstrate HR's interest in efficiency not in passing the parcel. It should take away (or at least limit) the excuse from managers that they cannot do people management processes because they lack time or skills. Well-designed e-processes should leave managers with less work.

EQUIPPING LINE MANAGERS TO SUCCEED

As to recalcitrant managers, most HR directors are likely to argue that their concerns are either overstated or can be overcome. Those managers that overstate the problems do so because they have not fully absorbed the kernel of the argument, namely that managers are responsible for employee performance. Being responsible for employee performance means dealing with all the facets of people at work – their health, welfare, safety and motivation, as well as individual and team performance. It is not HR's responsibility. If there are specific impediments to executing their people management duties, then HR directors would seek to remove them. Management development is a key feature in many organizations. Training is frequently on offer, especially for the transition to managerial posts. For example, the BBC offers a three-day coaching course for managers about to take on line responsibilities. There are also courses to deal with specific skill gaps. Programmes should ideally be based on what areas managers find difficult and on the areas where managers can make the most difference. HR effort should be targeted in these areas. IES research suggests that difficulties concern management style (selecting between soft and hard approaches), giving negative feedback (on attitudes, behaviour or performance), managing conflict and delegating work. Managers can help improve employee performance through building relationships with individuals. IES research points to managers successfully taking interest in their staff at a personal level, encouraging and coaching them, looking at their longer-term career aspirations, being available and building trust (Hirsh *et al.*, 2005).

Increasingly, managers can receive informal advice and coaching, if necessary, to give personal attention to their problems. The reorientation of HR so that there is greater emphasis on customer service and business sensitivity should mean that managers do not lack professional support through colleagues, helplines, intranets or written guidelines, unless there are structural impediments (which we discuss below).

Shell has made a 'systemic intervention' to raise the quality of leadership and develop managers' people skills in coaching, motivation and development. Future leaders will be selected and developed with people management skills to the fore under the Leadership Accountability Teamwork programme. Similarly, RBS revised its 'Management Essentials/First Line Management Development' programme in 2004 to give a sharper focus to people management. It covers:

- managing people
- developing high performance
- management practices
- coaching
- managing teams
- communicating and influencing
- delivering feedback
- managing and answering questions
- managing as a career coach
- managing change.

This approach ensures that managers know the basics; know where to find information and where/when to seek help. It then goes on to deal with the more sophisticated aspects of people management, such as delivering change.

DEVELOPING A PARTNERSHIP ON PEOPLE MANAGEMENT

If the style and nature of the relationship between HR and line management is a partnership, it means that it should be a two-way process, not just HR assisting the line, but the line assisting HR. This will come from managers being much more widely consulted on people management policy formulation than in the past. It will also come from policy development that is more attuned to business need, less concerned with HR best practice. It would suggest getting managers formally involved in steering committees overseeing HR projects or participating in them directly. Piloting new initiatives can give line colleagues a chance to influence final decisions. These methods, along with allowing managers greater space to adapt people management policies to suit specific circumstances, should engender both greater managerial ownership of policy and better alignment with business requirements.

Alan Warner describes a pragmatic sort of approach followed by Hertfordshire County Council. He accepts that the level of HR support will vary with the skills and inclinations of line managers. This means more intensive help for some rather than others. But he is very clear on the boundaries. HR sets the policy framework within which line managers operate. Compared with the past there is a lighter touch in policy-making. It is much less prescriptive than previously. There is deliberately more discretion available to managers because the space in which they operate is designed to be broader. There is less detail now, fewer 'embellishments'. It is now more of a question of the interpretation of guidelines to suit particular circumstances.

INSTITUTIONALIZING THE IMPORTANCE OF PEOPLE MANAGEMENT

We have already described ways of getting senior management on board with the importance of maximizing human capital. If executives accept the link between people management and organizational performance, they should support this by word and deed. They can signal their backing for people management processes, but, even more critically, they can agree to the alteration of the selection of managers. People management skills may currently be inadequate because those chosen for management posts are not selected with these skills in mind. The selection process does not look for ability in this area. Rather, it is likely to emphasize technical ability or a track record of delivering business results (narrowly interpreted). Instead, HR should be pushing senior management to put in place people with a disposition to encourage and motivate staff, and with an understanding that better results can be delivered if staff are managed properly. Achieving success via employees then becomes the norm, not the exception.

The right sort of selection can be reinforced by appraisal and reward. There are many examples of good practice now where the appraisal system reflects people management competencies (e.g. in interpersonal skills) and which try to identify deficiencies and seek to improve performance by dealing with them. There are some organizations that use 360 degree feedback mechanisms to identify those managers who, in the eyes of their subordinates (as well as peers or customers) encourage or discourage good performance. There are some that do take into account people management capability in their management selection process. There are fewer that link reward systems to people management targets. Some organizations reduce the rewards for those managers who drive for success, but neglect the people management aspects of their job or, worse, achieve their results through a bullying or dictatorial style.

Sir Fred Goodwin, RBS CEO, challenges direct reports on divisional performance on turnover (especially short term), on absence and on the results of the staff opinion survey. The fact that he holds those reporting to him accountable for their people management performance (with an associated proportion of bonus at stake) cascades through the organization with lower-level managers equally accountable for their area of responsibility.

GETTING HR'S GOVERNANCE ROLE RIGHT

This leads into the regulatory or governance question – whether it is right for HR to leave the line to get on with it or whether there are circumstances when it should intervene; when is it right for HR to advise and when to direct. Those who are in favour of HR as a service function would say that it is rarely appropriate for HR to direct or overrule the line. This may be seen as supportive of managers' own preferences. For example, a CIPD report on the public sector suggested that managers seek HR's involvement in specific areas, but otherwise, 'want to be left alone to be able to manage their teams' (CIPD, 2005c). Or, perhaps, such a view is a reaction to the professional authoritarianism that argues that there are correct ways of doing things that should be adopted by managers. Those that take this view have a clear sense of professional standards and practices that should be adopted. In the extreme version of this view, HR is loyal to the profession, not to its employer.

The latter approach is inconsistent with business alignment and is not one we would support. But one should not go to the other extreme. HR should neither be the master on people management practice nor the servant. There will be occasions where HR should intervene for the good of the organization, often because it is taking the long and wider corporate perspective in contrast to unjustified inconsistency which is being practised. The line cannot always be 'left alone' to get on with it.

The question is how does the organization decide when it is proper for HR to intrude on the manager/employee relationship? And who decides?

The sort of circumstances where HR might interfere are those where managers want to pursue a path that is illegal, threatens the integrity of the organization or is in violation of organizational values. The areas of discrimination and diversity spring to mind. More difficult is when managers do not abide by the agreed 'rules of the game'. Often the manager is seeking to satisfy their needs or solve their problem, but at the cost of others. Managers are taking a narrow, short-term, parochial perspective. When line management is clearly at fault, HR's objection may be easily sustained, but in the grey areas of interpretation line managers and their HR advisors may not agree. In which case someone should be able to arbitrate. In RBS's case, the HR director has this role under delegated authority from the CEO. Neil Roden offers the analogy of the third umpire at cricket or video referee in rugby. This role is to give a decision if the umpire/referee is in doubt over a decision. In fact, he would want to go further: he believes that both employees and managers can make an appeal if there is a dispute between the players and the umpire/referee. The emphasis is on the neutrality of HR, able to objectively and impartially judge between competing claims. Alan Warner makes the same point differently. He thinks that there are times when HR has to 'wear the police hat' to protect the organization from legal challenge or to uphold corporate requirements.

HR should similarly set standards on areas where line managers are using tools and techniques they have supplied, such as in OD, change management and resourcing. This allows a degree of quality assurance to be achieved, especially if there are periodic audits of practice. This enables HR to be more relaxed about blurred boundaries between what it does and what the line does. It means HR can worry less about, or even positively encourage, transfers in from other functions.

> Shell has change managers who frequently come from the line. HR is the 'keeper of change management skills' even if the tools from the toolbox are used by others. HR has to keep the tools in good working order and ensure that they are 'best in class'.

CONCLUSIONS

We believe the difficulties of devolution are largely solvable, but organizations need to recognize the potential problems and have the means to deal with them. If this is not done, they will find that either the standard of people management will deteriorate or HR will be drawn back into activities from which it has sought to withdraw. This may well mean proceeding with the process of devolution gradually and taking great care in considering who should undertake HR activities. This should include more clearly defining the relationship with line management. It means lots of listening to, and communicating with, line – hearing what is important to them and what HR is doing that is beneficial to them. For example, the CIPD research indicated that managers wanted practical help over resourcing and development; efficient administrative support; advice on difficult cases in the context of knowing their business (CIPD, 2005c). By asking managers what they want from HR and then, if need be, negotiating a deal, organizations are more likely to develop an enduring understanding of where HR's role begins and ends. But as we have emphasized, this deal is made between partners who recognize the primacy of the line's people management responsibility, but recognize too that HR has an interest and competence in ensuring that people management standards are met.

ACTIONS

So, what questions should organizations ask in thinking through what should remain part of HR's responsibility and what should move to line management:

* Organizational fit – What will go with the grain of the organization? In other words, is responsibility passed to line managers on other business activities, e.g. from Finance? Is there a general decentralization of accountability to operating units, and accompanying devolution of tasks?
* Managing difference – Are all business units of like mind or circumstance? Do some want devolution and greater responsibility for people matters or are they happy for HR to remove this 'burden'? Can the organization manage such differences in demand? Can individual line managers choose to buck the devolution trend, i.e. insist on HR participation even in activities deemed to be their responsibility (e.g. recruitment or discipline)? This may be a question of managers lacking time or skills, in which case remedial action can be taken. It could be a genuine reflection of the different business situations that justifiably require different HR solutions. Some managers in say Sales and Marketing may prefer a lot of personal dealing, but have little time for systems. Others in Production like to have clear rules. But it could be a more philosophical objection to HR withdrawing its expertise, and this will require serious debate.
* Line management capability – What skills do line managers possess? Are they equipped to deal with more people-related activities? Do they have the time and resources? Do they want more responsibility?
* Extent of e-HR – How much are line management actions facilitated by technology in a way that removes some of hard work from people management processes? This is likely to be more extensive in say an IT company than a retail one. It is also likely to be more culturally acceptable.
* Employee support – Are employees confident that managers are equipped to undertake people management duties in a fair, consistent and effective manner? What is the balance

between issues which can be tackled at the individual level and those which can be tackled at the collective level?

- HR commitment and capability – Do those HR staff who support line managers have the skills to advise, guide and encourage without taking over or abdicating responsibility? Do they agree with the move and have confidence in its success?

- What to devolve? – Do you devolve activities (doing things) or responsibilities (being accountable for things)? Do you take the same approach for each topic – do you treat conducting a training needs analysis the same way as undertaking a pay review?

- Budget responsibility – How much budget is transferred to line management in a devolved world? Some organizations have given the whole people budget to line managers; others have given specific parts to the line – resourcing or reward. Still others transfer the activity to the line, but keep the budget with HR. The assumption must be that full budgetary responsibility will become the norm for managers, but this re-emphasizes the need to decide whether there are any checks in the system and what they might be. For example, managers may exercise discretion to hire lots of temporaries (on the ground of cost). Is that acceptable corporately? On reward, there is the obvious question on whether equal pay rules are observed. This is a tricky decision. Giving managers responsibility for tasks but no accountability may incur their resentment. HR withdrawing entirely may be risky unless managers are skilled in exercising their duties wisely.

- How do you decide? – Which is the appropriate approach depends on the objective. If the aim is to drive through cost reduction in HR by devolving activities to the line, any debate will be on the 'how' not the 'whether'. If the aim is a genuine attempt to improve effectiveness (as well as efficiency) then line managers should be asked their views. But then, consultation has to be properly structured and meaningful. The aim is to discover what customers need, not want. This has to be teased out. HR may have clear ideas of where it wants to get to, but it may have to establish whether customers not only support the objectives, but also the detail of the proposals. The devolution of activities from HR to the line may be accepted in principle by line managers, but they may object on specific points.

- Measuring and controlling quality – How can you establish and keep managers to standards in the performance of devolved tasks? This may be an issue of good practice (differences may occur with managers on this point), legal compliance and adhering to organizational values. Is the organization able to keep sufficient track on people management performance when activities are devolved (and dispersed) to line management? For example, does HR retain an audit function? What processes does it put in place which allow debate and challenge?

With employees

We have said that HR's relationship with employees has changed over time, but the degree of change has greatly varied between organizations. In some, relationships with employees were, and still are, open and fruitful. In others, there is a perception that relationships have deteriorated. This feeling may be held by employees, HR staff or both. There is a third category where HR has never had much prominence for employees. It is the function that issues the employment contract and pays staff. All important decisions are made by others. This is the reaction that you would find (have found?) in those organizations where HR's role is less developed than elsewhere.

But whatever the status of the relationship, the question all too rarely asked in organizations is: what sort of relationship does HR want with employees? Does the view that HR is distant and uninvolved mean that devolution is a success? Should automation and e-enablement be pushed further so that there is less and less interaction? Does business alignment preclude any form of representative role of employees by HR? With the line manager as king in staff management, does that mean that HR is merely a courtier with no right to challenge? How is the collective dimension to relationships to be managed? Does HR have a more prominent role here?

One way of answering these difficult questions is by starting an internal debate. What view do the stakeholders have? Are managers and employees of like mind in relation to HR? It is easier said than done to have such a discussion in large, diverse organizations. Indeed, the response may be different in different parts, but that should not pose insurmountable problems if the organization accepts, as we have suggested, that a one size fits all HR delivery model is inappropriate. But the process of asking for views can be included in a customer opinion process through a survey or focus groups, as shown in the boxed example.

> Carlson asked its employees about their preferred form of communication. They were happy with e-mails where fast and timely messages were required, but overall wanted direct means of communication face-to-face with their manager or through team meetings (www.iqpc.com).

We should not prejudge the answer but the following might be a reasonable summation of HR's activities vis-à-vis employees (we discussed HR's role in relation to employees in Part 2):

- Allow employees to use HR as a source of help if relations with their own manager have broken down, but this role should be used sparingly.
- Accept that employee well-being is important to organizational performance. Staff will need counselling from time to time on personal matters that are impinging on work and on work-related stresses. Either provide such help through HR, in support of line managers, or contract the service out, but retaining a strong grip on the outsourcing process. HR needs to know what issues are emerging and whether employees are being properly dealt with.
- Ensure that any contact centre or advice lines are open for employees to use, just as much as managers.
- Ensure that employees' views on HR policies and practices are sought wherever necessary through 'town meetings', focus groups, surveys, e-response boards, etc.
- Have round table discussions with an open agenda to allow staff to set the terms of the debate or more formal question and answer sessions, such as 'ask the HR director', but where employees can raise whatever they wish.
- In service organizations, arrange for HR staff to meet customers to hear and discuss issues from their own standpoint.
- Enable information, consultation and negotiation fora to function effectively by giving them the necessary status and making sure that they are well managed.
- Encourage HR colleagues to participate in 'back to the floor' sessions, sitting in on a call centre, a processing unit, the hotel reception, etc.

Some of these tasks will be performed by business partners alone and some together with management colleagues. Many have the advantage of raising the visibility of the function and its leaders, encouraging employees to see its human face.

CHAPTER 1

13 *Challenges with the Operating Model: Structures and Roles*

Some organizations have read the textbooks and rather uncritically adopted the new operating model of HR, its structures and roles. They have accepted the logic of the argument but not thought through the consequences for their own organization's circumstances. Related to this point, some organizations have tended to impose the model on line managers without fully explaining the rationale. As we found when researching for our earlier book on shared services, organizations might well ask the customer what works well or not with HR, then go into purdah, only to re-emerge with a fully fledged design. In researching for this book, we still heard stories of line managers finding services previously offered by HR withdrawn without notice or explanation. We will detail here some of the negative consequences of this approach.

Structural issues

Whilst the new model has an apparent logic to it, there is a downside to its rationality, and that is the segmentation of the service into discrete operating parts. Many other difficulties stem from this source. Issues may fall through the cracks because they are not the responsibility of any one team. The tendency to apply a single approach exaggerates the impact from a customer perspective. In more detail, the problems relate to:

* boundary management
* service gaps
* poor communication and learning
* failing to recognize differing customer needs and expectations
* complex and multiple HR service delivery channels
* exploitation of the model by unscrupulous managers.

A number of these issues relate to the roles that individuals are expected to play. We will not dwell on them now, as we discuss them below; rather, we will make some general observations.

Boundary issues occur through the clear separation of tasks in the new model. Shared service centres should stick to information provision and transactional tasks, the business partner to strategic alignment with the business, the centres of expertise to policy development and high-level advice, and the corporate centre to HR strategy and governance. This means there are a lot of boundaries between activities that need to be managed. The interfaces that seem to cause organizations the greatest difficulties are between the following:

* Policy development and implementation, or even administration. Will the policy designer be fully aware of implementation difficulties if those surface in another part of the HR operation? These problems may occur during implementation or they might

surface sometime later. For example, are the payroll implications of reward modernization properly considered at an early enough stage?

- Need or problem definition and response – as the Absa example below shows, if an issue passes through a number of hands before being dealt with, there is the danger that the response is suboptimal, especially if some of the participants are not as skilled or knowledgeable as others.

- Administrative services from business partners – the delivery of most HR services comes from the shared services centre, but the principal interface (at a face-to-face level at least) is between the business partner and the line. SLAs may or may not be contracted between shared services and business units, but it may be that the business partner, as the visible representative of HR, is held accountable for the quality of services over which s/he has no, or little, control. Business partners may then end up as piggies in the middle between shared services and line customers.

- Strategic business support from consultancy/policy development – if consultants are not commissioned and/or managed properly by business partners, they may act too independently, developing approaches inconsistent with the business partners' aims. Similar boundary issues can arise between the business partner and centres of expertise. The former may get involved in policy development from a business unit perspective, cutting across the work of the centre of expertise. And what role does the corporate centre play, especially if the HR director is a person of strong views?

> A review of Absa's shared services model revealed the 'need to get better co-ordination between the commissioning of work to meet business needs, the design of appropriate responses and the delivery of projects' (Reilly 2004a). This problem was most in evidence in the area of learning and development. Account executives (business partners by another name) have on occasion commissioned the so-called 'delivery unit' to undertake training programmes without consulting the 'design and development group' (centre of expertise). If the account executive is not well versed in the learning and development field, the result may be a poorly specified commission.

If boundaries are not properly managed, gaps in the HR service can appear. One of the commonest is who delivers operational support to line managers. Business partners are not supposed to be involved in firefighting, nor are policy experts. They, together with the shared service centre, may not be sufficiently resourced or skilled to do this work. Of course, in some models there are consultants to draw upon, but they are supposed to tackle longer-term projects, not be available for immediate guidance. HR advisors or HR delivery managers have been introduced to respond precisely to these needs. The Immigration and Nationality Directorate of the Home Office (IND), for example, brought in HR advisors to deal with operational matters because the business partners were getting too involved in this area. The early signs were positive in the way the division of labour was operating (Kenton and Yarnell, 2005).

However, in solving one problem, another awkward boundary may be created. What is the separation between business partners and advisors or delivery managers? It may not be as straightforward as the IND has been finding. For example, in one organization, the jobs tackle the same content only the business partner worries about systemic issues and the delivery unit focuses on individual cases. Obviously, there is a link between the two activities. In another organization there is lack of clarity over what are the respective roles of the business partner and organizational change agents. If reporting relationships are not carefully drawn, business partners can find themselves having to manage their subordinates' operational problems.

Following on from the above point, communication, downward and across HR, can be ineffective. This is a perennial problem, but harder if the boundaries between parts of the function (i.e. corporate centre, business partners, centre of expertise and shared services centre) are too rigidly drawn. In particular, the informal transfer of knowledge may not occur and feedback loops may fail. Poor communication leads to poor learning. If problems that arise in one part of the HR service are not communicated to others in the team then the service will suffer. Business partners may not keep other members of the HR community aware of emerging issues – say, resistance to the implementation of a new people management policy. The shared services centre may not pass on feedback on individual cases or patterns of difficulty, picked up via the helpline. The net result can be that to the customer it seems as if the right hand does not know what the left hand is doing. So, far from offering an integrated service, HR delivers a fragmented one.

This can lead to tensions in the HR team. These can be worsened if one part blames another part of the service chain when problems arise, especially when criticized by the line. For example, business partners, rather than taking full accountability for the performance of the function, might disown the shared services centre if there is a service failure. From the customer's perspective, they want somebody to be accountable. Even though they no longer directly own the resources, business partners have to be seen to be supporting those providing the services.

The pressure to cut costs, which has often driven the introduction of a new HR structure, has meant that the key issue of how choice versus compulsion is managed has not been thoroughly aired. In other words, how is the balance to be achieved between putting customer requirements first and delivering cost efficiency? All too frequently a standardized service is offered, not the 'mass customization' promised. Instead of choice, the customer gets a take it or leave it offer. HR increasingly offers a uniform, 'best-practice'-type service. This may not be so bad in a simple business where the customer demands are likely to be the same. But is it right where the heterogeneity of business units suggests that a one-size-fits-all-model is inappropriate? The standardized approach may mean that HR staff are insufficiently attuned to the specific needs of the business. Advice services, in particular, can lack knowledge of the various business units. In some models, consultants' knowledge of individual business units too may be weak. All may lack the feel of what is going on in any particular business and may lack empathy with it. Therefore, HR staff may give generic rather than tailored advice, not adapting their guidance to suit individual needs. Local issues or circumstances may be ignored. The imposition of uniformity is not only applied across the organization, but across the range of HR activities. Having a common payroll is one thing, having a common employee relations method is quite another thing, especially in organizations which are heterogeneous by reason or geography or activity. It is in these circumstances that one experienced business partner described the tendencies of the shared services operation as 'monopolistic', with all the downside effects that this implies – especially poor customer service.

Moreover, from a customer point of view, the HR service delivery process can seem complicated and remote. Customers often resent the loss of their 'own' integrated HR operation and the need to deal with multiple HR services. Instead of walking down the corridor to your friendly, neighbourhood HR team you have to phone some distant office that may not be in your own country. Where in the past, there was a one-stop shop where all HR matters (transactional, informational, advisory or strategic) could be dealt with by a single team, whom the customer got to know well, now different units have to be approached for different things. Customers are required to look at the intranet for basic information, to use a distant call centre for a query and be passed through the escalation tiers for the answer to anything more complex. The business partner will handle strategic change issues, but that might involve the consultancy team if extra resources are required, or the corporate centre, if the issue is systemic, organization-wide or a challenge to the governing principles of people management.

Mischievous managers can exploit the division in HR responsibilities by using it as an opportunity to try out different parts of the function to get an answer that suits them. This so called 'e-bay' approach to getting advice can bypass those who are formally accountable, in the hope that the left hand does not know what the right hand is doing. And HR can make this easy for managers shopping around, if the policy-holder in the centre of expertise, the case manager and the business partner are not effectively collaborating.

The difficulty that HR has of playing the roles of both service provider and owner of corporate policy results in accusations either of inappropriate business solutions being levelled by the line or of inappropriate behaviour by management being levelled by HR. It is hard for the centre of expertise to uphold disciplinary procedures if the business is reluctant to take the advice given because of perceived concerns over impact on business performance. For example, there could be a tension between dealing with the inappropriate behaviours of a high-performing bully and not undermining their contribution to the business results. HR in its governance role might want disciplinary action taken. The desire of the line to deal with the issue may well be weak. The HR function may then find itself split: the business partner might support the line, the centre of expertise might want to uphold laid-down policies and procedures. In the traditional HR model, this disunity was less likely to manifest itself outside the function. Within HR's integrated department there would have either been no separate parties holding divergent views or, if there were differences, they would have been resolved internally. In the new model, tensions can arise from different organizational perspectives that may need to be resolved.

And to compound the threat of disunity, if performance objectives are set that emphasize the division of tasks, staff are rewarded not for pulling the organization together but for meeting their own narrow goals.

Issues with specific roles

SHARED SERVICES CENTRE ROLES

The role difficulties in shared services centres relate to the nature of their construction. By comparison with traditional administrative jobs, staff now find their jobs de-skilled and depersonalized. Those used to an all-rounder role, performing a range of tasks, may find themselves restricted to undertaking simple, highly circumscribed and monotonous activities, for example, only handling telephone calls or processing maternity payments. Previously, their job might have consisted of both dealing with queries on the phone and handling data input, as well as much else besides. Motivation and performance levels are hard to keep up if the jobs are badly designed and staff find the work repetitive and boring. Those who previously worked as personnel assistants in an integrated team may experience a lack of variety, especially if the tasks are heavily specialized.

As to depersonalization, instead of giving face-to-face contact, HR staff have to deal with managers and employees on the phone or via a computer. To make matters worse, call centres often have a bad name; they are seen as sweat shops, distant from the customers. Working there lacks 'kudos', especially if the drive is to reduce the amount of HR administration. Encouraged by consultants, there can be an almost messianic zeal to root out transactional work. It is not surprising that administrators themselves feel undervalued and threatened.

In the transition to shared services centres many HR staff left rather than endure the new structure. This was even truer where HR management was seeking interpersonal and call handling skills, not HR knowledge. The loss of historical understanding of HR policy and practice was sometimes found to be a handicap once the shared services centre was up and running. New staff do not always know how and why policies are interpreted in the way they are. This is naturally less of an issue if a policy overhaul is done before the shared services centre is set up.

Organizations that neglect these aspects of job design, that appear to denigrate administrative activities, will similarly suffer from job losses in the migration to the new model. Moreover, in the operation of the shared services centre, those staff who value variety will become demotivated if the roles are narrowly conceived: the resignation rate will rise once more.

BUSINESS PARTNERS

In the mind of Richie Furlong, the creation of the business partner role may turn out to parallel the transformation in the role of HR directors from the 1970s to 1980s, i.e. from being centred on industrial relations to generalist organization and management development roles. As then, there is no guarantee that those successful in one model will be successful in another. The size of the challenge faced by some organizations is described by practitioners such as Carol Wright. She believes the business partner role has often been 'oversold' to HR people. Consultants 'talk a good talk'. They present it as a 'high level role on an equal footing with the business'. The reality is frequently different: it is 'more operational than strategic in practice'. This is because in some cases (or to some degree) HR is indeed not sufficiently capable and/or the line managers want operational support not strategic inputs. Lawler and Mohrman (2003) came to a similar conclusion: HR may believe in the Ulrich model, especially the strategic partner role, but it is not clear they are operating it. The CIPD (2003a) survey makes the same point. Despite respondents' aspirations to be more strategic, they spend three times as much time on administrative activities as on strategic.

> At a government department the head of the business partner team tends to end up doing the strategic part of the role for the whole team because the individual business partners find themselves doing mainly operational work. This is partly a reflection of their skills and preferences, and partly due to the demands of line managers.

The business partner role is perhaps the trickiest to get right because of a number of interlinked design problems:

- poor initial specification of what the job entails
- weak definition of the boundaries/interfaces between it and other HR jobs
- failure to address the risk of business partners going 'native'

- lack of understanding (and support?) from line customers of what the role should deliver
- a location mentally or physically too far from employees to know their situation or have any empathy with it.

These pitfalls are compounded by the difficulties faced by incumbents in fulfilling the aspirations set for them, from a skills and role perspective. These will be covered in the skills section below.

The rush to create business partners, and the concomitant need to be more strategic, has led to roles being created on the basis of aspiration and superficial thinking rather than from the harder slog of seeing what the organization requires. So part of the problem of poor specification is that organizations have not thought through what they have created and, as described above, not given enough attention to how the links in the organizational chain will work. The very freedom there is to shape the business partner role is a strength with those who can mould it to deliver value, but in the hands of less capable performers, any framework to guide them will be insufficient, especially if not enough attention has been given to defining what being 'strategic' means. HR directors have not always been that much help to their colleagues; better at proclaiming 'get strategic' than in explaining what is required. HR wants to see itself at the centre of business activities, influencing decision-making, bringing people management issues to the forefront, but how is this best done? If you take the view that HR should be an indivisible element of a management team, then the distinctive nature of HR is lost. If you see HR in a customer/supplier relationship, then HR will continue to be relegated either to a support role or to merely being an agent of management – doing its bidding. HR may then fall into the trap of going 'native'. This refers, from a corporate perspective, to business unit HR teams which do not uphold organizational principles, policies and procedures: they develop their own to suit local needs. From the business unit viewpoint, HR might be seen as responsive and helpful. From the corporate angle, the business partners may be failing to keep up standards or increasing cost through their distinctive approach to handling 'unique' problems. Ironically, it has been this 'unnecessary' variation that has led organizations to centralize policy-making. One HR manager complained to us: 'Why is it we have six competency-based pay systems in this organization where one is quite sufficient?' In local government, for example, those in corporate HR have long complained about say the education or social services departments deviating from organizational norms.

So, the initial role specification has lacked foresight on the dynamics of how the role will play out in relation to other parts of the function. Equally, there has been insufficient discussion with customers about what they want from business partners. As the HR manager in a financial services company told us: 'Managers were surprised at the role being played by their business partners. They did not expect HR to behave in a proactive manner.' Whether this activism was welcomed is another matter. Certainly, in the same sector a company is considering abandoning business partners, at least in the way they are currently conceived, because they do not add sufficient value. Operational issues were more 'pressing' for managers so they are going to offer more 'practical support' to the line. Further evidence on this point comes from Buyens and de Vos (2001). In their study they found that, for a majority of line managers, the 'added value' of HR came from its administrative expertise and delivery of functional services, not from strategic contribution or transformational change.

Instead, as we described earlier, e-HR and devolution has left line managers to experience what they perceive as a greater workload and overly exposed to take responsibility for matters outwith their skills, with only remote and impersonal HR support, delivered, not face-to-face, but from a distant call centre. In these circumstances, the business partner being the only local HR representative is likely to be dumped upon by managers wanting operational (not strategic) advice and help. The line may believe (rightly?) that cost saving and functional ambition have come before customer service. If HR has not tried to build support for its objectives and the means to achieve them, then it is hardly surprising that managers may be doubtful about the benefits of the new operating model.

> A high-street retailer found that their business partners tended to get drawn into operational work, away from the strategic. The individuals were more comfortable with day-to-day firefighting than longer-term issues. This tendency was reinforced by inadequate technology that meant managers and employees got HR involved in form-filling because they could not complete them online. A further problem was that the business partner role was insufficiently defined. It was clear what shared services had to do, and this was reflected in their SLAs with the business. However, the business partners of the retailer operated without performance contracts, let alone SLAs.

The worst case scenario that emerges is of line managers or employees bringing administrative and operational work to the business partners who in their effort to please get dragged away from the higher-value-added tasks. This leaves little time to be properly proactive. When they are able to contribute to business team longer-term thinking, business partners may not be seen as able to offer much (positioned in managers' minds as only operational support). The business partners then find it hard to challenge their colleagues and make themselves heard. Acquiescence then follows and either people management issues do not get due attention or the managers do their own thing to suit the needs of the business, as they see it. This puts the business partners in conflict with the corporate centre, having already trodden on the toes of shared services through getting mixed up in transactional work. It can be a lonely job, being a business partner!

If the business partners successfully operate the 'pure' version of their role, but do not confirm it with their customers, the result may be that the line managers at middle or junior level see the business partner as distant, uninterested in their problems. This feeling may be even truer for employees. The business partner might have good relationships with senior managers in the business unit, but not with the body of the kirk. Employees are told that people management issues should be dealt with by the line, if they cannot be answered by searching on the intranet. In most companies they too have access to a call centre, but face-to-face HR involvement is denied them. Previously, involvement with transactional and operational matters gave HR managers (or their reports) more contact with a range of customers. The question is whether a loss of contact matters. The danger with this situation is that the business partners are only aware of issues as filtered through by their management colleagues. If the business unit is a harmonious, happy family, this may not be of concern. However, the unresolved issue bubbling below the surface might be missed. Distance from day-to-day issues may lead to business partners having a poor sense of what will play or not play with the workforce. They may lack information or a sense of how employees will respond to business change or new policies/procedures. Employees' responses may be picked up via employee surveys, but the business partner has no independent sense of the organizational health of their part of the organization. Employees and line managers may decide that the business partner is so associated with the long-term strategy that day-to-day matters are of little consequence. Employees, and indeed some line managers, may see HR as so focused on higher business issues that they have little inclination to discover their concerns and problems. As the business partner is the principal HR agent in their line of vision, employees and managers may conclude that this is what the function is all about. The rest of HR is tarred with the same brush.

THE ROLE OF EXPERTS IN THE CENTRES OF EXPERTISE

With the increasing desire for access to good practice and deeper specialist solutions, the HR function of tomorrow really does have to ask why it would continue to retain in-house capability when it may be more efficient to use the external consultant market. Firms such as Towers Perrin, Mercer, Hewitt and Watson Wyatt, as well as the usual more general consultant/audit firms, all have deep pools of specialist consultants who can bring both expertise and learning from having met the challenge of applying their skills in other organizations. Removal of fixed costs associated with employing permanent employees may justify the more expensive daily rates of external consultants, especially if their knowledge of good practice elsewhere allows them to bring better solutions quicker than an internal employee would be able to.

Another, almost contradictory, complaint about centres of expertise is that they all too soon become ivory towers separated from daily life. This is the consequence of their concentration on policy formulation and separation from execution. They may be too obsessed with strategic intention and insufficiently aware of operational necessity. They may think their job is done when they have constructed an elegant policy that is somebody else's responsibility to put into practice. They can be too preoccupied with developing best-practice solutions to problems, 'gold plating' their service, even to the extent of exaggerating the problems faced in order to justify the complex solution. As the HR manager of a shared services operation who made this observation said to us, the reason is that their centre of expertise has too much time because it is not directly responding to operational pressures. It is disconnected from the sharp end of the business. However, by inference, the same complaint of inefficiency was being made.

The twin challenges for the centre of expertise are therefore to ensure its knowledge of the organization (good awareness of policy and application) is vastly superior to that an external consultant could establish (outweighing the depth of technical knowledge and expertise of the external consultant) and that it has an efficient resourcing model. Should it fail to meet these requirements it risks falling foul of the HR headcount ratio challenge, especially if it is perceived as being a corporate overhead. The end result is that it will be reduced to a very small number of staff charged with engaging and managing the external consultants.

CONSULTANCY ROLES

The challenge faced by organizations is twofold with respect to their consultancy or project teams. The first is how does the organization size the resource correctly so that it is neither under-utilized nor rushed off its feet, and so that it has sufficient projects to tackle in an efficient and effective manner. The reaction in some organizations has been to create generalist teams to cover all business units and all topics. This leads to a second problem. Though the attractions of a consultancy or project pool are obvious, the downside is that the staff may become too generalist – insufficiently aware of specific business unit needs or without specialist knowledge in key HR areas. There is then a risk that the internal consultancy may give a less good service than an external consultancy, without the benefits of true resource flexibility. This is because those in the consultancy pool may have no knowledge of any particular business nor any experience of working with it: they can then only give generalized rather than tailored advice. They will be aware of the broader organizational objectives and sensitive to the organization culture, but they may well be unaware of local issues, ignorant of the local customs. Moreover, if the model used employs generalist content consultants, they may not be fully skilled in all areas of HR.

14 *Solutions to Operating Model Problems*

Customer dissatisfaction

As we have already said, some of the customer reaction to the new HR model is that it was imposed on organizations within insufficient consultation. Many shared services operations still favour efficiency over choice, but this may be a reflection of their stage of development. Driving down costs was the initial aim in developing the model; customization can follow later. If that is not the case, organizations must be careful not to impose over the long term a single operating model that does not fit the varied set of business circumstances. As we suggested earlier, the solution may be to adjust the model to distinguish between common and shared, compulsory elements to the service and separate, but tailored, optional elements.

Whatever the set of arrangements, HR and its customers need to have an explicit contract stipulating HR's role and activities, and what the responsibilities of managers and employees will be. This may well include a description of what specific roles will and will not do. This is particularly important to avoid duplication or confusion in the HR team. Moreover, HR needs to continue to work hard at communicating what the deal is. For example, HR should be emphasizing what shared services can offer, especially if customers have been critical of services delivered by HR in the past. A good shared services centre can promise:

- streamlined processes
- more comprehensive and readable policies and procedures on the intranet
- improved management information that can improve decision-making
- support over the phone over extended hours
- improved tracking of individual cases
- reference to expert help for tricky problems
- SLAs that specify fast turnaround times.

Thus, assuming HR meets its promises, managers and employees can expect faster, higher-quality services delivered in a more user-friendly manner. Customers may need to be reminded that they did not always receive an ideal service in the past. One service centre manager told us in response to a 'slow' call response: 'In my centre, callers may have to wait for four minutes for a call to be answered, and this is a problem; but callers must not forget that they might have in the past had to wait hours, days or even weeks (when the relevant personnel advisor was away) for a response.' Indeed, many shared services operations have obtained better feedback after implementation of the new model than before. As to the absence of the personal touch, this is obviously a downside where it occurs, but many staff and managers in reality never had it. Retail operations, for example, were too dispersed to justify a local presence. Only sites with large numbers of employees were likely to have had an on-site HR team.

In getting the message across, organizations with shared services centres have used a whole variety of different media to inform customers of the new model and to obtain their understanding, if not buy in:

- face-to-face briefings
- videos
- intranet, e-mail or written messages
- noticeboards
- booklets
- articles in in-house magazines
- mouse mats, mugs, plastic cups.

The content naturally has varied with the media. Background information on why the change is proposed, what is involved, what impact will be on customers and implementation plans have been conveyed via various of the above list, apart from those listed under the last point. Mouse mats etc. have been used to remind customers of contact centre telephone numbers or web addresses.

Segmentation and its ills

In tackling the various consequences of segmentation, and its associated problems of poor communication, boundary management and customer service, there are various actions organizations can take to ameliorate any deficiencies of the model that arise:

- Blur the distinctions between roles. For example, as is shown in the Marconi example in the box below, business partners should not be too precious about what they do. They may handle questions from managers that strictly should go to the shared services centre. Let the business partner get involved in a policy area. They could say take the lead resourcing issues. Allow contact centre staff to do more than log calls and pass them on. Permit some follow-up work. There are risks in this approach – that staff get dragged away from their primary duties – but equally customers (and HR colleagues) may be aggravated by the application of too rigid a model, and, for the HR staff, looser boundaries will mean more interesting jobs. The alternative is to be more purist in the division of labour. Take the approach employed by another company who talk about 'stamping out lurking transactional activities' wherever they are found outside the outsourced provider. Such organizations can claim to be better adherents to the model, but may suffer some service disadvantages.
- Give a lot of attention to communication across organizational boundaries. There may be formal mechanisms to advise other teams of issues, but informal communication can be vital in building organizational bridges. This might mean encouraging visits between teams so that personal relationships grow, and building 'communities of practice'.
- Facilitate job rotation. This may be for either short spells or longer assignments. Organizations have successfully encouraged those in the centres of expertise to experience time in the call centre to get a better appreciation of the types of enquiries received. This helps them understand the context of referrals in the escalation ladder.

- Organize joint project work, especially with respect to policy development. Project teams might include experts, business partners and administrative staff so that all the angles (direction of travel, customer reaction and implementation issues) are covered.
- Encourage HR graduates and other staff with potential to get wide exposure. To be able to perform well later HR graduates need to experience the different elements of people management, but in getting this broad work coverage they can help build bridges between different parts of the HR operation.

> Alana Collins at Marconi talks of not 'being over-bureaucratic about role definitions'. Moreover, such an approach helps business partners keep in touch with daily life. Otherwise, there is a real risk 'you don't know what's going on' (Smethurst, 2005b).

Solutions for specific roles

SHARED SERVICES CENTRE ROLES

Obtaining the support of the HR community may be harder than obtaining that of customers, which was described earlier. Jobs are likely to go or be radically changed. What is key is that the HR leadership remains positive about the importance of administrative work, the vital nature of the roles staff in the shared services centre will play and the learning opportunities presented. This message will be more difficult to sell if the centre is being outsourced (as this is likely to reinforce a sense of being marginalized) or if a new type of recruit, perhaps with only call centre experience, is being hired in (signalling that the existing skills are being devalued). It is particularly important that during the transition important knowledge, including tacit knowledge, is not lost. These staff have a longstanding awareness of HR policies and procedures: their origins and developments. They have established relationships with customers based on knowing the people and the culture. Ignoring this repository of experience risks a deterioration in the quality of service.

What may make the establishment, and subsequent running, of the shared services centre easier is giving proper attention to job design. Broadly, there is a choice between creating generalists or specialists in service centre work. Organizations can distinguish between the broad categories of work: telephone, records or payroll administration, and training/recruitment/ reward administration. Staff may be allocated to one of these functions or be encouraged to work across the boundaries. Generalist structures allow more resource flexibility in balancing supply and demand. They give more development opportunities and variety in the work. They are essential in small teams. Larger organizations can afford more specialization. Greater depth of knowledge can be obtained; the risk is more monotony, although this can be mitigated by job rotation.

The benefits of job rotation outweigh the disadvantage of lack of depth. We say this because it is the better way to keep staff motivated and work scheduling flexible. Moreover, broadening skills also helps with career development, and given the problems of career paths out of shared services, a subject we return to in Chapter 15, this is an important consideration. The clear exception to this statement is the complex areas of work, like pensions administration, that require extensive training and experience. And of course, what will also impact is the scale of the operation. In smaller units, generalist roles may be essential. In very large ones, specialization can bring rewards because of the volume and variety of the work.

There is little that can be done regarding depersonalization. If staff have been used to meeting customers, it is likely that this will happen less, except if the shared services centre is co-located with a large site operation. Powergen found benefits in their centre being situated in Coventry – a major company office. Some continuity can still be obtained, albeit remotely, if a case tracking system is used. This allows the call centre agent to have a full record of previous discussions, relieving the customer of having to repeat him/herself endlessly. An even better approach is to appoint a case manager to handle a complex and potentially long and drawn-out issue. This benefits the customer and the HR staff. RBS uses this approach explicitly to mitigate the effects of having a distant call centre. Much like the consulting pool solution we describe below, a service-oriented centre may choose to sacrifice some efficiency gains by having teams aligned to the different parts of the business. This builds back some of the lost HR/customer relationship. This was the approach adopted by the BBC in its earliest form of HR shared services.

BUSINESS PARTNERS

The business partner role is likely to be the pinch point in the HR function where the system breaks down because of poor role definition, made worse by poor appointments. Our suggestion is to avoid the hype and describe a job that is do-able. Yes, the job requires a strategic contribution, but organizations should interpret that broadly including strategy development and execution. Careful thought has to be given over whether the business partners give any sort of leadership on operational support and individual casework. If they do, they risk being dragged into a firefighting role. If they do not, and no other solution is found, there may be a gap in HR's service provision and customer frustration. We favour a single point of accountability in HR's relations with the line. This should rest with the business partner. This individual should not be involved in the nitty gritty of daily interaction. Having an oversight of operational support, however, will give reassurance to the line (and possibly to other HR colleagues), but it can also help the business partner learn about the pressing issues and get a feel for what is going on in their business unit. For this solution to be effective, proper resources need to be allocated to operational activities and individual casework, and a robust definition must be offered of how this support will be provided.

So a clear role definition of what is legitimate for the business partner to do and not do should put together. Reporting relationships and positioning vis-à-vis other HR colleagues should give an idea of what is required. A more detailed specification may be necessary. The MOD, for example, describes the content of the business partner job, but interestingly the organization specifies what it should not do. This includes administrative activity, casework and specific operational activities. This role clarity can be reinforced through setting personal objectives that reflect its key aims and offering rewards for delivering the right sort of results.

This introduces the wider question of customer expectations that have to be tackled. Do they share HR analysis of what the business partner's contribution should be? The best way to find out is to ask them what they expect. This should give the organization an idea of the degree of the mismatch. If a large proportion of managers see HR only as responsible for paying staff, issuing contracts of employment and updating records (as one HR director discovered when conducting this exercise), then there is a major task in convincing them that HR can be a strategic partner. Having good people in these roles will help shift views, but it may require time and patience. Organizations can also use the more 'enlightened' managers to support

HR's case. They can demonstrate to their peers the value HR can offer. This is especially true where there is divergence of opinion between newly merged organizations. An HR manager in a telecom company described to us how managers in a newly acquired business had a very limited view of what the function could do. Part of their integration into the main company involved getting the new managers to use HR in the way that was accepted in the acquiring firm.

The opposite problem can occur if managers are too keen to use HR, too dependent on them. Here the business partner may be suffocated by managers seeking help, advice or reassurance. This might be a broader cultural issue than simply relations with HR. For example, a government agency, charged with reforming the role of HR, faced a prevailing risk-averse culture. Managers wanted detailed rules, not discretion. They needed HR to endorse any actions to ensure they were being compliant. Without a wider programme of cultural change, it is hard, in this situation, to see HR successfully repositioning itself. The BBC is, at the time of writing, attempting such a move.

Regarding employees, the actions that the business partner can take are to a degree limited by time and devolution. None the less, they can signal their interest through choosing face to face means of contact. As we described on page 136, this might mean running focus groups, alongside company-wide employee surveys, especially where changes are proposed to HR policies. These can highlight not just views about the specific change in question, but about broader people management issues. Asking about a new performance appraisal may produce a reaction that is more related to management skills and interest, and less to do with the technical aspects of form filling. By these means, the business partner can get soft information to go with the hard survey data.

One tension in the business partner role, referred to earlier, is that incumbents are rightly pulled towards engaging with their business unit manager colleagues and taking forward the unit's ambitions, but at the same time they need to adhere to corporate requirements. Standardization is encouraging business partners to develop policy and process responses within narrow boundaries, even if this is disliked by their line colleagues. It has the advantage of pushing the business partners into more of the strategic and change management roles, and away from technical HR solutions. Yet business partners may need some help to balance local business pressures with corporate imperatives. Ways that may make business partners' lives easier include the following:

- Senior management commitment to upholding corporate requirements. In other words, senior managers must avoid undercutting business partner decisions if they have previously signed up to the rules of the game.
- Functional support from HR leadership and an understanding of the dilemmas that might be created. Simply blocking business unit initiatives will not do; HR leaders must help facilitate acceptable decisions that respect the different interests of the parties.
- Coaching from functional leaders to help business partners deal better with the tensions in their role and reconcile the wishes of different interest groups.
- Business partners offering informal assistance to each other, sharing the burden by recognizing common problems and offering solutions tried elsewhere.
- Involving business partners in people management policy formulation so that the interests of individual business divisions are properly represented.
- Offering role clarity, where possible, but especially with respect to the nature of their expected strategic contribution. (See the section on HR as strategist in Chapter 3 for what this might look like.)

- Dealing with tensions between centralizing and decentralizing tendencies in organizations. At present, the emphasis in many organizations is on selling the benefits of commonality. In Shell, for example, HR is helping to develop an 'enterprise first' culture that sees a virtue of doing things the same for the benefit of the corporation. Such a programme limits the chance of business-facing people to go 'native' after a while, adding back costs, previously taken out, through duplication and experimentation.
- Setting up career paths that move business partners around – moving between business units or between the business partner role and corporate HR.

CENTRES OF EXPERTISE

There is no question that organizations need the skills of deep experts. The debate is how best to resource the work. If the centres of expertise develop policy, then it is difficult to see how this could be contracted out. If they act as advisors to shared service colleagues on difficult cases of policy interpretation, again surely this should stay in-house. Where there is more debate is when they are playing more of a consultancy role. Here the use of external resources has more merit given the advantages in flexibility and bringing in extra capability. The balance must be between those benefits and those of the internal experts getting 'real world' experience through project working, to prevent them getting too theoretical in their thinking. This implies that the centres of expertise will provide the core resource, topped up by external consultants. We would suggest, though, that the numbers in the centre of expertise be tightly managed, both to avoid work creation to fill the day (leading to a greater risk still of over-engineered policies) and to force the use of third parties (who can bring in fresh thinking, pushing up the knowledge base of internal staff).

Where centres of expertise are more developed, large organizations may well choose to align the teams with business units to build better knowledge of those businesses and to understand the essential differences between them. Whilst some efficiency can be lost, the benefits in building expert knowledge attuned to specific organizational needs may be worth it. Moreover, it reinforces the decision to have an in-house resource, and not rely on external consultancy.

CONSULTANCY ROLES

The issues are much the same as the above: resourcing and organization. The response, however, can be more clear cut. Holding an internal consultancy pool to be available for project work can only be justified if it is cheaper than buying it in. Unlike staff at centres of expertise, internal consultants do not have another role to play in policy-making or as part of the contact centre escalation process. Organizations may benefit from internal knowledge (though they will do less so if the consultants are not structured on a business unit basis) and from some flexibility in deployment (management can despatch them where the need is on the basis of internal prioritization). However, as we have said, external consultants bring breadth and depth of expertise which internal resources are unlikely to match. The latter can be hired in as required, and, depending upon the form of contract, stood down as easily.

So to justify their expertise, internal consultants need to develop top-class technical skills and an intimate knowledge of their organization. This model may work best in homogeneous organizations large enough to justify skill segmentation in the consultancy pool, or in very big and complex organizations where each business unit can support a range of consultancy skills. Small organizations are better buying in consultancy. It is only really the *very large* organizations that can achieve sufficient business knowledge and professional know-how to make the internal consultancy pool work. It may also be that these types of organization have enough of a flow-through of project or change work to keep the consultants occupied.

Whilst large, multidivisional organizations can perhaps justify subject-matter consultants, aligned to the business units. There is an argument that they would receive greater benefit from having consultants who are shared across the organization. Through working on similar issues in other parts of the business, they can thereby bring better learning and solutions than can those who are aligned with business units.

15 *Challenges of Capability*

Generic HR skills

There is a widespread view that the lack of the right skills has been and will continue to be the principal reason for HR not meeting its own aspiration for repositioning or delivering against the promise made to senior management customers. Now that new structures have been put in place and processes reformed, attention has turned to skills.

The generally reported weaknesses cluster around such personal characteristics as:

- Risk aversion – do HR professionals tend towards the safe option rather than take the challenging option? Do they want watertight solutions to problems rather than to experiment with novel solutions?
- Drive – are HR staff sufficiently good at influencing, challenging and pushing their organization to give people management sufficient attention?
- Credibility – are HR staff respected as knowledgeable professionals who are able to apply their skills to business situations?
- Receptiveness – are HR staff able and willing to listen to problems, take on new ideas and address issues from a fresh perspective?
- Political awareness – how well are senior HR individuals able to build coalitions of support and find allies, but also identify the means to neutralize opponents?

As HR becomes more professional as a function, technical skills are becoming less of a problem. Increasingly, those joining HR have undertaken or intend to undertake CIPD study. This provides a good grounding in the content of HR work. The question mark is over whether HR people have the courage, drive and will to succeed.

The consequence of these deficiencies is to make HR less effective in the area where it most wants to be effective. Delivering good administration, professional support and advice should not be a problem – HR is well experienced and becoming increasingly well recognized for the quality of its input. Where HR falls down is in the area of high-level impact. A Kaisen consulting survey found that HR lacked the 'power' or 'confidence' to challenge the 'presenting problem'. The function's greatest needs were in self-belief, assertiveness and openness to others (Pickard, 2004b). It could do line management's bidding but it was less able to influence a change of direction. Performing an internal consultancy role is very difficult. External consultants can walk away; internal consultants have to maintain relationships with their colleagues. It is even less easy if HR has formed a partnership with the line, unless the quality of the partnership is such that disagreement does not have a terminal effect on the relationship. And HR has always had to contend with the problem that its power rarely derives from positional authority, but from its influence, based on expertise. HR in the organization of the future, if not always of the past, simply cannot tell the line management what to do, except in rare circumstances.

HR managers must cajole and persuade, with, at times (because this cannot be assumed), the implicit backing of senior management.

If HR is risk averse, tending to state difficulties rather than offering solutions or finding reasons in the law or corporate procedures to say 'no' also hinders the function's effectiveness. If managers get this sort of response they will look elsewhere for help. Of course, we are not arguing that HR ought to flout the law or ignore corporate policies and procedures, but it is about an attitude of mind. Are HR managers disposed to find creative solutions to problems, rather than assert the rules? If they do the latter it may be because they fail to understand the business realities properly. They may not truly empathize with the position faced by their line colleagues.

The unwillingness to change, to move outside the comfort zone, is one of the complaints made against HR, especially by management consultants. It is seen in resistance to structural and process change, in outsourcing and in devolution to line managers. HR may be happy to divest itself of chores through outsourcing or devolution, but not to lose important activities to the line or third-party providers. Consultants compare HR unfavourably with Finance or IT. This might be too hard in that it can be argued that HR processes (for the reasons set out at page 57) are more complicated and the development of human capital more complex than financial or technological management. None the less, the suspicion is that resistance to change comes from a combination of understandable self-protection with an over-inflated view of the uniqueness of HR, but also from a deeper suspicion of (or even objection to) the new business model. Phil Murray, at the time a consultant with Hewitts, suggests that HR is a vocation to many in the function and their view of the world as 'men of the people' inhibits them from taking tough business decisions. Indeed, support for this view comes from research by Buyens and de Vos (2001). The management of the employee was the area that HR staff cited as the most important for the function, above change management or HR as a strategic partner. Moreover, an IRS survey (Industrial Relations Services, 2004) found that 41 per cent of HR respondents and a SHRM survey (2004) 36 per cent cited 'wanting to work with people' as an important reason for working in HR. This group may well object to changes that reduce their contact with employees. This is especially true if it cannot be compensated for by an interest in business affairs. In the same IRS survey, 47 per cent admitted that a lack of business knowledge, and 41 per cent a lack of operational experience, was a barrier to career progress. Yet experience in generalist HR roles was seen as much more important to their career advancement than spending time in a line management or an operational role.

It is for these sorts of reasons that BT calculated that only a third of staff would be capable of shifting immediately to the new model and another third would need 'development to get there'. Deb Cohen of the US Society for Human Resource Management came to similar conclusions. 'Many executives now accept the importance of people to business performance. Some HR professionals get the need but continue to focus on the nuts and bolts, while others are still learning the critical role they can play in organizational success.'

To succeed in the future, HR staff will have to deliver by being competent in their profession and competent in business. They clearly must retain a sympathy for people issues, but this must be allied to an interest in, and a feel for, the business issues. It is in the business arena that HR has too often been found wanting. As one HR director said 'it is our biggest impediment that we think HR is a good thing in itself' (Lawler *et al.*, 2005).

Part of the reason for this state of affairs according to some in HR is that the professional training received by aspiring HR people is too narrow, too content focused and insufficiently attuned to business issues. For example, a survey of senior HR practitioners undertaken by

Industrial Relations Services (2004) elicited the response that getting hands-on experience was more important than gaining qualifications. The professional training is seen as too much oriented to theory and best practice, designed too much by academics and not practitioners. The risk is that this sort of training will produce those who see their profession as more important than the organizations they work for. An example of this view was given by the head of OD at a major US company: 'The profession of which I am part is bigger than the company. Therefore I represent one view about development, labor relations and human rights, and I am not going to knuckle under, regardless of whether or not they value my professional opinions' (Eisenstat, 1996).

An alternative academic direction – undertaking an MBA – has also been criticized as being a poor reflection of what goes on in real business life, especially if its teaching is done in functional silos (Partridge, 2004). Supply of MBAs now outstrips demand and there have been question marks on their quality as business schools have used them as cash cows (Arnot, 2006).

In both cases practitioners need to be able to think about the *application* of their knowledge in the diversity of organizational settings. So, should not learning in this area be more experiential than academic?

Business partner skills

As we remarked earlier, in many ways the business partner position is the most pivotal, but yet least well defined, of the new HR roles. Perhaps not surprisingly, there are widespread reports of organizations finding it hard to appoint the sort of quality they want for the role. And, as a McKinsey report (Lawler *et al.*, 2005) observes: 'The business partner model is fine but it assumes capable people – without that the whole thing falls apart.' Indeed, if those taken on as business partners are more comfortable with operational work and like to please the line manager customer by limiting work that they are doing to suit their preferences, it is hardly a shock if the business partners fail to fulfil expectations. Given that business partners will have to work in a matrix environment, there will be role ambiguities. If those who fill these jobs require complete role clarity, they will struggle. It is in this context that Richie Furlong poses the question of whether HR managers are both 'up for it, as well as up to it'. Is it a matter of disposition or a matter of skills and capability which needs to be addressed, or both? Are they competent to do the job and do they have desire to compete for what is a 'big' job against internal and external competition?

There is certainly a real question mark over how well HR can move to the new model in terms of skills and orientation. Previously, the HR manager had a team delivering an integrated service. Now they have to make an impact without resources to back them up. Then there is the challenge to focus exclusively on strategy and change management, rather than handle operational issues, still less administrative or informational ones. Do they have the capacity to do this?

Some seem to struggle with the business awareness dimension of their work, still emphasizing the professional aspects, still focused on HR-centred problems. For example, business partners at one organization we know did not see the need to discuss with line management, let alone challenge, business targets that were going to be used in a variable pay scheme. Similarly, if business partners cannot answer the majority of the questions listed on page 114, they are not acting as real business partners. They are pretenders of the old school. They are failing to demonstrate the USP that the new HR model offers: namely, the combination of people management expertise with business knowledge. Failure to offer this proposition to line management threatens not just HR's repositioning claim, but also internal HR's added value in the market. It is internal HR's knowledge of its own business and positioning that gives it competitive edge against external providers.

Conversely, there is a risk that, over time, business partners progressively lose their technical know-how, as they concentrate on business not professional skills. They rely more and more on the centres of expertise to keep them up to date with professional developments. This may matter less if they know where to go for help, but as the Absa example on page 156 showed, some business partners may seek to work independently. The go-it-alone approach may be driven by wanting to be seen as in charge or decisive in front of line colleagues, but, as the saying goes, a little knowledge can be a dangerous thing, especially if the business partner is unaware of the extent of their ignorance.

If you accept that the new business partner model focuses on organizational effectiveness, competition will come from business literate people from outside the function. From within the function, there is also already evidence that new recruits are being brought in to do the business partner role from outside the organization because internal candidates do not demonstrate the necessary skills. This is especially true if the skill bar is being raised and the content of the role transformed. (For example, there have been complaints about HR's change management and project management skills in the NHS, but there has also been realization that the function has not been asked to do such tasks before – Birchenhough, 2004.) It is very hard for people in these circumstances to shift from being an advisor or expert to being a business partner. It is particularly difficult make such a move within the same organization, which might explain the search for talent externally. Where these new recruits are getting the skill development is a moot point. Perhaps their employers are living off the talent that was developed under previous HR models. Moreover, whether these external appointments will work sufficiently often to make recruitment the preferred resourcing method is also questionable. The absence of organizational knowledge and the need for cultural fit are barriers to success: so much so that one HR director has taken the view that it is safer to bring in people from outside the company to specialist posts and too risky for generalist roles like the business partner.

Those new into the role may not have these transitional difficulties, but they still have to define the role. Do they know how to be strategic? Do they know when to make the right interventions? Change management tasks may be more obvious, but, again, do the business partners have the necessary skills to be effective? Can they affect the business plan and ensure that people management issues are to the fore? Are they sufficiently business literate to see opportunities and thus make a professional contribution that is relevant to business needs? Have they got the honed diagnostic skills to spot trends, identify problems and come up with solutions? If their analytical skills are weak, according to Claire Aitken at RBS, they will fail in the role. In her view, these skills are closely related to intellectual calibre and have a significant bearing on who will succeed and who will not.

HR leadership

Minimizing the importance of the HR role or of the contribution employees can make to the organization impacts on HR's credibility. So can weak leadership of the function. Too often in the past HR has not been blessed by the best of leaders. Alan Warner complained of their lack of imagination and drive. This may have a number of causes. The HR community itself may have lacked quality, or may simply have had good Indians but few chiefs. It has certainly been because the function has not been taken sufficiently seriously by CEOs. The quality of what HR got by way of leadership has been a reflection of the importance attached to the function by the CEO. It has been used to house failed executives with no other home to go to; or at least to deal with homeless, if deserving, souls who had fallen on hard times. It has been used as the last stop before retirement. How often have you heard the complaint: 'Oh no, not him!' The then CEO of Carlsberg Tetley made this point starkly at a business dinner: 'HR is seen as an exit door rather an entry gate in professional development.' Or as Dave Ulrich (1998c) even more brutally put it: 'Too often HR departments are too often like computers made up of used parts.' If it is indeed a retirement home for failed executives, this sends a signal both to the function and to the wider management community that HR has limited clout. The best and the brightest will therefore avoid the function on their route to the top.

Alternatively, non-HR leaders have been parachuted in because they were regarded as 'people friendly'. Either way there was no guarantee that they understood HR or realized the complexity of the work. They were very dependent on the effectiveness of their subordinates, hoping they did not tire of bailing out yet another HR novice.

Of course there are successful home-grown HR directors, developed through the function. But they, like leaders brought in from other areas, are under enormous pressure to succeed. HR directors tend not to be performance managed on their professional or functional performance. The definition of success may not at all be in delivering good human capital performance, but in cutting costs and in improving efficiency. There has certainly been one recent example of an HR director leaving their job for this reason and there are fears of the increasing 'politicization' of the HR director role. To operate in an unsympathetic environment, these directors have primarily to satisfy their CEO's requirements, however narrowly constructed these may be. This may cause them to ignore good people management precepts; damage their function in the search for efficiency; adopt the latest fad or fashion that takes the eye and seems to offer a 'quick win'. In other words, instead of considering how to organize people management in a way that increases organizational value, the search is for short-term, gimmicky measures that will keep the boss happy. This in turn may lead to initiative overload in a frantic attempt to deliver value and service. Moreover, especially if the HR director is not an HR professional, there is a further risk that s/he may have a poor understanding of what the function is trying to achieve. This means its objectives and initiatives may be poorly defended in the boardroom.

Careers

One of the all-too-apparent downsides of the HR model we have been describing is that traditional career paths are unlikely to operate as before. The risk is that internal development of people may be restricted. This may prevent the growth of the leaders we describe above as being vital to the success of the organization. It may also severely restrict the building of expertise by shared services staff that would allow them to fill more senior positions later. And how will business partners and experts emerge, if there is no feed from below?

If staff cannot be home grown within HR, they will have to be bought in. But which organizations will be undertaking the necessary training? Employers cannot rely forever on those trained in the past. Failure to develop, in particular, HR leaders and business partners will again give rise to imports from outside the profession.

Precisely this problem has been found in the banking industry. It is much harder, because of job segmentation, to develop well-rounded bankers with broad experience and understanding of how a bank works. In the past there was a rotation of jobs through back office processes before customer-facing roles were offered to employees. All these moves took place under the eyes of the same manager. Now, these roles have been separated and are separately organized under different management structures.

In the pyramid shown in Figure 15.1, you can see that staff could enter the function in personnel assistant roles. These were often generalist positions, involving a wide variety of administrative tasks. Job holders might have been school leavers, from secretarial, clerical or administrative posts or the shop floor. The interpersonal skills, record-keeping experience and procedural competence gained in a wide variety of administrative posts served these people well. If individuals proved themselves to be any good, and showed interest and initiative, more work could be delegated to them. They could be trusted with some advisory responsibility. Should they wish to, they could participate in projects on wider HR issues. Through these means staff could develop themselves into personnel officers, and then further up the organizational pyramid in competition with graduate entrants.

In the new model in many organizations such movement is much more difficult. Getting from a shared services centre to any other HR post is quite a leap. One needs specialist expertise for the centres of expertise, consultancy skills for that type of work and business knowledge and strategic capability for the business partner roles. How is one to acquire the knowledge, skills and experience in the shared services centre to fulfil the requirements of these posts? Moreover, geography can play a part. If, as is the case in many organizations, the shared services centre is in one location and the centres of expertise and corporate centre in another, then internal transfers may be uneconomic for junior staff. This is especially true if the shared services centre is in a low-cost location with the corporate centre/centres of expertise in a big city HQ like London. RBS has the geographical divide between an HR shared services centre in Manchester and specialist roles in Edinburgh. As a result, organizational movement tends to be either divisional (i.e. within a division based at that location) or within one HR unit. A high-street retailer described to us precisely the same problem.

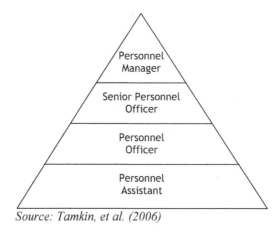

Source: Tamkin, et al. (2006)

Figure 15.1   Traditional organizational hierarchy

> One financial services organization admitted to having no formal career management processes in place for HR shared services. It had concentrated on getting the structure and staffing right. Evidence from exit interviews suggested that lack of career opportunities was the primary reason for resignations. The company has now, four years after set-up, decided to give attention to career management (McLaren, 2005).

Those coming from the shop floor (rather than from secretarial and clerical jobs) might fare better. These staff could, and still can, become technical trainers. Using their knowledge of products and processes, they can induct others. Whether or not technical training is part of HR, individuals can move across to general development roles. Another path was to switch from being a trade union representative to being an employee relations advisor – from poacher to gamekeeper. This is still possible if there is a small employee relations team in the centres of expertise.

Although it might seem easier to move around the new model as a graduate entrant, it is also not as straightforward as in the old model. Where do you start? If you apply the pure model there are now no development positions. Each role has its own expertise – in administration, a subject-matter area, consultancy or strategic business partnering. For graduates, development positions can always be created, but not on a large scale as a feature of standard career paths. Figure 15.2 indicates the broader problem. Movement in or out of the corporate centre should be relatively easy. Those coming from the centres of expertise will have deep knowledge in a field which could be relevant to corporate centre work. For example, if executive remuneration is located in the corporate centre and general reward work in the centres of expertise, a transition from one to the other could be straightforward. Whether it is depends on the gap between a corporate role (dealing with executive remuneration) and the tasks of the centres of expertise manager. In some companies the transition is so great that external appointments are always made. A business partner role can prepare someone for a strategic contribution in the corporate centre. The transfer can work in the opposite direction. Someone in the corporate centre should have the sort of business and people management overview that could be applied in a business setting. The parallel situation applies to those who lead a shared services operation: they have the sort of

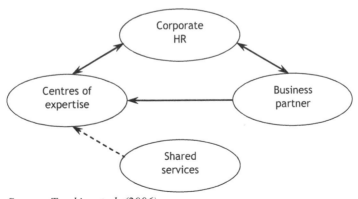

Source: Tamkin, et al. (2006)

Figure 15.2   Career map in new HR operating model

commercial skills that would allow a move to a business partner role – as the career of one of the authors illustrates.

Those who do a particularly good job in business partner roles may find that their very success limits further movement. They may find themselves tied to their business unit because of line management reluctance to lose somebody tuned into their needs. The same risk applies to specialists in the centres of expertise. Their knowledge of the intricacies of past policy development is such that there may be pressure to retain it in the same role over an extended period.

The limitation of the above career paths is that there are few jobs available, certainly in the corporate centre and centres of expertise. The option of adding a third path from centres of expertise to business partner is problematic. Jobs in centres of expertise are for specialists and business partner jobs for generalists. Of course there will be exceptions, due to particular personal attributes, but it is hard to develop deep knowledge, skills and experience in a generalist role, whilst those in the centres of expertise may not have the profile of skills to fit business partner.

There are two further challenges with respect to career paths. Should the shared service centre be offshored, it is hard to imagine internal transfers to HR posts outside the shared services centre. For example, IBM (Pickard, 2000) used graduates in its call centre (making use of their language skills). Whether this will be so easy given its relocation to Hungary is a moot point. This problem is even clearer with outsourced administration: there will be no source of upward movement within the client organization, unless those working for the outsourced provider transfer to it. They, too, would face the question of where they would fit in, as well as having to make the adjustment to a different employment culture. Recruitment, either from the service supplier or otherwise, would be straight to business partner and centres of expertise positions, making it more likely to come from the external labour market. This is unless the jobs are filled by internal, non-HR people. This brings us to the second further challenge: in the view of many, business partner, OD or change management expert roles can just as easily be filled by line managers. Figure 15.3 makes the point graphically. Indeed, this may be something that is encouraged. Line managers bring useful knowledge of the business, lots of practical experience of change management and of people management. The alternative view is that, if these roles can be done without HR expertise, are they really HR roles? If they

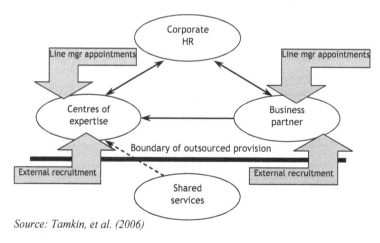

Source: Tamkin, et al. (2006)

Figure 15.3   An HR career map with the impact of outsourcing and line transfers

are truly part of the HR family and exemplify HR's USP, how can organizations expect non-HR people to perform them? These transfers in may be for development purposes or they may be to bring expertise to the role – or both. Whichever it is, there are fewer posts on offer to HR professionals. The risk from an HR perspective is that those in the function get marginalized to specialist or administrative roles. The 'sexiest' jobs, those with the highest profile, go to those from other functions. If it is they that get the plum jobs, the signal to those working in HR is that professional knowledge, skills and experience are not that important to success. To get on, you need to get out of the function.

16 *Capability Solutions*

In this section we will look at the development of capability through the acquisition of the right sort of skills, with a brief discussion in the specific context of the business partner and HR leadership roles, and via career management, as some of the problems in capability stem from the lack of the right sort of preparation.

Skills

There are two strands to the solutions we suggest for skill gaps: one relates to improving the flow of talent into the function, the other to improving the existing capability. From a practical perspective, organizations are likely to tackle the second element first, before looking to the external labour market. However, it should be noted that in many of the HR change processes of recent years there has been quite a throughput of resources. From shared services centre administrative staff to business partners, organizations have brought in many new employees. In RBS, for example, over the past five years, a substantial number of business partners have been either new recruits or transfers in, and an even greater proportion of those in shared services came from outside on the back of growth more than as a result of churn.

In an ideal world organizations should begin by being clear about requirements for each role. This should encompass the knowledge, experience, skills and competencies (i.e. the hard technical skills and soft behavioural competencies). This may also cover qualifications. It should detail minimum requirements, but also what a fully effective performer might possess.

> Shell has developed a competency framework that lists a range of HR skill areas – from implementing people management through attracting/interviewing candidates to supporting mergers and acquisitions. These then can be assessed at five levels of proficiency. Job profiles take the competencies and proficiency levels and then apply them to dozens of generic jobs at different grades, organizational locations and 'competency groups' (e.g. industrial relations or talent management).

Entry requirements in such competency descriptions are useful for resourcing purposes. They should specify in clear terms what those taking on these jobs should be able to offer. Producing the framework should provoke some debate about what is really needed in the job as opposed to what is desirable. Is it essential to have a degree to be an HR expert or business partner? Surely not. Is it essential to be a full CIPD member for the same roles? This is certainly questionable for the business partner, because having CIPD membership would exclude line transfers.

Having descriptions of what full competence looks like is useful not just for continuing performance appraisal purposes, but also for establishing whether HR has the requisite quality in its resource at the outset of a change process. It enables a gap analysis. This can be done

RBS has a competency model that is used for all professional appointments and for their training and development. It covers such topics as:

- change agency
- managerial skills
- value delivery focus
- diagnostic/advisory skills
- communication/influencing skills
- enhancing professionalism.

Potential recruits are put through an assessment centre that tests applicants under these headings. Only the top quartile performers will be considered for an employment offer.

in a broad brush way to give an impression of collective shortfall or at an individual level for specific responses to specific needs.

The response to gaps will vary if the analysis is that the problem is endemic or confined to certain employees. It will vary if the difficulty relates to a lack of experience or knowledge, shortcomings in skills or competencies. Experience can be gained by giving employees the relevant exposure through short-term projects, longer-term (but temporary) assignments, job rotation, etc. For example, IBM used small projects for call centre staff, taking them away from the phone 20 per cent of the time (Pickard, 2000). Knowledge gaps can be tackled through formal classroom-style training (internally or externally provided) or informal knowledge-sharing sessions to discuss how to deal with non-standard or new problems. RBS has 'lunch and learn' sessions on specific topics. An electronic 'chatroom' for HR staff was a helpful feature at Telewest Communications (Incomes Data Services, 2001) that allowed questions to be posted and answers received where people were uncertain on company policy. Sheep-dip style training can be used to at least in part to remedy collective skill deficiencies. Thus a lack of commercial awareness or customer-facing skills can be responded to through some group training.

One manufacturing company was sufficiently concerned with the variability of the HR contribution to the business planning process for the HR director to decide that the HR managers acting as business partners needed skills training. He observed that, whilst some of his colleagues were able to introduce people management issues into the plans, others appeared to be ineffective – judging by the results. The training examined the role of HR in the strategic planning process.

Away days have proved good at team building and some of the content has been devoted to updating knowledge or awareness. Siemens Business Services, for example, periodically has team away days that cover such issues as the business strategy, the role of HR and specific HR topics where work is required, e.g. workforce planning.

There are also examples of joint learning with HR and line managers present. The BBC used a joint approach to the setting up of their HR shared services operation in 2001. HR and managers worked through different scenarios of process issues to see how the different roles played out. The benefits are clear from the DWP boxed example.

The Department for Work and Pensions has used two-day 'partnership for business results' workshops. Interestingly, business partners and their line customers came together to these sessions to work on live business issues. They were, thus, able to build relationships and learn about each others' skills, whilst doing useful work on real problems (CIPD, 2005c).

But some skill or, as likely, behavioural shortcomings need to be approached at the individual level. This is best done through normal performance management processes with the immediate line manager as coach. The difficulty occurs either if the manager is not a good coach or if s/he suffers from some of the same problems as the managed. If s/he has a closed mind, fixed on delivering the right HR answer, then it will be difficult to move to a situation where his/her staff are prepared to take risks, try out novel solutions, orient themselves to what the business requires or wheel and deal to get their ideas accepted. This may lead organizations to think of ways of bypassing immediate management, maybe by giving staff broader exposure through working on projects outside their own immediate area or by visiting other organizations. Of course, this still leaves the unresolved issue of what to do with the ineffective line manager, and whether the organization can tolerate poor people management skills in HR as elsewhere.

Organizations will have to work particularly hard to tackle the personal, as opposed to professional, gaps in capability. By the time of recruitment to the organization much has already been determined in terms of disposition and preferences. Organizations can develop knowledge, technical skills and experience, and tackle skill deficiencies in certain areas, but problems with attitudes and behaviours are less susceptible to training. As the saying goes: 'If you attract the right attitude, you can train the skills.' So, organizations should not be overly ambitious in trying to effect cultural change through the alteration of deep-seated individual habits.

What HR management can do is create a climate in which staff are encouraged to face up to what is expected of them to meet organizational needs now and in the future. This means getting them out of their comfort zone, encouraging them to stand up to and challenge 'scary managers' and to push their ideas forward, and ensuring that new policies are effectively delivered. The organization can give them the 'licence to learn' and indeed 'fail', as a BT HR manager put it. This means offering a safety net to experimentation.

Through this sort of intervention the organization can signal that to succeed individuals will have to try to adjust thinking and behaviour. The direction of travel will be indicated and support offered for those who struggle to arrive at the final destination. In the end though, it may not be possible to effect change with the resources the function has and new resources may be needed. Self-evidently, improving the collective capability of the HR function in these circumstances requires a flow of good-quality people into the profession. This will be achieved when the HR brand is seen as of high value in the external and internal labour market. People need to be clamouring to get into the function. It should be seen as a good career in itself or good route to the top: 'a key business slot', according to a US consultant. Organizations must then facilitate entry by internal candidates, finding ways to allow talented individuals who have a feel for, and interest in, people management to transfer in to appropriate roles. Organizations must also recruit externally at non-graduate and graduate levels. Non-graduates are likely to be recruited to administrative and informational roles in the shared service centre. Graduates can be accommodated in a variety of roles, if they accept that they will have to learn the ropes. Having a graduate programme is important as it signals that HR is as important as other disciplines in developing a management career. At present only 1 per cent of graduate jobs are in HR, according to the Association of Graduate Recruiters. Yet the success of the HR graduate entry scheme in the NHS proves that there is a market for HR jobs. There were 16 places in NHS HR graduate programme in 2004 for which 700 applied. The following year 1420 applied for 28 places. The scheme is part of 'Building HR Capacity', which is precisely what organizations should be doing. If organizations can successfully acquire quality recruits for HR, a 'virtuous circle' develops: more talent will apply because of the organization's reputation and having a quality resource makes it more likely that a better function will emerge. The opposite is of course true – a vicious circle of poor performance driving away potential recruits.

Having entered the profession, the new recruits need to establish an initial basis of knowledge that allows them to be credible and effective. This can be achieved through internal organizational recognition schemes, as in the box below, or through external accreditation.

Alan Warner is about to introduce an HR 'driving licence' at Hertfordshire County Council that gives the bearer permission to practise. This will be at a number of levels, so only the equivalent of HGV 1 licence holders can handle the most difficult problems. This he hopes will make it is easier for managers to locate those who can help them. By the same token, the scheme might reduce the tendency of some managers to shop around until they get the right answer.

The MOD, in the early stages of its transformation process, introduced:

- 'foundation' training for basic knowledge across HR activities
- a 'specialized' programme with modular training in HR content areas
- support for the acquisition of vocational qualifications or CIPD membership.

An e-test was available to check whether knowledge has been successfully absorbed. The MOD's Certificate in HR Practice was given to all those in the function who had completed the foundation training, had successfully passed the e-test and had received their manager's endorsement that they were putting knowledge into practice.

A fresh look at meeting the personal and professional development needs for MOD HR staff is under way as a result of the major changes to HR roles, service delivery and the comprehensive overhaul of HR policies and processes.

As far as the external accreditation is concerned, there is already a recognition that CIPD courses have to adjust to meet the criticisms made earlier, though, as the box below shows, improvement has started with broadening the nature of the management standards. Further development from CIPD could be to move beyond courses to offering more flexible (modular) forms of professional development. This might be in terms of content (technical specialist and general business), forms of delivery (via new media) and timing (early and mid-career). Accreditation for knowledge obtained via other relevant qualifications (e.g. MBAs) is also being extended. There is now a plethora of short courses. All these initiatives might help both the wide range of those in the function and those coming into the function from outside. It would be an appropriate response to changing career patterns.

> New leadership and management standards are being launched by CIPD (Whittaker and Johns, 2004). They cover:
>
> - managing in a strategic context
> - managing information for competitive advantage
> - managing and leading people
> - managing for results.

None the less, the burden of getting HR professionals exposed in practice to business issues, perhaps not unreasonably, falls on their employer. This may be achieved through experiential learning. Some organizations have specific development programmes, especially for graduates, that will be described in the careers section below. As to more formal learning, doing an MBA can support the job experience; it has the twin advantages that it gives those born and bred in HR the chance to understand better other aspects of organizational life, and conveys the message to line colleagues that the student (or degree-holder) is serious about looking at issues from a business perspective. As with CIPD qualifications, it seems that providers are addressing the question of making MBAs more relevant to organizational life (Arnot, 2006).

What may be more lacking in some organizations is a real commitment to continuing professional development (CPD). Having helped the individual get their driving licence there is a tendency to assume that no further testing or help is required. Certainly, in middle-graded jobs, in the middle years, most (if not all) development is through learning on the job. There may be the odd course on legal changes or the odd conference on a relevant topic on offer, but little broader knowledge or skills exposure. Senior people may be better catered for if the interest in executive coaching continues, and there are various HR director clubs or fora that provide opportunities for learning. However, structured learning for HR directors to figure out how to deal with situations where strategy hits business realities or strategic intent has to be translated into real results may be in shorter supply than executive coaching. And this is where many of the problems occur. The CIPD Reward Survey (2005a), for example, reported that four fifths of respondents had difficulties linking pay with performance.

> The LEAP programme has been offering senior HR managers in local government the chance of strategic coaching. Run by the Employers' Organization for local government in partnership with IES, it was designed to offer skills and build confidence in strategic management.

There are of course exceptions to this observation, as the LEAP example indicates, but good quality CPD should be the norm. There is a lot of training for business partners at present. Lynda Gratton provided a bespoke HR leadership programme for RBS. The civil service is now offering a Masters degree in HR strategy and change at Kingston University Business School, which is aimed at helping senior HR managers to become 'true business partners to their organizations' (Pickard, 2004b). There are similar degrees offered at other universities, like Bath and Kings London, often credited against CIPD qualifications. Centrica has teamed up with Roffey Park for business partner training. The MOD is using external support in order to help provide initial training for its new business partners.

Some organizations are also offering broader professional development. Rolls-Royce has strongly linked its professional development framework to CIPD membership. Over three quarters of its professional HR staff are chartered members or fellows. The company uses internal mentors and encourages the use of 'development diaries' for recording training and development evidence. Its competency framework describes in a hierarchical ladder the internal competencies required and supporting development options, but also parallel CIPD qualifications and courses (Simms, 2005).

RBS offers 'master classes' in technical areas of HR and an Advanced Business Consultancy course to develop skills especially in analysis and diagnosis. Rolls-Royce has run programmes to develop knowledge and expertise in particular content areas.

BUSINESS PARTNER SKILLS

Many of the above solutions apply to business partners, as much as to any part of HR, and a number of relevant points have been made in the section on the business partner role. The key additional skill issue is whether business partners are sufficiently business aware. Do they know enough about the activities of the business unit they are part of to make a full contribution? Are they able to answer the sort of questions listed on page 114?

HR LEADERSHIP

According to Neil Roden, HR directors need to obtain positional authority and gain influence through reporting to the CEO with a seat on the executive committee or wherever the real decisions are made. (Membership of the board to him is largely irrelevant.) The real solution to any perceived problems with HR leadership is to appoint the right quality of people in the first place. Those who will succeed will be those who find out pretty quickly how to operate the levers of power. Preferably, they will either be HR professionals or, at least, those with significant HR experience. Once the importance of human capital and people management policies and practices is accepted, the most talented will seek to be appointed to HR director posts. They will have the skills to network and influence and ensure the right reporting relationships. HR will have really arrived when the HR director position is one of the most sought after in the executive team.

Another key dimension of HR leadership identified in our discussions is the extent to which the HR director takes charge of the relationship between HR and the rest of the organization. In particular, with the challenges the new operating model offers in terms of delivering customer value, whilst containing cost and in the dispersion of HR delivery streams, HR leaders really do have to be of 'the top order', according to Mike Watts (Director, HR Transformation, Cabinet Office), to ensure the model works. They must be active supporters of their function, ensuring it has the resources (people and technological) to deliver and do a good job, but also be prepared to challenge performance or practice if it is not up to standard. Given HR's role ambiguities, the HR director must set a clear course for the function, setting it stretching but achievable goals that will move the organization forward in line with the business strategy.

For HR to succeed it has to have leaders who are:

- active not passive
- pushing change within HR not reacting to directives from elsewhere
- seeking solutions, not acting as 'abominable "no" men' (Alan Warner)
- balancing business need with organizational governance
- creating a learning organization by listening to others

- leading by example within the function
- showing courage in tackling difficult problems
- managing the politics of the organization so that it moves forward rather than be dogged by endless debate or in-fighting
- encouraging change in other organizations by acting as an exemplar (especially true in the public sector)
- creating a vision to inspire others
- realizing that people management is not an end in itself, but a means to deliver returns to shareholders, services to customers, a contribution to the community, etc.

Careers

The basic solution to problems with HR career paths is more active career management. The CIPD's Managing Employee Careers report (2003b) pointed to the difficulties with the current dominant model of career self-management. The theory is that the employer will offer advice, training and support on career issues to back up individual efforts. The reality is often that this infrastructure is absent. It is seen as a 'nice to have' rather than an essential activity. The result is that many HR staff are receiving fairly limited career advice and support and a significant proportion of HR staff worry about their career direction. A SHRM survey (2004) found nearly a third of respondents identified the absence of a clear path in HR as an obstacle to advancement. Some organizations are of course offering more appropriate levels of career counselling, and these will be described here.

One way of helping HR colleagues navigate their way around is by formally describing the possible career paths. As shown in Figure 16.1, Centrica has set these out in a model that shows the possibility of movement from bottom to top of the hierarchy, and between generalist and specialist lines of development.

Such descriptions have to be realistic so as to avoid false expectations being generated; not so specific that they relate to precise jobs that quickly go out of date with the next reorganization. (Indeed Centrica will have to adjust its model with the decision to outsource its shared services.) They also have to be acted upon. There is the risk that glossy documents end up gathering dust if line managers do not use them. One way of ensuring that this does not happen is to have a positive approach to career management. In particular, organizations need to identify those with the capacity for growth to higher levels and then provide opportunities to facilitate this development. It may mean that the occasional gamble is taken to push forward someone who has talent, but is not completely ready.

The description of role competencies at different grade levels, which we described earlier in the section on skills, can also be useful for career management purposes. This allows people to peer over functional and geographic boundaries to see what opportunities there are on offer elsewhere. It means they do not have to be constrained by the limitations of their part of the business. For competency statements to work best in career management terms, they should cover knowledge, skills and experience, as well as behavioural competencies. In other words, professional expertise and personal characteristics need to be described.

Centrica, for example, has used competencies to underpin its career path model. The company makes a distinction between behavioural (business knowledge, strategic contribution, personal credibility, HR delivery) and technical (employee relations, developing the organization, HRIS) competencies. It encourages self-assessment against the framework,

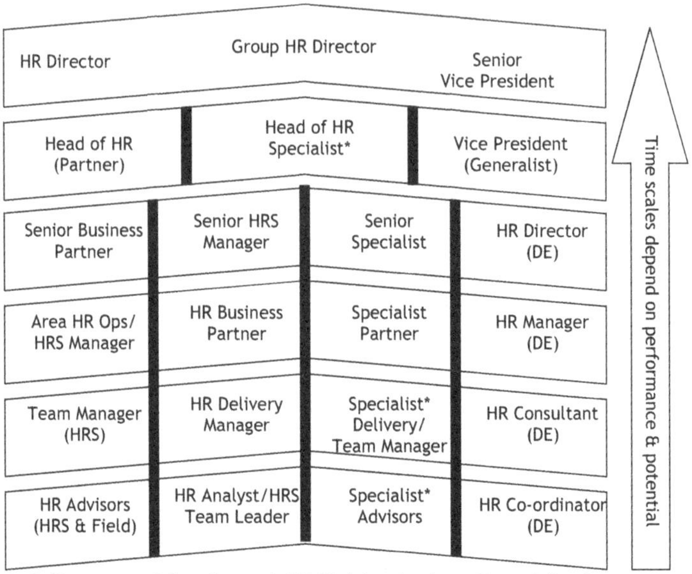

*   Indicates a specialist role, e.g. L&D, Training Academy, Reward, Pensions,
    Resourcing (list not exhaustive)
    Source: Centrica plc

Figure 16.1   Centrica career paths model

Shell has produced a development model to help with individual career management decisions for HR staff. It suggests that a development plan should have six stages:

1.   What does my job require?
2.   What career path do I want to take?
3.   Where am I now?
4.   What competencies and experience do I need to add?
5.   What action do I need to take?
6.   Am I on track?

To assist individuals to carry out this exercise, HR staff may use a number of tools like the 'experience navigator', 'education and learning curriculum', job profiles and competency framework (see Figure 16.2). The navigator describes a range of 57 'job experience opportunities', including those for specialists and generalists. Each opportunity is described in terms of what experience can be derived from each job and whom it would suit.

discussion with the line manager and appropriate development action. Shell has created a range of ways of assisting career development, as shown in the box above.

RBS is thinking about creating role families within HR to help those with jobs with the same cluster of skills and competencies to see what development path they have. The model might have three families – technical professional, consulting, and partnering/relationship management. As with competency frameworks, the model allows staff to see what is required in the other families. This helps them think through whether a switch of family would be possible or desirable. In the RBS structure a move from consulting to relationship management

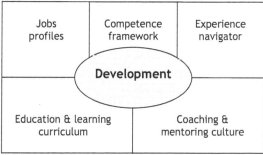

Source: *Shell HR Functional Excellence*

Figure 16.2   Career toolbox at Shell

is easier than some moves because part of the relationship management skill set includes consultancy skills. The difference is in the environment in which the consultancy is delivered – as a third party or as a member of the team.

The use of some form of skill/competence-based progression could be applied as a further option. This would offer a sense of making progress and might provide extra pay, as individuals enhance their capability. McLaren (2005) describes the 'gate' system whereby as advisors learn to handle more complex cases they pass through a higher gate.

How else can functional management ameliorate difficulties with career paths? There are two broad clusters of solutions: staff development (especially experiential) and structural adjustment to the operating model.

Without disturbance to the structure, organizations can help develop staff. We described earlier methods of formal and informal learning. Organizations can assist this process by sponsoring talented staff on CIPD courses or degree programmes. Learning through doing can also be encouraged. Lead administrators on a subject basis (recruitment, reward, maternity policy, etc.) can be selected to induct new starters, help the team develop understanding in their particular area and be available to deal with queries from colleagues. Depending upon its size, the shared services centre may offer temporary spells of supervision to cover holiday or other absence, such as maternity leave or extended sickness. Assignments can be organized where individuals can see how they like and are suited to different types of work; and the organization can likewise evaluate progress. WMC Resources Ltd (an Australian metals firm), for example, allows shared service staff to fill temporary HR positions at its sites (www.iqpc. com).

Another approach for all staff in the function is to use short-term projects to grow knowledge, skills and experience, while at the same time testing ability. So, for example, the person in the shared services centre responsible for leading on a topic, say flexible working hours, could join the policy expert in centres of expertise and a business partner or consultant in a review of that policy. The gap between policy and implementation can also be eased if the delivery team is widened in a similar way. By these means organizations can see whether there are talented administrators with the potential to develop, or whether there are business partners with an aptitude for policy work or individuals in the centres of expertise with the capacity for a more generalist role.

Other ways to assist this transition are to cycle people quickly through their initial jobs or create some development positions. On the first point, JP Morgan assigned staff to their call centre for only 9–12 months at a time before moving them on to new jobs (Pickard,

2000), precisely to avoid their getting stuck. This may be sensible for call centre work, but organizations might not want to see such churn in all their shared services centre jobs – the loss of continuity would be damaging. Such a system works better with jobs with limited HR technical know-how and so suits call centre roles where the emphasis is on customer handling skills, not HR knowledge. As to development positions, we remarked earlier that graduates may be offered roles in which they can develop. Centrica, for example, gives HR graduates a one-year exposure to business activity, followed by a move into HR delivery roles. If such programmes exist, they are a good way of getting generalist HR experience. RBS has a three-year graduate programme that offers the chance of 12 months in a business-facing HR team as well as spells in other key areas – corporate HR, shared services and centres of expertise. There is no reason why development positions cannot be created for other staff. This might be for generalists to have exposure to specialist work or for specialists to rotate through a range of roles in the centre of expertise.

Modifying the structure is, of course, more fundamental. Rather than having the flexibility of adding or removing temporary positions, the organization can be more radical in adjusting its structure to permanently take account of these difficulties. It may be asked: does this not mean that the tail is wagging the dog – that the ideal structure to meet business needs is being tampered with just to satisfy the career aspirations of HR staff? Would this be allowed for other functions? If organizations change their structure just to ease career paths, it is bold and brave step, but, as we noted above, there are problems of segmentation with the new HR model that can be dealt with in a way that helps effectiveness and functional careers. Thus, assistant business partners can be introduced either to ease the load of their business partner boss or to get a better fit with the business unit structure. Assistant business partners could be given a small business unit to look after, under the guidance of the senior business partner. Similarly, there can be junior members of centres of expertise or corporate centre teams with responsibility for an easier policy area. The Prudential, for instance, allows transfers from the Ask HR helpdesk to an employee relations advisor, with the employee relations consultant role the next step up (Tamkin et al., 2006).

Without institutionalizing these structures, organizations can create temporary posts of, say, assistant business partner, trainee consultant or a deputy head of reward. These posts can be introduced to meet the needs of individual staff, and can be cut when they move on.

> At BOC Gases in the USA, a business partner has filled an assistant's role with a mature graduate. In exchange for helping with basic administration, the assistant gets involved in project work, especially regarding data collection. Having such a role, and having a high quality of incumbent, allows the business partner to deflect some of the 'grunge' work that comes his way without being unhelpful to his line customers. In particular, running the bonus scheme is a task that can be successfully delegated. It offers good learning for the assistant and some relief to the business partner.

We believe great care has to be exercised if these modifications to the most efficient structure (i.e. the minimum possible manning) start to cut across some of the clear boundaries set between transactional and transformational work, or even between policy development and execution. Those that have put administrative staff with business partners with the aim of deflecting transactional tasks away from the business partner that were not reaching the shared services centre, have found that business partners still get dragged into this kind of activity.

But without doing anything too drastic, job design can be influenced by giving staff interesting and worthwhile work to do, or, if that is difficult in the nature of the role, at least some job satisfaction. Not all staff hope to progress up the career ladder, but it is likely that they will want to enjoy their work. Too narrowly constructed posts may cause disenchantment and lead ultimately to a higher resignation rate. Conversely, through the structural change, if better-described roles emerge, with appropriate challenges to them, then retention rates may improve. This is what happened in the state of Massachusetts: reorganization brought individuals 'more varied and broader responsibilities to make work more interesting for them'; and this was in the context of a 25 per cent staffing reduction (Bramson, 2005).

As to taking business partners from line management, we remarked earlier that there is a benefit in having a balanced team in HR comprising business knowledge and HR expertise. Some business partner jobs are in particular suited to those with a business background. It should also be recognized that HR has to refresh itself by accepting new staff into the function. These people may be external recruits, but they can be transferees from line or general management. Remember that not all HR professionals are HR 'lifers'. Many of those currently regarded as part of the HR community started out in other areas and either deliberately chose HR or fell into HR by accident.

Nevertheless, care has to be exercised with resourcing decisions. If HR professionals think that all the good jobs go to outsiders (be they internal line appointments or external recruits) this will be dispiriting. It will result in good people leaving, frustrated by career blockages, or approaching their job in a more transactional manner.

Movement in should be balanced by movement out: HR professionals should be able to move to non-HR positions. In the past this has been difficult, and it still is for specialist posts, but business partners should have got a general business awareness that makes them well placed to move to operational roles. The spectacle of professionals from HR landing good jobs in the business does much for the credibility of the function. Assignments in from the line can have a similar effect as long as they are successful.

Changes to roles and structures in HR certainly pose the question of what an appropriate career path might look like for those with potential to move to senior HR positions. For the top generalist posts, such as senior business partners or HR directors, is specialist experience in a functional expert area (reward or learning and development) required? If candidates for these posts do not have some subject-matter expertise, do they risk being jacks of all trades – and does that matter? In the past industrial relations experience was essential, some now argue that learning and development or OD expertise has replaced it as the essential background to have. Do aspiring HR directors need to have done a non-HR job in a business unit or corporate role? There are those who argue that transfers of this sort are no longer necessary because business partners can get sufficient exposure to business issues through their current job. Then there is the balance between HR corporate and business partner roles. Most organizations would probably want to see experience in both, so that senior people have looked at the organization from different perspectives.

17 *What Can We Learn From Other Functions?*

In addressing a number of skill challenges described above, HR might reasonably look at how other functions have tackled some of the same problems. This will go some way to reducing a tendency towards insularity that has weakened the function's capability to transform itself. Good HR people look to other functions to see how they have developed. More commonly HR is in follow-my-leader mode. How often have you heard at external conferences the refrain that HR 'is of course merely following what X function did 5–10 years ago'? The most oft-quoted is that outsourcing HR transactions is much like the outsourcing of IT services of 10–15 years ago, when many large organizations, both public and private, contracted out the management of their IT infrastructure. We cover this in more detail, as well as giving other examples, including:

*   What can we learn about reporting and decision support from Finance?
*   What can we learn about employee segmentation and product development from Sales and Marketing?
*   What can HR learn about professional project management from business consulting?
*   What can we learn about HR operations from service providers?

What can we learn from Finance?

We identified earlier that the need for robust monitoring and reporting of the people measures or key performance indicators (KPIs) was critical to the changing role for HR departments in the move from administrators to strategic contributors. This step change in the expectations required from key functions by senior management of course has been seen before, in the manner that Finance sought to make a similar journey some time before HR.

Indeed, the journey made by Finance has some other similar marker posts on the way to those now being passed by HR. Firstly, the back office processes such as accounts payable and monthly preparation of management accounts were centralized to facilitate the opportunity to free up the finance director to act in a more advisory capacity and be less burdened by reconciliation issues. More recently this centralized production has morphed into Finance shared service functions in many private and public sector organizations.

Secondly, centres of expertise were created in areas such as tax, audit, treasury/cash management and, in larger commercial concerns, corporate finance capabilities emerged focusing on mergers and acquisitions and restructuring expertise. More recently, the centralization of decision-support reporting into either functional hubs or enhanced shared service operations has moved more activity away from the finance director.

If this combination sounds familiar, it should do, as many HR departments have since followed suit in centralizing back office HR processing, creating centres of expertise and, again in some cases, moving 'advisory' HR activity into a shared service centre.

So if HR is following Finance's path, what is there to learn from Finance's experience? The key lesson for HR is that it must obtain the same standard of quality in its decision-support and reporting as Finance. The finance function has built a credible reputation as the guardian of the corporate capital base by introducing and then owning the process of capital utilization metrics that any new investment must be judged against. Different enterprises will set their targets at different rates (e.g. setting a minimum rate of return at 12 per cent). The finance function often not only sets this minimum rate of return, it also designs the methodology for presenting the business case and the process for obtaining board-level approval. These mechanisms are used for IT investment, forays into new markets or products, acquisitions and even HR capital investment. Organizational performance is then measured against the metrics set by Finance. This process can be extended so that all management reporting is integrated into single document, allowing 'joined-up' thinking in understanding how the business is performing.

By owning the governance structures, approval processes and the underpinning theories around strategic investments, Finance's seat at the table as a key part of the decision process is a given. The challenge for HR is to create a similar level of authority in its sphere of operations, so that it is part of the decision-making process, not just involved in the implementation. In our experience there are few examples of where HR plays this role. Indeed, in many organizations it is not obvious that people management data is seriously reviewed by the senior management team. Why is this the case? There are a few factors:

* HR professionals do not have the skill set in undertaking data analysis and diagnosing issues to the same degree as accountants.
* Many organizations have been more reluctant to invest in appropriate technological solutions to help the systemization of people management reporting than they have been with financial reporting.
* Organizations may take this approach because they take financial information more seriously than that relating to employees or because HR has not produced a sufficiently strong business case. In truth, especially in private sector firms, financial data drives the business in a way that people management data does not.

It has not been previously so necessary for the HR function, valued for its technical capabilities in areas such as industrial relations, remuneration or training, to be effective in management reporting at the same level as Finance. However, given the repositioning of the role of HR, the growing interest in human capital and the coming adoption of more rigorous 'accountancy-type' reporting, the need for good HR decision-support has increased significantly. This would help identify investment possibilities and rates of return on investments. Putting the benefits in numerical terms may be attractive to decision-makers conditioned to evaluate quantitative data. The emergence of a more structured form of reporting and, with it, changed relationships with its key stakeholders, may be leading to a real paradigm shift in allowing HR to be on the front foot driving change in the organization based on improved management information.

With this in mind, the HR function of the future will need to follow in Finance's footsteps and address its skills levels, its data collection methods and its technology. Learning from Finance could indeed be enhanced by acquiring the relevant skills (especially diagnosis) from those with Finance backgrounds. Moreover, with the true integration of enterprise-wide solutions such as SAP, Oracle and Peoplesoft, which can all cover Finance and HR needs, the opportunity for integrated decision-support reporting is already available.

What can we learn from Sales and Marketing?

With the changes to the profile of the working population described on page 90, as we have noted, the view that a 'one-size-fits-all' employment proposition can be used looks increasingly out of touch. Some organizations responded in the early 1990s by adopting cafeteria-style benefit packages to allow some tinkering and customization of terms and conditions. Allowed, perhaps, was the trading of pensions for shopping vouchers by younger employees, or cars for extra cash by those who had no need for a car. The scope of the offering did not really facilitate any proper differentiation between employees. Since then, the idea of personalization of benefits, so that staff can choose the package that suits their circumstances, has grown in number and complexity, aided by better technological decision and administrative systems. None the less, for many organizations the extent of flexibility is limited by cost and the range of benefits on offer.

But some organizations have gone further than this over the last five years. Companies, led most famously by Tesco, have used finely honed sales and marketing skills to segment their employee groups much more specifically and to improve product packaging. The People Insight Unit at Tesco has been created to examine how employees could be viewed more like customers. This is an approach, taken from Sales and Marketing, which relies on gathering detailed evidence on customer/staff preferences, permitting much more customer differentiation. It has allowed the creation of broader, bespoke offerings, not limited to reward-type benefits. Included have been focused career development, flexible employment terms and conditions (including bespoke working hours) and tailored communication, as well as the more usual benefits.

In some companies employee benefits are 'sold' to staff. Such an approach is not new, as it is used by banks in their customer products, such as packaged bank accounts, credit cards and loans to aid customer retention. You may ask, though, what this is to do with HR? Interestingly RBS has found that the more products staff take under its employee benefits programme, the greater their propensity to remain with the company. In other words, product marketing has helped deliver one of HR's key goals of staff retention.

> RBS sells its RBSelect benefits scheme by bundling products into packaged products such as its 'YourCar' offer (competitive insurance from its Direct Line or Churchill subsidiaries, breakdown cover from Green Flag and car leasing through its own car division) or using direct sales techniques, such as benefit mailshots, on specific products (e.g. Apple products such as laptops and i-Pods or special wine offers).

Some companies are even now considering approaches based on the notion of a market of one. In other words, if organizations want to connect to employees they need to understand that, however much they segment their approach by some form of categorization, they are still grouping together individuals with different needs and interests. The challenge is then to find ways of designing offers on this basis that do not become too costly to administer.

So what other skills can we lean from marketing to add greater credibility to the changing HR role?

Data-mining skills can be used to manipulate the organization's employee data much more rigorously. This can be in areas such as skills profiling, development needs identification, past experience tracking and so on. This can allow far better career management and decision-making on resources. It facilitates making finely honed job offers, instead of taking the open 'grapeshot' approach that many organizations use today in appointing staff internally.

Marketing has applied techniques in direct mail and general promotion that could be used in enhancing employee communication on key policies, issues or business changes. A wider range of media beyond paper, such as internet, mobile texting and video streaming, can be exploited.

Employee attitude surveys can be improved by considering customer surveying techniques. Moreover, in certain organizations, results from customer surveys can be powerfully combined with those from employees to understand better the link between staff engagement and customer satisfaction (see, for example, Barber *et al.*, 1999; Robinson *et al.*, 2004).

Market sampling and testing skills applied to pilot new HR practices or products can be employed before general release. This is particularly important in that not all HR initiatives use 'market research' techniques to establish what customers want before launching them. Using pilots can allow the organization to gain good feedback on the potential value and pitfalls of what is being proposed.

Promotion of the HR function itself would benefit from sales and marketing techniques. In particular, following improved definition of customer needs, which we have argued is essential, HR can tailor its offering to match. It then should spend time in devising approaches that will show to customers that it is responding. As we described earlier, launching the new operating model has allowed HR both to describe the new services and to market them.

We know that some of the elements of these marketing methods will be found in the very large, commercial organizations. However, taking advantage of such skills and experience would, for the majority of HR functions, be good policy.

What can HR learn from business consulting?

With the use of business partnering and consulting pools and the interest in applying robust analysis to understand the link between business and HR metrics, it would seem obvious to look at how professional business consultancy deals with these issues. However, in our experience, few HR functions have thought about, let alone adopted, the key principles of the business consultancy operating model, especially the management of projects. Inputs from this source might well help the business awareness, commercialism and, ultimately, the credibility of the HR function. There are probably five key principles of a business consultancy model which HR functions should seriously consider adopting:

1. Making sure the senior 'partner' owns the client group and is primarily rewarded by delivering value. We talk elsewhere of the role of the business partner in the HR model; there is still much to learn from the way in which the equivalent in a big consultancy would be positioned and operate. They would be experienced, credible individuals with a certain gravitas.

2. Investing in good analytical skills to build a coherent picture of business problems. The emergence of human capital reporting offers a more holistic measurement tool and is helpful in that it pushes the HR function towards the level of skill and expertise expected in external business consultancies. Perhaps because many large consultancies are linked to accountancy firms, they have put a premium on numeracy and have hired maths/science graduates to provide the deep analysis needed to support consultancy.

3. Ensuring rigorous time allocation and resource planning tools are embedded in the systems that help manage the use of consultants. These will not just facilitate time and resource management on existing projects, they will also provide good management information to inform line colleagues on the use of their resources and to estimate future projects. Being realistic with clients about completion dates helps reinforce HR as a business-aware function. Being clear how it spends its time should demonstrate the value HR is adding.

4. Requiring consultants to follow good practice in project management, e.g. using the concept of a project 'life cycle'. The creation of formal proposals of work activity, setting terms of reference and project plans, stakeholder mapping (to identify key people to influence), risk and issue logging, structured project governance and regular reporting are all aspects of a good project discipline that should be used more widely than they are. Such an approach not only offers a vital tool in effectively managing projects, it also adds to the professionalism of the way assignment is conducted. Failure to adhere in practice to these principles is likely to show up HR as poor at running its projects and lacking the necessary discipline. It then gets criticized for slow delivery, partly because it has not kept stakeholders aware of any complexities and well briefed on progress.

5. Conducting formal post project reviews. These can capture the learning from the project. For external consultants, this information is used to help future client 'pitches' and is a critical way of getting future business. Internally, HR staff, be they from the consultancy pool or from the centres of expertise, should similarly identify lessons from successful and less successful projects so that this can inform how best to support clients in the future.

A sixth area where HR could take advantage of business consultancy experience is managing charge-out regimes. However, we recognize that such a mechanism is not always attractive, as we described in Chapter 7. It may produce unwelcome bureaucracy. But for those organizations that do have a more commercial model, again, business consultancy has much to offer in terms of tools, techniques and mindsets.

What can we learn about HR operations from service providers?

As some organizations have already done, HR can also learn ideas on how to run its back office operations, such as shared service centres, from practices commonplace in commercial service centres. Many contact centres have adopted such techniques as call management, call monitoring, telephony-based customer service models and workflow to refer more specialist queries, call tracking and reporting, adoption of service levels and so on.

More recently, organizations such as GE are examining at how to adopt 'lean' manufacturing techniques in their HR functions, following from work already completed using Six Sigma techniques. Six Sigma is a quality improvement methodology. It focuses on functional conformity and has been used to check on the extent to which products meet specification. Its ideas have been extended to other environments, not wholly straightforwardly.

> WMC Resources Ltd uses Six Sigma to improve its processes in HR and other functions. Project teams are asked to define the problem, measure its effects and test potential solutions before implementing them. The authorization of their domestic travel policy was an example of simplifying a business process (www.iqpc.com).

Ideas from supply chain thinking can also be utilized to HR operations. Firstly, the notion of re-engineering to reflect end-to-end processes can be applied to the employee life cycle (from entry to exit). Secondly, organizations can recognize the collective buying power of the organization is so much stronger than that of individual business units operating independently. Just as logistics have leveraged organizational scale, so can HR. For example, centralizing the purchase of recruitment services may lead to large cost savings.

What can we learn about BPO from IT?

We sense that, in considering HR outsourcing in the twenty-first century, HR functions have understood some of the lessons from IT's experience in the twentieth. Messages from their experience include:

- Conduct a risk assessment which considers the technological, operational and legal implications of outsourcing.
- Undertake a full estimation of the cost/benefits of outsourcing, including the non-financial, e.g. skills impact, cultural effect. This to be done on a long-term as well as a short-term basis.
- Bring an end-user perspective to contract specification and selection so as to minimize the sense that this is HR looking after its own interests, not those of customers.
- Do not outsource if there is not a flourishing external market. Competition drives down the price: monopolies have the opposite effect.
- Do not lock the organization into long and inflexible contracts that will be expensive if changes are ever required.
- Do not outsource problems. Improve processes before outsourcing, otherwise the supplier will make a financial killing.
- Fully understand service costs after process improvement before testing the market. Remember that the contractor has to make a profit, so see where they would find scope to improve on the reformed model.
- Ensure there is sufficient internal expertise to manage an external contract. The danger is that contractors will run rings round inexperienced HR representatives.
- Set up proper monitoring systems to flag up any performance failures early enough for them to be rectified without too much damage.
- Offer rewards to successful contract performance, as well as penalties for failure.
- Ensure there is good communication between the parties. This means both regular formal meetings and informal discussion.
- Take care with the transition to a new service provider so that the service level is maintained and that skills and knowledge are not lost.

Certainly, there are examples where these messages have been learnt. For example, Ian Muir, in discussing Cable & Wireless's experience of minimizing risks in outsourcing (Scott-Jackson *et al.*, 2005), asserts that 'a broken process will get worse, not better, if you outsource it'. He also points out the need for contractual flexibility, rewards for successful contractual performance, retaining 'tacit' knowledge of those leaving the company, and managing stakeholders' objections.

Conclusion

We wrote this book because, having written one on HR shared services, we were conscious that many organizations were more concerned with processes and structures, and less with content and skills in their search for strategic added value. Perhaps the first is a necessary precursor to the second, but it is not sufficient. Research by Lawler and Mohrman (2003) suggests that, on its own, the repositioning of HR through structural change, outsourcing and e-HR is not enough to achieve the goal of strategic repositioning. Time and energy may be released from changes to structures, roles and processes. What is critical is how this time is used. If HR is to be a strategic contributor, not merely an efficient administrator, it has to ensure that it has the capability to use the time to deliver the necessary results.

HR in large complex organizations has achieved a lot in cost reduction and focus through consolidation, standardization and automation. The segmentation of activities that has separated administration, expertise, governance and business partnership is a logical approach. Bringing information and administration together via service and call/contact centres allows for economies of scale with benefits that can flow from the use of standardized processes. Ensuring that HR retains deep technical know-how through the creation of centres of expertise is vital when organizations are becoming ever more sophisticated in their policies and practices on reward, resourcing, learning and development, etc. Business partners are critical to HR's success in aligning what HR does with what the organization requires. And a corporate centre must maintain adherence to values and mission, to the overarching strategy and to overall, holistic organizational need.

So far so good! There are problems with the operating model that we have covered in the book. Its very logic contains the seeds of its own difficulties. Segmentation can mean isolation, poor communication and learning. In operating this model, HR has to be very mindful of the need to integrate: to link policy with implementation, individual business alignment with the corporate perspective, problem logging at the contact centre with policy development in the centres of expertise, and so on. Of perhaps greater significance is the 'polo' problem: the gap in the middle. Is HR giving sufficient support to line managers on operational HR matters? What do we mean by that? Is HR helping with the difficult, individual cases, concerning attendance or discipline? Is it giving what the line wants by way of support on recruitment, performance management, training and development, etc.? There are two ways of answering these questions: looking at whether HR is set up to assist and whether it should be. Taking the practical issue first, the new HR model can struggle with operational HR work. Business partners, certainly, should not be involved. If they are, there is no way that they can do the strategic task with which they are charged. Centres of expertise are designed to develop policy or to give high-level advice, not to provide day-to-day support. A contact centre can give line managers information and interpretation on policies and procedures. Again they are not, generally, geared up to give continuing assistance. Some organizations have consultancy or project pools, but their focus is on longer-term, systemic intervention.

To meet this need for operational support, some organizations have made adjustments to the 'pure' model. They have given a casework role to the shared service centre. Time can be spent dealing with individual issues, brought by line managers or employees. This is an easy adjustment to the model. It still can mean a remote and ad hoc service. It is not a personalized or regular source of advice and guidance to line managers. Other organizations have introduced 'delivery' units or HR delivery managers. These provide much more operational support. The former gives resourcing flexibility, as it is another pool of HR advisers. The latter offers more permanent provision, in that the delivery manager is assigned to a business unit(s). The problem that then presents itself is: to whom do these people report? If it is to the business partner, surely they will drag him/her into firefighting, operational issues? If it is not to the business partner that they report, then to whom? None of the other HR units (centres of expertise, shared services centre or corporate centre) make much sense if the delivery managers are organized by business unit. Although, having said that, a proportion of the MOD's shared services agency (PPPA) will be located in the business units to offer line managers casework support. It will be interesting to see how this works out: whether it is a temporary feature to ease transition to a new devolution model or whether it becomes a key element of HR service delivery.

The second way of answering the question of operational support is to challenge whether it is necessary in the first place. Those organizations that have seen devolution of people management responsibility to managers as a primary aim, may well not see it as desirable to return to 'supporting' the line in this way. The argument is that once HR starts to help with case management, or with processes such as recruitment, it will soon become a 'prop' for managers to lean on.

This debate introduces another of the big questions: what is the role of HR? Organizations have been keen to redefine themselves in terms of being more strategic, adding value, being business aligned and so on, but have they thought hard enough about the relationship to management and, indeed, employees? There is the longstanding concern that HR should avoid being management's servant, doing its bidding. Yet all the pressure is on HR to become more customer focused. If this is not a master/servant relationship, then it is a client/service one. Taking that position to its logical conclusion, HR should indeed provide what line managers want. If they need help with people management or recruitment, they should have it. If they want HR present at disciplinary interviews, HR should be. Line managers retain (obtain in some organizations) the authority to decide what to do with staff, but HR can be there as consultants, advisors and gofers. This is a far cry from business partnership.

In a strange way, coming to HR's aid in this debate is corporate management. It is attracted to devolution as it can justify cutting HR numbers and costs. Similarly, e-HR will be backed in so far as it delivers reductions in expenditure. Some (many?) senior managers are not that interested in the philosophical debate about HR becoming more strategic and managers taking on their people management responsibilities. The top brass is concerned merely with efficiency; or, if they are concerned with effectiveness, it is in a different way. They may see outsourcing as another means of driving down numbers, if less obviously costs. It is the combination of these thrusts (cost-driven devolution, automation, self-service and outsourcing) that led some to be so worried about HR's future. In the words of Paul Birt, General Manager – HR Shared Services, at Siemens: 'HR will have its legs cut off.' It will have a strategic role, but no means of performing it. It will lose its ability to integrate people management activities. Its ability to know what is going on in the organization will be threatened, being too far removed, at the strategic level, from the daily happenings of organizational life. This fear is not so very different from Tyson and York (2000) talking about the risk of the 'balkanization' of the HR role, as more and more bits are externalized. Or John Philpott's (2001) concern that organizations 'risk throwing out the strategic people management baby with the administrative bath water' by viewing HR too narrowly and outsourcing administrative activities. Similarly, Pfau and Cundiff (2002) worry that: 'The recent emphasis on strategic at the expense of operations has hurt HR. In their rush to become strategists, HR executives and managers have dropped the ball on some fundamental aspects of HR.'

So HR is now faced with the conflicting pressures of a cost-reduction agenda from senior management encouraging HR's withdrawal from day-to-day people management activities and a consumerist model that suggests that HR should meeting the customers' stated needs. Fortunately, over the hill comes the Seventh Cavalry in the shape of the people management agenda. Coming together is the combination of a tight labour market, with employees who are more self-reliant and less deferential and a knowledge economy that demands quality inputs from a well-educated and motivated workforce. This presents a new management challenge. To help meet it, a whole raft of research emphasizes, amongst other things, that engaged employees will offer greater commitment and performance; that line managers have a critical role to play in generating the right employment climate; and that people management practices (such as employee involvement, work discretion, sharing in organizational rewards, etc.) help deliver superior performance. Whether this is described as a human capital agenda or as one of its subsets – talent management, employer of choice – it puts employees at the heart of business success.

Not all senior management may yet have been won over by the argument that employees can really make a difference to business success, but it gives HR a robust platform to work from. Far from being 'human remains' or 'an endangered species', HR can argue that it is the part of the organization that can orchestrate the employee performance. It will not play all the parts – line managers will largely do that – but it can conduct, so that the sum is greater that the parts. It can ensure, keeping this metaphor going, that there are no discordant notes. The performance will be ruined if there are too many players playing off key or hitting bum notes. This image of HR conducting the orchestra, performing the employee engagement suite, does give some answers to the difficult role questions we have raised.

Line devolution is essential because it is the managers who have responsibility for their staff. They should do all the tasks necessary to ensure employees know their work, the purposes of the organization and their role within it. They should recognize and reward staff's achievements, motivate them when necessary, chide them if their performance slips and be available if they have problems. HR should be there in reserve if managers need some professional advice or merely a second opinion. But HR should all the time be encouraging greater self-reliance. As managers become more skilful in people management, then HR should withdraw more. What HR should not tolerate (and this is clearly where HR is not management's servant) is either managers abrogating their people management responsibilities, since that prevents the necessary bond with employees being established, or managers taking action that violates the organization's values or principles. Moreover, in our opinion, HR would be justified in intervening if managers, far from building human capital, were depleting it. As Neil Roden says, 'HR is right at times to interfere in the employment relationship. It can't afford line managers screwing up on precious talent.' So, managers who demotivate staff, and/or cause absence or resignation rates to rise, should be challenged. Managers who risk legal action because they inadvertently favour one group of staff over another, or who fail in their duty of care, can also expect to be challenged. The conductor would always be justified in objecting to a player whose instrument was badly tuned because their performance damages not just their own contribution, but the success of the whole performance. So it will be right on occasion for HR to oppose management practices, which might be ill thought through, parochial or short-term focused. In these situations, HR should not simply bend the knee, but assert corporate principles or perspective. The key is in getting the balance right between intervention and non-involvement.

Why describe HR as the conductor of the people management piece? It is the function best placed to oversee the whole people management effort. It may not be the best musician, most able to play the people management tune, but it can be the best co-ordinator and integrator. HR can demonstrate that its role is legitimate through having the requisite knowledge of the research and good practice in people management. It should know about what in general terms (not individual – that is the line manager's responsibility) is likely to attract, retain and motivate staff to be productive and aligned with business goals. This is why we describe the content of its work around the organizational proposition, capability and effectiveness. With the conviction (justified by evidence) that increasingly business success will be based on good employment relationships, HR should grab hold of the people management theme. It should be the function that guides the organization in terms of describing and branding the employment offer, setting out a skills growth programme, institutionalizing development measures, testing employee opinion, building social capital, putting in place mechanisms that encourage staff to be valued and involved. The model shown in Figure 4.1 describes how HR's lead on people management policies and practices offers a framework within which line managers act.

This brings us back to the relationship between HR and the line. If all the effort with individuals is for managers to discharge, with HR to support as necessary, the same logic applies to operational support beyond case management. The line should be as self-sufficient as possible, but, for reasons of time, skill or expertise, it is perfectly legitimate for managers to call upon HR's involvement. In conducting a recruitment selection process or training exercise, the line may reasonably ask for assistance. HR should be geared up to provide it either directly or via trusted suppliers. Help should not be universally on offer, it is a matter of horses for courses. In some parts of the organization it is in everyone's interest if HR is more involved; in others, the line should be encouraged to trust its own judgement.

But how in the new world does HR relate to employees? If case management is a line activity, then what role does HR have beyond providing an intranet and call centre? And this is an important question because HR's claim to fame is that it knows about employees' wishes: it needs to be able to take the temperature of the organization. Firstly, HR should not underestimate the importance of designing, presenting and interpreting policies with the employee perspective in mind. As a BT manager says: HR 'needs to remember that employees are at the end of the policies HR designs'. This should be self-evident, but too many organizations have become excessively management focused in policy development.

Secondly, HR can use the improved management information to assess trends in employee attitudes and behaviour. People management metrics need to get better – to be more predictive – but even now organizations do not sufficiently exploit the data they have. As we have said earlier, some organizations suffer from data overload, but focus and action are in short supply. Organizations should be looking at two areas of performance in two dimensions: the efficiency and effectiveness of people management and the efficiency and effectiveness of the HR function. Efficiency measures have tended to predominate. Although they are important, metrics should be shifting away from concentrating only on process mechanics to human capital type metrics, as Dean Royles argues: 'How do you measure the contribution of people to the success of the organization?' Information on resignation, absence or health and on employee attitudes may be inputs to this key outcome measure, and it is line managers' responsibility to examine the implications from their own business unit perspective. HR should be taking the organizational learning from the data, before guiding the organization on what actions managers should take. It should then be checking whether these actions have been successful, not just from the organizational, but also from the employee, perspective.

Thirdly, our view is that HR is not employed to represent or champion employees, but, as we have said, it should intervene if individuals are suffering from poor management. At a corporate/business unit level, HR should assist management colleagues in understanding how business decisions will affect the workforce. This suggests that HR should be bolder in its education role, telling managers the facts about how valuing and involving employees can deliver positive business results. HR should not be shy to press the message that talent is an asset to the organization. It is not just precious, but precarious. It can walk or sulk. It can engage or disengage. Its problems may be work related or purely personal. So people have to be nurtured. HR can be more assertive about the risks managers may run in sailing close to the legal wind: the thought of an appearance at an employment tribunal should concentrate their minds.

If HR performs its role in the right way, it can be strategic, professional, an effective regulator and a change agent. But success will only come from carrying out the complete range of activities in a holistic manner. This requires a model that links HR work to line managers' people management efforts and both of these to business performance. This can be described as 'a human capital model', 'an employee engagement model' or 'the service/profit chain': it does not matter what it is called as long as it integrates the people management effort and gives it a purpose. That is why we emphasized organizational proposition, capability and effectiveness. Attracting people into the organization should be facilitated by a brand that describes the organizational vision. The capability required needs to reflect business demand, though in some cases it drives business activity. And organizational effectiveness ensures that staff have the right environment in which to perform with the correct balance between management control over their activities and freedom for them to shape their work.

This interlinked chain should not be regarded as an academic construct. It should be a description of what HR ought to be doing. It should be action oriented. This brings us back to strategy: if HR is to be strategic, it will work in the way we now describe. Strategic contribution has to be at a number of levels. It is about setting corporate direction, but it is also about implementing strategy which might be about translating a strategic intent on people into a workable reality, monitoring performance and evaluating the results. As we described in the section on HR as Strategist, the strategic contribution should both explain the human capital model at the outset and then make it happen. This includes dealing with the content elements described above.

We regard the task that HR faces as exciting and challenging. Our only doubt concerns whether HR has the capability to deliver. We are less concerned with the overall structure, more about the skills to perform the business partner role in particular. Even Dave Ulrich has conceded that: 'All my life, I've tried to build organizations as systems, but … I've not thought as much about people' (Conley, 2005). Shared services operations, if well designed, give important economies of scale so long as they link in well with other parts of the function. Centres of expertise should provide technical professionalism, all the more necessary with a sophisticated workforce. They need to guard against getting too isolated, becoming filled with policy wonks who have little grip on the reality of organizational life and are driven by notions of functional best practice. The corporate centre has important roles to play in regulating and auditing practice across the organization. It must find the right balance between a centralizing tendency towards consistency through uniformity, and decentralization pressure to respond to specific business unit needs. The current concentration on standardization means that the former pull is the stronger at the moment. The corporate centre must take care that the pendulum does not violently swing the other way, because centralization has been pushed too hard, since this will lose all the benefits of commonality. This is a tough job in dealing with the inevitable corporate politics, but one HR directors are used to playing.

The real concern is the business partner role. We agree with Kevin Green at Royal Mail who said that the 'jury is still out' on the business partner role, not because the 'aspiration was wrong,' but because of implementation. 'In many cases HR directors have simply rebranded their HR managers and have not developed the capability to play these roles' (Green, 2005). The detail of the role has been insufficiently thought through, discussed with customers and debated with the potential incumbents. Organizations have latched on to the S word – strategic – without defining what is meant by it. Or, if they have tried to, they have been in some cases handicapped by a desire on the part of the business partners for a comprehensive answer, where only an outline is possible. In general terms, it is right to have embedded HR managers with their line manager colleagues, but it is a tricky role for them to play. There is the risk of going native, as some embedded US journalists were accused of being in the Iraq war. They do not see the bigger picture and view the world from a narrow perspective. Always asserting the corporate view will equally fail, since the business partners will be seen less as colleagues than as fifth columnists. The happy medium – where, as we have said, HR should on occasion challenge because managers are getting it wrong, and help when the request is *reasonable* – demands real skill, especially judgement. Adapting Caldwell's description of Ulrich's whole model to apply to just the business partner element, he challenges that the business partner offers 'an extraordinary idealised vision' where HR is 'an agency of competitive success, organizational change and human progress' (2001). In other words, the business partner is expected to be fully conversant with the business, but professionally competent; capable of being a coach to the line, but also of being a regulator of management behaviour; not a deliverer of services, but a broker for services s/he does not control; a strategic player and change maker. These activities should be focused on achieving greater organizational performance through people. All these challenges have to be met between 9 and 5! It is no wonder that it is hard to find staff to live up to this aspiration.

Instead, organizations report that they are finding it difficult to identify internal candidates for business partner roles or even to recruit successfully externally. This is not surprising. It is especially difficult for colleagues to suddenly change their modus operandi and, more importantly, relationships, and be able operate in the new manner. If you have been schooled in being customer responsive, operationally alert, there to put out all the fires or be on hand whenever there is a problem, it is hard to shift to the new role. This requires rather more distance from the customers, operating on a higher plane, giving oneself time and space to think and network so that interventions are well considered and address deeper-seated or longer-term issues.

External recruits do not have the problem of shifting an established set of relationships with colleagues and they may have the advantage being unconstrained by cultural norms, but where have they developed their strategic thinking skills? The danger is that organizations will be chasing the small number of people who have the talent to operate in the new way and have had sufficient experience to develop their capability.

We suggest that organizations be a bit more modest in their ambitions and allow a bit more time before passing judgements. Firstly, as we have said, the business partner role may need some adjustment, primarily to satisfy line management needs, but also to be within the compass of what staff can currently do. Secondly, organizations should invest in enriching their internal resource through education and training, as some leading edge organizations are doing. This will improve the stock. The third change is to tackle the flow by encouraging quality people into HR. The business partner role offers a great opportunity for those who want to combine technical skill and business awareness in a way that drives the organization forward. HR directors should be creating the right brand for their function, as of the organization as a whole. It should be realistic it what it offers, but that does not mean it cannot be exciting. HR should be more positive about proclaiming the benefits of working within it. Variety, challenge, access (to senior management) and organizational overview are some of the elements that successful HR managers get from their work. The fact that 83 per cent of those currently working in the function would choose jobs in HR if they had their time again (Tamkin *et al.*, 2006) says it all.

So, taking the long view: upskilling managers so that there are better people managers, and improving the stock of HR talent and the flows into the function, will enable the business partner role to meet its promise. Critical to this aspiration is making career development function better within HR. The new operating model threatens traditional career paths. Organizations are only getting round now to thinking of how to tackle this problem. There are a number of solutions we described earlier, but it is the philosophical point we want to get across here. Organizations will not be able to build the business partners of the future if they do not invest in career development. By that we mean consciously looking at how individuals will get the requisite experience. Better CIPD courses (in the sense of being more business attuned) and a wider range of CPD initiatives are necessary to improve capability, but they are not sufficient. A lot of HR learning is on the job. So, organizations should be examining what sort of career paths will deliver specialists (for the centres of expertise) and what will help generalists (for business partner roles) to grow. Because of the segmentation, organizations need to use bridging mechanisms to allow people to gain experience so that they can move from service centres, consultancy roles or expert positions. This may mean temporary assignments, secondments or projects. More permanent adjustment to the model (e.g. through delivery managers) may also deal with customer reservations about the new model.

And outsourcing should be viewed in the context of skill development too. Finding external suppliers for specific tasks may make economic sense and in some cases deliver improved service. Contracting out large swathes of HR operation has to not only pass more stringent efficiency tests (because it is harder to reverse direction), but also to prove that it will not impair the growth of HR talent. Fragmentation is already a risk with the new model in service delivery terms, making it harder to develop and share skills weakens the model still further.

It is interesting, in relation to our view that it is the skills of staff in the HR function which will unlock the door to success, that Dean Royles's definition of success has a large number of skills-related elements to it. Within the NHS, HR will be seen to have arrived where there is always an HR director on the board, a fair proportion of ex-HR people are appointed as CEOs, line managers want to go into HR as a career development move, HR is seen as the expert on organizational change, and that change is being managed in a positive manner. The first half of this list is all about getting the quality of people into the function so that it can claim senior posts. Success will breed success, encouraging others into the function. With these skills at its disposal it can tackle the key tasks, such as change management, which are the organizational priority.

So to conclude: the HR teams in organizations are generally moving in the right direction, but they need to give closer attention to the following:

- Better defining the role of the function and, in particular, in its relationships with line management and employees. HR teams should secure the support of executive management for the purpose and aims of the HR function and be more proactive in getting people management more firmly on the organizational agenda. They should ensure that the devolution of people management responsibilities is working effectively, but that HR has the means to understand and describe employee opinion. And they should be prepared to intervene, where necessary, in manager/employee relationships to protect the overall interests of the organization.

- Being clearer on the key areas of HR activity. We suggest focusing on developing capability, ensuring that it is properly utilized and that staff are sufficiently engaged that they do a good job. These activities encompass strategic direction, change management and the deployment of professional expertise. Areas such as CSR, knowledge management, employee well-being, OD and social capital will merit more attention in the future. Much of the effort will be directed towards facilitating line management's maximization of the employee contribution. Sometimes, instead, HR will need to act as the corporate 'regulator', described above.

- Designing an operating model that combines cost efficiency, through obtaining economies of scale and working with well-constructed processes, and providing a quality service which meets customers' needs. This will require bringing customers on board with the model by communicating more effectively HR's ambitions, listening to their requirements and checking that HR is delivering. An approach that insists on the standardization of key processes and services (e.g. payroll, records, information provision), but gives flexibility to how business units resource others (e.g. recruitment, training or employee relations) might offer the best solution to the choice versus compulsion dilemma.

- Limiting the risks of service segregation and poor communication, by more clearly specifying the nature of the key roles within the function the relationships between them. HR should give particular attention to the business partner role by describing activities that allow a strategic contribution to be made, but also an integrated HR service. This may require the creation of roles (or parts of existing roles) dedicated to providing operational support to the line.

- Taking care to invest in technology where it supports helpful standardization, cuts costs and improves service, but not in such a way (or at such a pace) that it becomes a case of the tail wagging the organizational dog. Manager self-service and employee self-service should reduce administrative effort not redirect it – away from HR and onto the line and staff.

- Choosing to outsource when there is a clear cost or quality advantage, taking into consideration both long-term and short-term effects and non-financial implications. HR teams should be very wary of outsourcing where the market is immature or organizational circumstances are dynamic. This suggests selective and progressive outsourcing, where it makes sense, rather than wholesale externalization.

- Building up functional capability through training, development and improved career management in order to fulfil existing roles and build up expertise for the future. These interventions should concentrate not just on technical skills, but on business awareness/ sensitivity and the personal characteristics which will make for confident, impressive and robust practitioners. Professional development is not just for those new to the function, nor just for those with the potential for senior positions, but should be available to all so that they can become more effective. HR should learn from what other organizations do well and should take relevant ideas from other functions, such as Finance and Marketing. Moreover, good practice ought to be disseminated within HR itself.

- Making sure that the function is measuring the right things for the right reasons, attributing responsibility to those that can make a difference. This means monitoring not only the efficiency, but also the effectiveness of the HR contribution, distinguishing it from the part played by people management (largely the responsibility of line management) and establishing the extent to which the function is achieving the positioning it seeks, especially its strategic input.

- Evaluating the results of any people management policy or practice initiatives to aid future learning. And ensuring that action (not just words) follows any measurement or evaluation.

By these means HR can make itself the strategic business contributor it wants to be.

References

Age Wave and The Concours Group (2005) 'Attitude and Engagement creates Turbulence in Corporate America'. management-issues.com, posted 23 June.

Arnot, C. (2006) 'How the MBA Brand has Lost Value', *Guardian*, 3 January.

Augar, P. and Palmer, J. (2003) *The Rise of the Player Manager*. Harmondsworth: Penguin.

Barber, L. and Wolfe, H. (2005) *CSR: Doing Good or Doing Good Business*. The Institute for Employment Studies: www.employment-studies.co.uk.

Barber, L., Hayday, S. and Bevan, S. (1999) *From People to Profits*. The Institute for Employment Studies, Report 355. Brighton: IES.

Barber, L., Hill, D., Hirsh, W. and Tyers, C. (2005) *Fishing for Talent in a Wider Pool*. The Institute for Employment Studies, Report 421. Brighton: IES.

Barney, J. (1991) 'Firm Resources and Sustained Competitive Advantage', *Journal of Management*, 17, (1).

Bartlett, C. and Ghoshal, S. (1992) 'Beyond Strategy to Purpose', *Harvard Business Review*, November/December.

Becker, B. E., Huselid, M. A. and Ulrich, D. (2001) *The HR Scorecard: Linking People, Strategy and Performance*. Boston, MA: Harvard Business School Press.

Bevan, S. and Hayday, S. (1994) *Towing the Line*. The Institute for Employment Studies, Report 254. Brighton: IES.

Birchenhough, M. (2004) 'A Change is Good as a Rest', *People Management*, 20 May.

Booz Allen Hamilton (2004) G A Survey. www.boozallen.com.

Bramson, R. N. (2005) 'A Sequel to Shaking up the State Workforce, An HR Shared Services Model', *IPMA News*, January.

Brenner, L. (1996) 'The Disappearing HR Department', *CFO*, Vol. 12, No. 3.

Brocket, S. (2004) 'Becoming a Business Partner: HR at Coca-Cola Enterprises', *Strategic HR Review*, Vol. 3, Issue 2, January/February.

Brown, D. (2005) 'Is CSR the New GDP?', *Personnel Today*, 9 August.

Buyens, D. and de Vos, A. (2001) 'Perceptions of the HR Function', *Human Resource Management Journal*, Vol. 11, Part 3.

Cabrera, A. and Cabrera, E. F. (2003) 'Strategic Human Resource Evaluation', *HR Planning Society*, Vol. 26, March.

Caldwell, R. (2001) 'Champions, Adapters, Consultants and Synergists: The New Change Agents in HRM', *Human Resource Management Journal*, Vol. 11, No. 3.

Carter, A., Hirsh, W. and Aston, J. (2002) *Resourcing the Training and Development Function*. The Institute for Employment Studies, Report 390. Brighton: IES.

CBI/Alba (2004) Off-Shoring Survey. Available from: http://www.personneltoday.com/Articles/2004/11/08/26582/UK+business+under+pressure+to+relocate+overseas.htm

CIPD (2003a) *HR Survey: Where We Are, Where We're Heading*. London: CIPD.

CIPD (2003b) *Managing Employee Careers, Survey Report*. London: CIPD.

CIPD (2005a) *2005 Reward Management Survey*. London: CIPD.

CIPD (2005b) *HR: Where Is Your Career Heading?* London: CIPD.

CIPD (2005c) *Fit for Business: Building a Strategic HR Function in the Public Sector*. London: CIPD.

CIPD (2005d) *Making CSR Happen*. London: CIPD.

Clake, R. and Robinson, V. (2005) 'Stay Tuned', *People Management*, 19 May.

Conley, L. (2005) 'The Once and Future Consultant', *Fast Company*, August.

Connolly, T. R., Mardis, W. and Down, J. W. (1997) 'Transforming Human Resources', *Management Review*, June.

Cunningham, I. and Hyman, J. (1999) 'Devolving Human Resource Responsibilities to the Line', *Personnel Review*, Vol. 28, No. 1–2.

Dalal, J. (2003) 'Strategic Offshore Outsourcing: Taking Full Advantage', BPO Outsourcing Africa Conference, 6 October.

Dempsey, K. (2005) 'HR Must Abandon Hope or Become Human Remains', *Personnel Today*, 17 May.

Department for Trade and Industry (2003a) *Services and Offshoring: The Impact of Increasing International Competition in Services*. London: DTI.

Department for Trade and Industry (2003b) *Accounting for People Report*. London: DTI.

Eisenstat, R. A. (1996) 'What Corporate Human Resources Brings to the Picnic: Four Models for Functional Management', *Organizational Dynamics*, Vol. 25, No. 2.

Donkin, R. (2003) 'Money Men see Beauty in Human Capital', *Financial Times*, 5 March.

Donkin, R. (2004) 'How to Run a Tighter Ship: Rent a Boss', *Financial Times*, 15 April.

Elkington, T. (2005) 'Bright future for online recruitment,' *Personnel Today*, 1 August.

Francis, H. and Keegan, A. (2005) 'Slippery Slope', *People Management*, 30 June.

Gladwell, M. (2002) 'The Talent Myth: Are Smart People Overrated?' *The New Yorker*, 22 July.

Gratton, L. (1997) 'Tomorrow's People', *People Management*, 24 July.

Gratton, L. (1998) 'The New Rules of HR Strategy', *HR Focus*, June.

Gratton, L. (2000) 'A Real Change', *People Management*, 16 March.

Gratton, L. (2003) 'The Humpty Dumpty Effect: A View of a Fragmented HR Function', *People Management*, 1 May.

Green, K. (2005) 'Unless HR Treats Business Partnership as More Than a Name Change, It's Only Window Dressing', *People Management*, 19 May.

Griffiths, J. (2004) 'Civil Unrest', *People Management*, 29 July.

Griffiths, J. (2005) 'The Man from Auntie', *People Management*, 19 May.

Guest, D. (1994) 'Important Players in a Different Game', *Personnel Management*, Vol. 26, No. 13, December.

Guest, D. (2000) 'Piece by Piece', *People Management*, 20 July.

Guest, D. and Conway, N. (2002) 'Communicating the Psychological Contract: An Employer Perspective', *Human Resources Management Journal*, Vol. 12, No. 2.

Guest, D. and Conway, N. (2004) *Employee Well Being and the Psychological Contract*. London: CIPD.

Hall, L. and Torrington, D. (1998) 'Letting go or Holding on – the Devolution of Operational Personnel Activities', *Human Resource Management Journal*, Vol. 8, No. 1.

Hawksworth, J. (2005) 'Impact of Offshoring on the UK Economy', *PricewaterhouseCoopers UK Economic Outlook*, March.

Higginbottom, K. (2001) 'BP Learns Outsourcing Lesson', *People Management*, Vol. 8 November.

Hirsh, W., Silverman, M., Tamkin, P. and Jackson, C. (2005) *Managers as Developers of Others*. The Institute for Employment Studies, Report No. 407. Brighton: IES.

Hirsh, W. and Reilly P. (1998) 'Cycling Proficiency', *People Management*, 9 July.

Hoffman, L. (2005) 'Going Global: Outsourcing HR Offshore', *Human Resources Magazine*, 27 July.

Holbeche, L. (1998) 'Too Close to the Client?', *People Management*, 24 December.

Huselid, M. (1995) 'The Impact of Human Resources Management Practices on Turnover, Productivity and Corporate Financial Performance', *Academy of Management Journal*, Vol. 38.

Hutchinson, S. and Wood, S. (1995) *The UK Experience in Personnel and the Line: Developing the New Relationship*. London: Institute of Personnel Development.

IBM Business Consultancy Services (2004) 'Debenhams Invests in Improved HR Delivery with the Help of IBM', www.ibm.com.

Incomes Data Services (2001) *HR Service Centres*. Report No. 707, April.

Industrial Relations Services, (1994) 'The Centre Cannot Hold: Devolving Personnel Duties,' *Employment Trends*, No. 566.

Industrial Relations Services, (1998) 'The Evolving HR Function', *Management Review*, Issue 10, July.

Industrial Relations Services (1999) 'IBM Delivers International HR,' *Employment Trends*, No. 689, October.

Industrial Relations Services (2003) 'Absence Management Still a Challenge', *Employment Review*, Vol. 775.

Industrial Relations Services (2004) 'Hands-on Experience is Key to Career Progression Issue', *Employment Review* Vol. 814, 24 December.

IPMA (2005) 'IPMA-HR Award for Excellence'. Unpublished. Alexandria, VA: IPMA.

IPMA (2006) *IPMA News*, 27 January.

Johnson, G. (1987) *Strategic Change and the Management Process*. Oxford: Blackwell.

Kaplan, R. and Norton, D. (1996) *The Balanced Scorecard*. Boston, MA: Harvard Business Press.

Keenoy, T. (1989) 'HRM: A Case of the Wolf in Sheep's Clothing?', *Personnel Review*, Vol. 19, No. 2.

Kettley, P. and Reilly, P. (2003) *E-HR: An Introduction*. The Institute for Employment Studies, Report 398.

Brighton: IES.

Kenton, B. and Yarnell, J. (2005) *HR – The Business Partner*. Oxford: Elsevier Butterworth-Heinemann.

Lawler, E. E. and Mohrman, S. A. (2003) 'HR as a Strategic Partner', *Human Resource Planning*, Vol. 26, No. 3.

Lawler, E., Mueller-Oerlinghausen, J. and Shearn, J.A. (2005) 'A Dearth of HR Talent', *McKinsey Quarterly*, No. 2.

Legge, K. (1989) 'Human Resource Management: A Critical Analysis', in Storey, J. *New Perspectives on Human Resource Management*. London: Routledge.

Legge, K. (1995) *Human Resource Management: Rhetorics and Realities*. Basingstoke: Macmillan.

Lentz, S. S. (1996) 'Hybrid Organization Structures: A Path to Cost Savings and Customer Responsiveness', *Human Resource Management*, Vol. 35, No. 4.

Lonsdale, C. and Cox, A. (1998) 'Falling in With The Out Crowd', *People Management*, 15 October.

Lynch, S. (2003) 'Is it Safe to Hand HR Tasks Over to Non-experts?', *People Management*, 11 September.

Mankins, M. C. and Steele, R. (2005) 'Turning Great Strategy into Great Performance', *Harvard Business Review*, July/August.

Martin, G. and Beaumont, P. (2003) *Branding and People Management: What's in a Name?* London: CIPD.

Mayo, A. (2005) 'Serious Behaviour', *People Management*, 7 April.

McBain, R. (2001) 'Human Resource Management. Culture, Commitment and the Role of the HR Function', *Henley Manager Update*, Vol. 13, Part 2.

McGovern, P., Gratton, L., Hope-Hailey, V., Stiles, P. and Truss, C. (1997) 'Human Resource Management on the Line?', *Human Resource Management Journal*, Vol. 7, No. 4.

McLaren, F. (2005) 'The Impact of Career Management on Shared Services: A Practical Solution for Royal Bank of Scotland.' Unpublished management report for Masters degree.

Michaels, E., Handfield-Jones, H. and Axelrod, B. (2001) *The War for Talent*. Boston, MA: Harvard Business School Press.

Mintzberg, H. (1994) *The Rise and Fall of Strategic Planning*. New Jersey: Prentice Hall.

Murray, S. (2004) 'Self service tools bring instant revolution', *Financial Times*, 29 April.

Partridge, S, (2004) 'Given the Third Degree', *People Management*, 12 August.

People Management (2005) 'HR Suffers From Low Self Esteem', International News, 24 March.

Personnel Today (2005a) 'HR is the Unhappiest Profession in the UK', 14 June, Personnel Today Online.

Personnel Today (2005b) *Employer Branding is Key in Fight for Talent*, 17 May

Pfau, B. N. and Cundiff, B. B. (2002) '7 steps before strategy', *Workforce*, Vol. 81, November.

Philpott, J. (2001) 'No 11's Way to a Winning XI', *Guardian*, 12 April.

Pickard, J. (2000) 'Centre of Attention', *People Management*, 6 July.

Pickard, J. (2004a) 'Should I Stay or Should I go', *People Management*, 25 March.

Pickard, J. (2004b) 'One Step Beyond', *People Management*, 30 June.

Pickard, J. (2005a) 'Time to Measure up to Business Needs', *People Management*, 21 April.

Pickard, J. (2005b) 'HR is Changing at an Unprecedented Rate', CIPD Annual Conference newspaper from *People Management*, 28 October.

Pollard, E. and Willison, R. (2005) *Beyond the Screen: Supporting eLearning*. Institute for Employment Studies Report 425. Brighton: IES.

Prahalad, C.K. and Hamel, G. (1994) 'Competing for the Future', *Harvard Business Review*, July/August.

Prahalad, C.K. and Hamel, G. (1990) 'The Core Competence of the Corporation', *Harvard Business Review*, May/June.

PricewaterhouseCoopers/Economist Intelligence Unit (2005) *Offshoring in the Financial Services: Risks and Rewards*. www.pwc.com.

Purcell, J., Kinnie, N., Hutchinson, S., Rayton, B. and Swart, J. (2003) *Understanding the People and Performance Link: Unlocking the Black Box*. London: CIPD.

Purcell, J. (2001) 'The Meaning of Strategy in Human Resource Management', in Storey, J. (ed.), *Human Resource Management: A Critical Text*, London: Thomson Learning.

Purcell, J. (1994) 'Personnel Earns a Place on the Board', *Personnel Management*, February.

Purcell, J. and Ahlstrand, B. (1994) *Human Resource Management in the Multi-Divisional Company*. Oxford: OUP.

Radcliffe Public Policy Center (2000) *Life's Work: Generational Attitudes toward Work and Life Integration*. Cambridge, MA: Harvard University Press.

Reilly, P. (2000a) 'Flexibility at Work: Balancing the Interests of Employer and Employee', Gower, Aldershot.

Reilly, P. (2000b) 'Called in to Question', *People Management*, 6 July.

Reilly, P. (2004a) 'Into Africa', *People Management*, 15 January.

Reilly, P. (2004b) 'Defining the Human Capital Agenda', *Strategic HR Review*, Vol. 3 Issue 2 January/

February.

Reilly, P. and Tamkin, P. (1997) *Outsourcing: A Flexible Option for the Future?* The Institute for Employment Studies, Report 320. Brighton: IES.

Reilly, P. and Williams, T. (2003) *How to get Best Value from HR: The Shared Services Option.* Aldershot: Gower.

Reilly, P., Phillipson, J. and Smith, P. (2005) 'Team Based Pay in the United Kingdom', *Compensation and Benefits Review*, July/August.

Renwick, D. (2003) 'Line Manager Involvement in HRM: An Inside View', *Employee Relations*, Vol. 25, No. 3.

Rick, J., Tamkin, P., Tackey, N. and Pollard, E. (2000) 'Institutional Racism: Where's the Prejudice in Organizations?' Paper presented to the British Psychological Society Occupational Psychology Conference, Brighton, January.

Robinson, D., Perryman, S. and Hayday, S. (2004) *The Drivers of Employee Engagement.* The Institute for Employment Studies, Report 408. Brighton: IES.

Rucci, A. J., Kirn, S. P. and Quinn, R. T. (1998) 'The Employee-Customer Profit Chain at Sears', *Harvard Business Review*, January–February.

Russell, R. and Harrop, D. (2005) 'Staffing the Human Resources Function', www.rsmmcgladrey.com

Shared Services and Business Process Outsourcing Association (in association with ADP) (2005) HR Transformation Survey, www.sharedservicesbpo.com.

SHRM (Society for Human Resource Management) (2002) *The Future of the HR Profession.* Alexandria, VA: SHRM.

SHRM (Society for Human Resource Management) (2004) *The Maturing Profession of Human Resources in the United States of America Survey Report.* Alexandria, VA: SHRM.

SHRM (Society for Human Resource Management) (2005) *Special Expertise Panel 2005 Trends Report.* Alexandria, VA: SHRM.

Scott-Jackson, W., Newham, T. and Gurney, M. (2005) HR Outsourcing: The Key Decisions, CIPD Executive Briefing.

Simms, J. (2005) 'High Rollers', *People Management*, 14 July.

Smethurst, S. (2003) 'Pooling Resources', *People Management*, 1 May.

Smethurst, S. (2005a) 'The Great Beyond', *People Management*, 27 January.

Smethurst, S. (2005b) 'The Long and Winding Road', *People Management*, 28 July.

Smith, L. (2005) 'We are Part of the Solution', *Guardian*, August 27.

Storey, J. (1989) *New Perspectives on Human Resource Management.* London: Routledge.

Storey, J. (1992) *Developments in the Management of Human Resources.* Oxford: Blackwell.

Storey, J. (1995) *Human Resource Management: A Critical Text.* London: Routledge.

Syedain, H. (1999) 'Why Getting to the Board Does Matter', *Human Resources*, September.

The Conference Board (2002) 'HR Outsourcing Trends'. www.conference-board.org.

The Conference Board (2004) 'HR Outsourcing: Benefits, Challenges and Trends'. www.conference-board.org.

The Work Foundation (2003) *Managing Best Practice*, No. 107: Outsourcing in HR. London: The Work Foundation.

Taylor, R. (2003) 'Generation Next', *People Management*, September 11.

Tamkin, P. (2005) *The Contribution of Skills to Business Performance.* London: DfES.

Tamkin, P., Reilly, P. and Hirsh, W. (2006) *Managing HR Careers: Emerging Trends and Issues.* London: CIPD.

Thornhill, A. and Saunders, M. (1998) 'What if Line Managers Don't Realize They're Responsible for HR?', *Personnel Review*, Vol. 27, No. 6.

Torrington, D. (1998) 'Crisis and Opportunity in HRM: The Challenge for the Personnel Function', in Sparrow, P. and Marchington, M. (eds) *Human Resource Management: The New Agenda.* London: Pitman Financial Times.

Torrington, D. (1989) 'Human Resource Management and the Personel Function'. In Storey, J. (ed) *New Perspectives in Human Resource Management.* London, Routledge.

Towers Perrin (2005) 'HR Outsourcing: New Realities, New Expectations', study of HRO effectiveness. www.towersperrin.com.

Tyson, S. (1994) 'Getting Into Gear: Post Recession HR Management', *Personnel Management,* August.

Tyson, S. and Fell, A. (1986) *Evaluating the Personnel Function.* London: Hutchinson.

Tyson, S. and York, A. (2000) *Essentials of HRM.* Oxford: Butterworth Heinemann.

Ulrich, D. (1995) 'Shared Services: From Vogue to Value', *Human Resource Planning*, Vol. 18, (3).

Ulrich, D. (1997) *Human Resource Champions: The Next Agenda for Adding Value and Delivering Results.* Boston, MA: Harvard Business Press.

Ulrich, D. (1998a) 'HR with Attitude', *People Management*, 13 August.

Ulrich, D. (1998b) 'Intellectual Capital = Competence x Commitment', *Sloan Management Review,* Winter, Vol 39, No. 2.

Ulrich, D. (1998c) 'A New Mandate for Human Resources', *Harvard Business Review*, January–February.

Ulrich, D. and Brockbank, W. (2005) *The HR Value Proposition*. Boston, MA: Harvard Press.

Watkin, C. (2005) 'Standing Out From the Crowd.' Management Consultancy, VNU Business Publications, March.

Whittaker, J. and Johns, T. (2004) 'Standards Deliver', *People Management*, 30 June.

Whittaker, S. and Marchington, M. (2003) 'Devolving HR Responsibility: Threat, Opportunity or Partnership', *Employee Relations*, Vol. 25, No. 3.

Wigham, R. (2005) 'Reap the Benefits', *Personnel Today*, 27 September.

Williams, A. (1993) *Human Resource Management and Labour Market Flexibility*, Aldershot: Avebury.

Wilson, A. (2003) 'Double Vision', *People Management*, 9 October.

Workplace Employee Relations Survey (2006) Department of Trade and Industry, Essex University Data Archive.

Index